Minorities
in South Asia and in Europe

Minorities in South Asia and in Europe

Edited by

Samir Kumar Das

Samya

MINORITIES IN SOUTH ASIA AND IN EUROPE: A New Agenda
was first published in 2010 by SAMYA,
an imprint of Bhatkal and Sen,
16 Southern Avenue, Kolkata 700 026

ISBN 978-81-906760-3-8

The research leading to these results has received funding
from the European Community's Seventh Framework programme
[FP7/2007-2013] under grant agreement no 216072.

Eurasia-Net Partners
Accademia European Bolzano/Eurpäische Akademie Bozen (EURAC)—Bolzano/Bozen (Italy), Brunel University, West London (UK), Johann Wolfgang Goethe-Universität, Frankfurt-am-Main (Germany), Mahaniran Calcutta Research Group (India), South Asian Forum for Human Rights (Nepal), Democratic Commission of Human Development (Pakistan), University of Dhaka (Bangladesh).

Design by Compuset International
85 Park St, Kolkata 700 016
and printed by Bengal Phototype Co,
46/1 Raja Rammohon Sarnai, Kolkata 700 009

Published by Mandira Sen for SAMYA,
An imprint of Bhatkal and Sen,
16 Southern Avenue, Kolkata 700 026.

Dedicated to the memory of Cristina Boglia (1965-2010),
an invaluable colleague in our work on the
Protection of Minorities in South Asia and Europe.

CONTENTS

PREFACE

The book is a part of the Eurasia-Net project on the protection of minorities in Europe and in South Asia that Mahanirban Calcutta Research Group (CRG) was involved in during the last couple of years. In a sense, the project stands in continuity with CRG's earlier works on issues of forced migration, autonomy, rights and justice, and so on, including, of course, the minorities. The project gave CRG the precious opportunity of working in partnership with some of the best academic institutions of both South Asia and Europe. We thank all the partners, the European Academy in Bolzano, Italy, in particular, for extending all kinds of help to us. I have myself benefited by the advice and contributions of Günther Rautz and Ranabir Samaddar at different points of time and remain indebted to them. The rough contours of the book were planned in a rainy evening at Güenther's place in Bolzano in late-August 2008. I am thankful to Alexandra Tomaselli who has ungrudgingly familiarized us with all the necessary project details. I recall with great pain the tragic loss of Cristina. We had received so much support from her in our collective journey through the project.

The ideas gradually took concrete shape in course of the deliberations held during a series of project steering group meetings organized in New Delhi (February 2009), Kathmandu (August 2009) and Dhaka (November 2009). My interactions with the colleagues of the European Academy during my study visit in August-September (2008) helped me a great deal in shaping some of the ideas pursued here. We particularly thank Tapan Bose of South Asia Forum for Human Rights, Nepal, Kamran Arif of Democratic Commission of Human Development, Pakistan, Borhan Uddin Khan of the University of Dhaka, Javid Rehman and Harriet Hoffler, Brunel Law School, Brunel University, Rainer Hoffmann and Ugo Caruso of the University of Frankfurt, for their inputs that went into the preparation of this book. Much of the Introduction to this book is adapted from the inaugural address that I delivered to and the discussion that followed the workshop on 'Minorities and Their Alienation' organized by CRG in Kolkata on 8 August 2009. I take the opportunity of thanking all of them, CRG's young research team, in particular, for their comments. I am proud to be a part of a wonderful academic team and I must confess that without the help of Paula and Sabyasachi's the book could not be completed. We also thank Samya for its support.

Kolkata, January 2010 SKD

INTRODUCTION

SAMIR KUMAR DAS

THIS BOOK INTENDS to study minorities of South Asia and Europe from a comparative and transnational perspective. While country-specific studies in minorities are by no means rare, their comparisons within a region (like South Asia and Europe) or across them are almost non-existent. This is so because the history of the formation of minorities in many ways coincides with that of the formation of nation-states in both these regions. As modern states emerge and their boundaries are drawn in fairly neat and precise terms, minorities are created, if not 'trapped' and 'colonized', within them.[1] International boundaries have often been drawn both in postcolonial South Asia or in post-war Europe in ways that have not only dismembered the hitherto homogeneous groups into minorities dispersed over two or more nation-states but also brought about newer sources of division amongst them. Insofar as they operate within two or more national milieus, each distinct from the other, they get configured in similarly distinct ways. Minorities, as we will see, are 'minorities' only with reference to the national body within which they constitute themselves as minorities.[2] Contemporary writings on the emergence of modern nations in different parts of the world particularly in Southeast Asia point out how nations played a great role in liberating them and delivering them from the medieval evils of minority intimidation and persecution.[3] Modern minorities are the product of nationalist discourse. For, it is in relation to that body that one is a majority or for that matter a minority.

Unlike in the modern times, minorities in the Middle Ages were called so insofar as they were perceived as a threat to the sovereign—an emperor, a king or a sultan—and the aristocracy. While sovereignty now circulates within the national body, sovereignty during the Middle Ages, as Foucault's monumental work tells us, was concentrated in the person of the sovereign. Modern minorities in that sense are part of the sovereign and those who refuse to be identified with them, either with the majority or with the minority, *as it were* do not exist. They are the people—who in the parlance of contemporary radical theory—may be 'killed with impunity'. Such homogenizations of geopolitical space achieved in Western Europe during early modern times[4] and in South Asia after decolonization[5] hardly leave room for non-national minorities. While incorporation of the minorities into the sovereign body of the nation contains its own 'contradictions',[6] dissent against the nation has a disempowering effect in a world that has become overwhelmingly nationalized; it divests one of one's citizenship rights and renders one 'stateless'. Statelessness is considered the bane of today's world. Nearer home, the plight of the stateless 'Biharis'—the non-Bengali Muslims—who had decided to migrate to predominantly Bengali-speaking East Pakistan/Bangladesh during the tumultuous days of Partition (1947) and their descendants who have been staying in camps since the formation of Bangladesh serves as a case in point. They remain perpetually stranded between two nation-states. While their Islamic identity pushed them towards the then East Pakistan, they became thoroughly disillusioned as Bengali nationalism started taking shape and eventually led to the creation of Bangladesh. Examples of statelessness are by no means peculiar to East Pakistan or its successor state, Bangladesh. Many of the minorities whether in South Asia or in Europe live in a state of virtual statelessness. For, they are systematically dispossessed of their rights. In recent times, such dispossession—as Paula Banerjee's essay, 'Mapping the Minorities', shows—has taken on an extremely violent character. Extreme violence exercised more often than not in collusion with the instruments of the state aims not only to denigrate citizenship rights of these minority groups but to eliminate and exterminate them altogether. Extreme violence in short seeks to create a nation *without* minorities declaring them as nations. Or, wherever they are not rendered effectively stateless, they are forced to assimilate themselves into the national mainstream. The 'Georgianization of Abkhazia' in the former Soviet Union as portrayed by Benedikt Harzl in 'Kosovo in Abkhazia or the Universality of De Facto States' in this volume serves as a case in point. This was closely followed by the Georgian policy of ethnic cleansing after the Soviet collapse. On the other hand, a 'majority of Catalans'—as the Catalan leader Argemi tells us in his interview with Thomas Benedikter, 'Expanding Catalonia's Autonomy'—consider Catalonia of present-day Spain as 'a nation', notwithstanding the cultural and linguistic diversities that mark the region.

Contemporary researches on the minorities of the Middle Ages, particularly in Europe, reveal that there was hardly any fixed and immutable 'persecuting discourse' on the minorities. The exact target, nature and intensity of this threat perception would however vary from one context to another. As Nirenberg argues:

> The notion of a 'persecuting discourse' requires qualification. Such a discourse about minorities was but one of those available, and its invocation in a given situation did not ensure its success or acceptance. The choice of language was an active one, made in order to achieve something, made within contexts of conflict and structures of domination and sometimes contested.[7]

Determination of one's status as a minority is always a sovereign decision; whether of the sovereign people and the nation as in modern times or of the sovereign person or the king as a person during the Middle Ages. But what sets apart the minorities of modern times from those of the Middle Ages is the persistence of the nationalist discourse as the 'persecuting discourse'. Minorities of the Middle Ages were defined more by the contingent decisions of the sovereign king than by any preponderant and consistently woven discourse of the time.

The imperative of governing the minorities in India, as Samaddar's essay tells us, was felt for the first time by the colonial rulers in late-nineteenth century when they were alarmed by the growing Wahabi threat to their sovereign power. The essay traces the shifting strategies of governing the minorities in India since the colonial times and focuses on the paradoxical relationship that obtains between the imperative of exercising sovereignty and that of governing the minorities. As he sums it up: 'Without the government functioning in a rational way the sovereign power cannot operate for long. Yet as the insistent existence of minorities *qua* minorities poses challenge to sovereign power, it appears that sovereignty cannot exist without being shared. This is where governmental operation becomes critical. It creates the impossible: sovereignty seems to dissipate in the deep waters of micro-management of society, without necessarily dissolving the power to coerce.' This should be read together with his essay, *The Materiality of Politics*, published earlier, in which he pointed out how minorities have been the objects of care and how care for the minorities is implicated in the exercise of governmental power.[8] Strategies of governing the minorities have their implications for the exercise of sovereign power by the state.

Besides, studying the comparative status of minorities within the respective state boundaries has become an object of diplomatic offensive—at times, real wars—between states. The 10-month long civil war in East Pakistan unleashed against the Bengali-speaking minority was followed in quick succession by the Indo-Pak war of 1971 resulting in the 'liberation' of Bangladesh. Comparisons therefore are regarded as too politically volatile a subject to be encouraged by the nation-states, the donor agencies, other multilateral bodies or even by the universities. Thus, there are excellent comparative studies in minorities safely 'distant' from each other, say, the minorities of India and Malaysia,[9] but not of, let us say, India and Pakistan precisely because the former comparison is regarded as politically benign and the latter is not.

Today the reasons for comparing the minorities across nation-states have become far more compelling than what they were two decades back. The forces and processes of globalization have as it were flushed the minorities out of the 'trappings' of their respective state boundaries. Minorities are increasingly seen to be involved in establishing and harbouring translocal and transnational linkages in their attempts at mustering political power and transforming themselves from minorities to 'unrepresented nations', that is to say nations denied or awaiting their membership to the United Nations, or even 'peoples'. The right to self-determination has gathered certain momentum in recent years. Groups, which were hitherto regarded as 'national minorities', refuse to identify them as such and clamour for reconstituting themselves as 'nations'. Or those who do not prefer to tread the extreme path or simply lack the resources necessary for pursuing such a political agenda, want to be recognized as 'peoples', as per international law, instead of being reduced to minorities and therefore 'second class citizens'. Similarly, these forces and processes have in a sense contributed to the disaggregation, if not fragmentation, of minorities. If dalits (literally the downtrodden) are considered as a minority in India, then the dalits and the dalit women cannot be treated at par with each other. Dalit women are far worse off than the dalits in general. Dalit lesbians amongst the dalit women could be treated as yet another category separable from both the dalits and the dalit women in terms of their deprivation and vulnerabilities. It will be more apt to describe the dalit women as a minority *within* a minority, suffering the double jeopardy of being dalits and being women. The women are to be considered as a minority only in that sense: first, as a group that suffers from the generalized discrimination against women in society by virtue of being women, and second, as one that suffers from the double jeopardy by being part of some particular ethnic or communal minority. Pfaff-Czarnecka's essay, '"Minorities-in-Minorities" in South Asia' shows how privileging of the 'minorities' as a category in South Asia through such forms of political intervention as reservation, positive discrimination and affirmative action, and so on, obliterates and levels off the 'minorities within minorities' and contributes to their homogenization. Her essay may be read as a clarion call for deconstructing 'minorities' as a category and initiating the legal reforms that it entails. As the minorities of Europe and South Asia come into contact with each other and set up solidarities that seem to transcend the state boundaries while negotiating with and alleviating their minority status, nation-states have not become obsolete, but have certainly become inadequate in responding to the changing requirements of time. As the framework of nation-states proves to be inadequate to the changing demand of the minorities, as the book advocates, it needs to be supplemented by a transnational or even a transregional platform.

In other words, a plea is being made for making a paradigmatic shift in state responses in this context. State sovereignty that still theoretically marks each of the member states of the United Nations is sought to be redefined in international law today more as a 'responsibility' towards its own citizens than as a power that is situated over and above ('a determinate human superior' as Austin would have us believe) and therefore alien to them. The more sovereignty is redefined as responsibility, the more the states are subjected to supranational or multilateral sanctions and obligations. The probability of securing funds by Bangladesh from the donor states and regional organizations including the European

Union depends among other things on Dhaka's track record of treating its tribal minorities in Chittagong Hill Tracts (CHT).[10] In many ways, traditional post-Westphalian system of nation-states proves to be ruefully inadequate to respond to the claims of these new solidarities. State responses moulded in the post-Westphalian framework have already become inadequate. There is no end to the process of formation of new states in response to the growing minority demands for national self-determination as the recent past experience of Europe would bear out.[11] State boundaries are bound to produce minorities within them. As there are minorities within minorities, formation of nation-states as a response to increasingly strident minority demands would be like peeling an onion. While right to self-determination was considered as a democratic right, the international community in the recent past seems to have conceded to the demand only as the last resort. But we have reached a moment when the question today is not one of keeping the order of nation-states intact but of devising ways by which we can put in place a regional or a transregional platform with necessary mechanisms for minority protection. The agenda of establishing a transregional platform depends in its turn on our ability to draw lessons from past experiences, to make a thorough audit of the protective mechanisms that are already in place within the nation-states and also without and, most importantly, to negotiate constantly with the given order of nation-states.[12] Such negotiations by all indications are unlikely to make the order of nation-states extinct, at least in the near future. But they will certainly attempt to respond to the inadequacies built in that order. The transregional platform comprising a plethora of voluntary initiatives, networks of universities and research bodies, human rights and activist groups, even public intellectuals and others is required to function as a vigilante mechanism insofar as the protection of minority rights is concerned. Protection of minority rights in other words has become too serious an agenda to be relinquished to the sovereign prerogative of the nation-states. It is in this spirit that Basu Ray Chaudhury's essay, 'An Indian Charter for Minority Rights', formulates a South Asian regional charter of minority rights.[13] Compared to South Asia, Europe has already made considerable headway in this regard. The essay by Lantschner and Eisendle, 'Minorities of Europe: An Overview of National Regulations' presents an overview of the relevant national and regional laws of minority protection with particular reference to six European countries: Hungary, Romania, Slovakia, Slovenia, Austria and Italy. Thus, to cite an instance, the Organization for Security and Cooperation in Europe (OSCE), created in 1992, has the office of the High Commissioner for National Minorities. Its main tasks are to provide early warning and mediation procedures whenever tensions involving minorities seem to threaten peace and stability in the continent. Again, Bojan Brezigar's essay on 'Transnational Minority Networks and Mobilization in Europe' makes a detailed stdy of two 'relevant' non-governmental organizations in Europe. Bilateral agreements between countries on the issue of minority protection, although a much-publicized practice in Europe, are by no means a rarity in South Asia, as the essay by Das and Samaddar points out.

This book seeks to respond to this challenge by sensitizing us to the lessons of minority experience in a cross-national and cross-regional perspective. It is prepared in the framework of the Eurasia-Net project that the Mahanirban Calcutta Research Group (MGRG) had had the opportunity of working on, in collaboration with the partners of both South Asia and Europe. This obviously calls for a paradigmatic shift. The hitherto existing modes of understanding the minorities are increasingly becoming inadequate. As we will have occasion to see later, these modes of understanding continue to exercise their influence on the academic and activist landscape and are premised either on any given nation-state or on the given order of nation-states. Das and Samaddar's essay, 'Hundred Years of Research on Minorities in South Asia: Towards a New Agenda' reviews a century of research on the minorities in South Asia in general and India in particular and proposes to draw only the bare outlines of a future research agenda along these lines.

The year 2009 marks the twentieth anniversary of the publication of late Professor Myron Weiner's provocatively titled essay, 'India's Minorities: Who Are They? What Do They Want?'[14] The essay is commonly regarded as a critical milestone in our understanding of the status of minorities of South Asia in general and India in particular. Although an earlier version of this essay was published in 1986, the one just cited was published three years later and is considered one of the most complete statements on the status of minority research and practices in India and South Asia in the late 1980s. His central argument is that the institutional capacity for managing the minorities in India in the 1980s has been severely depleted by *(a)* the decline and fall of what once was known as 'the Congress system' that could absorb all oppositions within itself and its growing inability to accommodate the ever-strident minority demands; *(b)* ethnicization and communalization of the governing institutions: of the police and the paramilitary forces in particular as the reports on recent ethnic and communal violence in South Asia bear out; *(c)* the rise of territorial nationalism amongst both the majority and most of the minorities; *(d)* the emergence of minority coalitions and alliances that are of international character; *(e)* the federal rearrangement that used to work reasonably well since Independence (1947) through the 1950s and the 1960s has fallen into disuse with the effect that the state governments do not seem to act as 'viable' unit; and *(f)* the emergence of majority 'self-awareness' and their demands. The list is by no means exhaustive. But it obviously gives us a sense of Professor Weiner's anxiety that the paraphernalia of governing institutions might in future be swept away by the increasing violence and militancy that have come to mark minority politics in South Asia. Although never explicitly mentioned, the incommensurability that he points to—of political institutions with the rising levels of political mobilization—owes much to the early writings of Samuel P. Huntington. All these taken together, according to Professor Weiner, are likely to 'worsen majority-minority relations' and threaten to tear the body politic apart. Though not a doomsday prophet, his essay on the minorities takes him perhaps closest to that position.

I think researches on minorities, albeit sporadically conducted, say, during the last twenty years since the publication of his famous essay, have gone a long way in setting forth a new research agenda on minorities. The present book intends to take a stock of the post-Weiner researches and experience with minorities in South Asia and Europe. These researches to my mind have made departures in at least three very important areas from Professor Weiner's landmark essay. That is precisely the reason why it continues to serve as a reference point for any understanding of the minority situation, particularly during the last two decades.

First, minorities, according to him, are defined as those who 'lack power' and 'who do not share what they regard as the central symbols of the society'. He does not probe into how certain symbols acquire a pride of place within any given society, and turn into 'central symbols' while dislocating and displacing many others. In other words, the way by which the so-called central symbols acquire their centrality also tells us the secret story of how the majorities perpetrate their hegemony over the minorities; a hegemony that also makes the minorities 'voluntarily' use and share these symbols by 'universalizing' them.[15] The spreading of a national language serves as a paradigm of all these symbols. These symbols help in organizing the society into a single whole by establishing their hegemony and centrality, in short by producing a nation of which both the majority and the minorities are inseparable parts. A good deal of anthropological studies has been conducted both in South Asia and in Europe to show how the modes by which certain symbols acquire their centrality are implicated in the power relations, and how these symbols being 'central' to the society, get organized around a 'centre' and thereby contribute to the centralization of symbolic power. It is, as we have argued, only in relation to 'society', the larger social whole or the nation, that one is considered a majority or for that matter a minority. This may sound intriguing but is nevertheless true that minorities are not nations per se but are only national minorities.

Second, democratic institutions are believed to lie outside and remain untainted by the sometimes messy nature of majority-minority relations. Professor Weiner's optimism that the minorities can be accommodated more or less by the existing political institutions is in a sense obsessive. For, he does not call for any major institutional change; the same institutions, according to him, will be able to take care of the minority problem, provided they are allowed to perform in their letter and spirit. In fact, he argues in one of his essays contained in the same collection that notwithstanding serious depletion of institutional capacity, the existing network of institutions is sufficiently strong to withstand the crisis that it was facing. His faith in the secular nature of democratic institutions and their capacity is unwavering. The argument is turned upside down thanks to new empirical evidences that are coming to light. The involvement of the state—particularly its politicians and security forces—whether by commission or by 'active inaction' in the ethnic and communal riots in different parts of South Asia and in the post-socialist states of Eastern Europe points to its unmistakably communalized and ethnicized character.[16] While for Professor Weiner it is the politicians, bureaucrats and the security forces who fail our secular, democratic institutions, contemporary researches on the subject under review point out how such institutions simultaneously function as critical nodes of minority exclusion built in their very fabric. The systemic and institutionalized nature of contemporary exclusions reminds us of Tocqueville who more than anyone else in 1835 warned us against the 'tyranny' of the majority in a democracy. This deficit, according to him, is intrinsic to any representative democracy governed by the principle of majority rule and he was keen on putting in place a series of apparently 'counter-democratic' institutions that would act as a check on their tyranny.

Professor Weiner's dilemma is that he insists on reconciling the interests of the majority and the minority without initiating any major institutional change. His concern in simple terms is 'to accommodate the demands for substantial administrative decentralization and prove skilful at reassuring minorities without threatening the cultural identity and interests of majorities'. Democracy, as this book argues, is not about simple accommodation; it is over and above about reorganizing the institutions in a way that will not privilege the majority. This perhaps calls for a 'shared' notion of sovereignty in which any minority by being entitled to a share of it can elevate itself into a 'people' in the sense of renegotiating the terms of its relationship in the political dispensation hitherto dominated by the majority. Minorities for their protection seem no longer to insist on 'accommodation' defined by the given institutions, but to fundamentally redefine the very institutional terms and conditions that provided for such 'accommodation'. Minorities can be 'accommodated' only as a contracting party: as an equal partner to the contract that brings the political dispensation into existence.[17] Such demands for renegotiation and redefinition are unprecedented whether in the postcolonial history of South Asia or in the post-war history of Europe and have made up the new agenda of minority politics in both these regions. I have shown elsewhere how the act of making the Constitution in India was at the same time an act of constituting a social whole with its implicit rules of minority exclusion.[18]

By contrast, the recent constitution-making experience in Nepal is instructive in this regard. By all indications, the country is poised up for new federal experiment in recognition of its multinational character. Constitution being defined as a political contract is believed to have 'trapped' the minorities within a dispensation the terms of which have been preset for them. All over the world, the common trend has been to renegotiate these terms so that the minorities do not feel constrained to acquiesce to them. For instance, the inclusion of Naga Hills of the then undivided Assam at the same time constituted the Nagas as a minority whether within Assam or within India. The outbreak of Naga rebellion in the early 1950s is a testimony of how many of them were resentful of their minority status. Indeed, it will be more accurate to say that the Naga rebel discourse is characterized by a resolute denial of their minority status for it prefers to view the Nagas as a 'nation'. A section of Naga rebels today demands 'special federal relationship with India' in which Nagalim (the land of the Nagas) will first of all be constituted as a separate political entity (the Government of India has so far recognized the 'unique history' of the Nagas and the peace talks have been initiated since 1997) and then only negotiating on the exact institutional form of their relationship with India as an 'equal people' without being reduced to a minority. Nagas are a people who have a right to negotiate their terms of inclusion in India and not a minority to be 'accommodated' into it within the given terms. These situations have set off a series of experiments with institutional forms and Benedikter's essay in a broad canvas gives us a glimpse of some of these experiments particularly in the European context. But, the institutional experiments, as Lantschner and Eisendle warn us in the context of six countries of Central and southern Europe where these have been carried out with incredible pace, particularly since the formation of the European Union, will have to provide 'innovative solutions' rather than easy and 'weak compromises'.

Third, Professor Weiner notes that the 'international coalitions of minorities' are a newly emergent phenomenon. Such international coalitions in essence remain 'international' and minority relations across the nation-states are usually mediated through nation-states. Of course, there have been exceptions. Thus, bilateral agreements on the question of minorities (like Nehru-Liaquat agreement, Shastri-

Bandarnaike pact, Indira-Mujib agreement or a successive series of agreements from Versailles in 1919 to Dayton in 1995) are agreements signed by the respective nation-states. But on the other hand, transnational networks of the minorities, of course, in their varying states of formalization seem to have released the minorities from the shackles of the nation-states. The term that is widely used to capture this new development is 'Minority discourse'. Minority politics exists more as a discourse producing its effects and resonances across the boundaries of nation-states than as a given entity still trapped within them.

Never before in its history has the nation as a point of reference for determining one's status as a majority or as a minority faced so much challenge as it does now. For one thing, globalization has resulted in a certain disaggregation of levels of governance and political and economic power. The nation, in other words, is no longer the only relevant level of governance where a group is constituted as a minority. The national minority may be a minority at the national level; but may not be so within a given locality, neighbourhood, constituent state or region. The local has perhaps emerged as the irreducible unit of global politics in the sense that the control of the national over the levels over or below it is increasingly wearing thin. Thus anthropological studies conducted in recent years suggest that New Delhi had very little control over the streets of Delhi after the assassination of Mrs. Indira Gandh, the former prime minister of India, and the anti-Sikh riots (Sikhs constitute about 2 percent of India's total population) that followed it immediately in 1984. The functioning of the local as an autonomous entity does not represent an extension of the state, but it certainly bears the 'signature' of the state.[19] Similarly, excesses committed during the national emergency declared during 1975-1977 point to the multiplier effects of the otherwise centrally sanctioned abrogation of rights in the localities and neighbourhoods of Delhi. What we call the multiplier effect is always demonstrated in excess of the central sanctions.[20] Similarly, who exercises control over the streets of Mumbai in India, gun-running in Peshawar, Pakistan, or over land to be inundated with saline water for cultivation of exportable shrimp in Khulna, Bangladesh, becomes as much important as winning national elections in their respective countries.[21] The newly resurgent gang wars for control over localities and *mohallas* are indeed a product of globalization and the loosening of the grip that the national governments had hitherto enjoyed within their respective nations. The majority that rules the country from the legislative bodies of New Delhi, Islamabad or any of the European capitals finds it difficult to establish its authority over the streets and localities of their own countries. As democracy gets disaggregated into various levels of governance, each retaining its relatively distinct and autonomous character, such terms as 'national majorities' or 'national minorities' have lost much of their relevance. The proliferation of levels is likely to render these coinages redundant in no time. The agenda of minority politics, as the book argues, oversteps the national boundaries and spills into regional and transregional spheres.

While it is imperative to form transnational platforms in keeping with the changing configurations of majorities and minorities in an increasingly globalized world, any plea for transnational activism cannot be indiscriminate by nature. It is true that the minorities are, as it were, released from the 'trappings' of the nation-states. Not all minority interests are reconciliable with each other or even with the transregional agenda, let alone with that of the global multilateral agencies. The aggregation of essentially non-aggregatable interests may compel the minorities to function in ways that are detrimental to their own interests. Minorities being caught in the whirlpool of global politics sometimes do not know how to retain the autonomy of their social and political agenda.

This book seeks to tell us many stories of how minority interests may be a casualty of transnational activism. The sudden surge of minority activism in simple terms may not eventually serve the long-term minority interests and may remain tied to the strings of donor agencies. The setting up of a transregional platform must ultimately stand up to this challenge. At a more general level, Negri warns us against the 'imperial' nature of our resistances in global times. 'Counter-imperialist ontology', to borrow the phrase from him, contributes to the accretion of an empire that it seeks to resist and steamrolls diverse minority interests into one and levels off their differences.[22]

Minority politics today is clearly at a crossroads. While there is the need for understanding it *also* outside the order of nation-states, the transnationality or transregionality is yet to acquire any definite shape. Minorities are caught between the given order of nation-states on one hand and their transnational or even transregional campaigns and programmes, on the other. In that sense, the book, while drawing our attention to the changing nature of minority politics, does not or, more aptly, cannot, give us the sense of direction that it might take in future. The future is still uncertain. In simple terms, this book proposes to sketch only the outlines of a new agenda of minority research in South Asia and Europe. MCRG will feel rewarded if the book brings about any refreshing change in our understanding of the minorities in these two regions and offers some useful guidelines for future research in the area.

NOTES

1. I borrow this usage of the term 'colonized' from Ranabir Samaddar. See Ranabir Samaddar, 'The Last Hurrah That Continues', in *Divided Countries, Separated Cities: The Modern Legacy of Partition,* edited by Ghislaine Glasson Deschaumes and Rada Ivekovic (New Delhi: Routledge, 2003): 22.
2. Thus, a commentator on ethnic politics in India, writing in 1978, for instance, defines the minorities as 'an appreciable subsystem' within

'an environing society'. See, R. A. Schermerhorm, *Ethnic Plurality in India* (Tucson: University of Arizona Press, 1978): 16. I have discussed elsewhere how minorities have emerged in postcolonial South Asia through the event of Partition (1947) and the consequent reorganization of international borders in the region. See Samir Kumar Das, 'Governing Minority Rights?' in *Political Governance and Minority Rights: The South and South East Asian Scenario,* edited by Lipi Ghosh (New Delhi: Routledge, 2009): 199-216.

3. Summing up this literature, Balakrishnan observes: 'At its best, imagined nationhood in all its crudity has been the entry ticket for the wretched of the earth into world history'. See Gopal Balakrishnan, 'The National Imagination', in *Mapping the Nation,* edited by Gopal Balakrishnan (London: Verso, 1996): 212.
4. This period has been chronicled in Tilly's classic work. See Charles Tilly, ed, *The Formation of National States in Western Europe* (Princeton: Princeton University Press, 1975).
5. In South Asia, nations did not create borders; borders created nations. Critical studies in borders are slowly appearing now. The works of Ranabir Samaddar and Sanjay Chaturvedi deserve special mention.
6. Some of these 'contradictions' have been highlighted in the debate on sovereignty in the South Asian context intermittently serialized in the pages of *Economic and Political Weekly* during July-December 2005.
7. David Nirenberg, *Communities of Violence: Persecution of Minorities in the Middle Ages* (Princeton NJ: Princeton University Press, 1996): 6.
8. Ranabir Samaddar, *The Materiality of Politics,* vol.1 (London: Anthem Press, 2007): 133-88.
9. See, for instance, Ratna Naidu, *Communal Edge to Plural Societies: India and Malaysia* (New Delhi: Vikas, 1980).
10. In South Asia, such terms as 'tribe' and 'tribal' are freely used both in official circles and in popular parlance without necessarily any of their otherwise derogatory meanings.
11. See Samir Kumar Das, 'Identity and Frontiers in International Relations Research', in *Understanding Global Politics: Issues and Trends* edited by Anindyo J Majumdar and Shibashis Chatterjee (New Delhi: Lancer Books, 2004): 97-122.
12. At a more theoretical level, the exercise was made by Saskia Sassen. See Saskia Sassen, *Territory-Authority-Rights: From Medieval to Global Assemblages* (Princeton: Princeton University Press, 2006): 289-90.
13. S. Basu Ray Chaudhury, 'An India Charter for Minority Rights', in *Key Texts on Social Justice,* vol.4, Sage Series on State of Social Justice in India, edited by S Roohi and R Samaddar (New Delhi: Sage, 2009): 334-72.

14. In Ashutosh Varshney, ed. *The Indian Paradox: Essays in Indian Politics* (New Delhi: Sage 1989): 39-75.
15. For a very crisp statement of how the 'central symbols' diffuse themselves in a hegemonic manner across the body politic irrespective of the social divisions that mark the majorities from minorities, see David Forgacs, 'National-Popular': Genealogy of a Concept', in *The Cultural Studies Reader* edited by Simon During (London: Routledge, 1993): 178-90.
16. I borrow the phrase from Amarjeet Singh Narang, who used it in his keynote address to the workshop on 'Minorities and Their Alienation' organized by CRG in Kolkata on 8 August 2009.
17. See, for instance, Ranabir Samaddar, ed, *The Politics of Autonomy: Indian Experiences* (New Delhi: Sage, 2005).
18. Samir Kumar Das,: 'The Founding Moment: Social Justice in a Constitutional Mirror', in *Justice and Law: The Limits of the Deliverables of Law,* edited by Ashok Agrwaal and Bharat Bhushan (New Delhi: Sage, 2009: 64-99).
19. Veena Das, 'The Signature of the State: The Paradox of Illegality', in *Anthropology in the Margins of the State,* edited by Veena Das and Deborah Poole (New Delhi: Oxford University Press, 2004).
20. See Emma Tarlo, *Unsettling Memories: Narratives of India's 'Emergency'* (Delhi: Permanent Black, 2003).
21. A good deal of literature is centred on these themes. See Thomas Blom Hansen, *Urban Violence in India: Identity Politics, 'Mumbai' and the Post-Colonial City* (New Delhi: Permanent Black, 2001). Malini Sur presented her findings at a workshop on 'Gender and Non-Traditional Formulations of Security in South Asia' organized by Women in Conflict Management, Security and Peace in New Delhi on 24-25 September 2006. Studies by Bertil Lintner and others on the drug barons and arms syndicates in North Western Pakistan, Afghanistan, in Myanmar and Thailand attest to the autonomous nature of their functioning.
22. Michael Hardt and Antonio Negri, *Empire* (Cambridge, Ma: Harvard University Press, 2000): 413.

Part I

Minorities of South Asia

1

HUNDRED YEARS OF RESEARCH ON MINORITIES IN SOUTH ASIA: Towards a New Agenda

SAMIR KUMAR DAS and RANABIR SAMADDAR

EMPIRES OR IMPERIAL states always had an awareness that several communities, some major, some minor, inhabited imperial societies, and besides the subjects professing the religion of the state there were other faiths and other religious communities as subjects of the empire. These other groups, 'the minority religious communities', would at times get special favourable treatment from the emperor and the imperial administration, at times be subjected to harsh treatment, particularly when suspected of disloyalty or of hiding wealth. The histories of the Ottoman, Austro-Hungarian, Mughal empires (the empires of the late Middle Ages and the early modern age), bear this out. We can also say that while this was a situation bearing out the existence of proto-minorities, yet the societies and states were not majoritarian societies and states, and official majority-minority situations and policies did not exist. We can call this policy and situation as being produced out of a reason of state (raison d'état). This reason of state had more to do with considerations of the empire's security, occasional requirements relating to revenue and taxation, and the anxiety that the divine power the empire represented must not be threatened by any other notion or belief in divinity. This was the divine reason that mixed with imperial reasons and produced the reason of state. Even if the state in question was not an empire, but a monarchy, it would always and invariably be a strong centralized state. Reasons of state, laws, centralization (which meant the gradual formation of standing professional armies) went together.

We are, however, discussing not an issue exemplifying the reason of state, but *reason of government:* minorities being produced not as a consequence of raison d'état, but out of governmental history. Governmental reason has relation with state reason, which overlaps, but governmental rationality has its specific ways of functioning, such as reasons of managing culture, turning an anonymous mass of population into identifiable, governable population units, laying down norms of representation through elections, combining the policy of guaranteeing rights with ensuring methods of control of the subjects who are becoming citizens, an agenda of creating a society that would be synonymous with a governable whole, adding political value to number (statistics), and so on. Security, taxation, and revenue-raising still remain important, but they now become parts of a vast repertoire of governing methods and technologies of rule. The significant question here is: Where does the nation stand in this division of state reason and governmental reason (and transformation from the former to the latter)? We can guess the answer, namely, that the nation as a form of political society stands on the divide, the intersection of the two. It means that it builds on both kinds of reason. Considerations of national security, national representation (known as national will), and national administration and governance, all these three factors, predicate the emergence and the perpetuation of the modern minority problematic. There is a factor, however, that marks the histories of all these three considerations: the colonial past, which is a part and parcel of the nation question. In this respect the histories of Europe and South Asia bear similarities. Both regions carry the *post-colonial predicament,* which is as follows: how to democratize the nation/region to such an extent that minority as category of powerlessness vanishes (that is, numbers lose political value). We are aware that democracy and modern nationhood, having roots in the colonial past, create what may be called fictive ethnicities, majority-centric values and passions, and hierarchic structure with regard to access to resources—in short the minority question.

We must keep in mind these dynamics in order to appreciate how knowledge of minorities has been produced, what and how policies have guided the research agenda, and how changes in these policies have occurred. While this chapter deals with the Indian situation in particular, readers of this book will find similarities and commonalities with situations in other South Asian countries. Equally significantly, the readers will realize the closeness with various European situations in which the once-colonized *other* finds its past as well as possible futures.

Thus as we begin this report with a brief description of India's colonial past whence began the project of 'knowing the minorities', it will be good to recall the European situation in order to be cognizant of the likely directions that the postcolonial project of 'knowing the minorities' can take. We must not be astonished at the fact that the compulsion to 'know the minorities' is the same in both cases, in India and Europe: namely, retaining liberal democracy, nationhood, and encouraging trans-national links. The question is the same (of course, again broadly speaking): Can liberal democracy abolish the 'minority question' while retaining its principal modes? This question propels most of the researches. At the same time, for us the more specific question will be: What specific rationality today determines the existence of the minorities as a problem and thus what is the specific reason guiding today's researches on minorities?

Europe, as we know, produced its minorities out of the long religious wars, Napoleonic wars followed by other national wars, collapse of the two empires (Austro-Hungarian and Ottoman), and then the inter-state wars of the nineteenth and twentieth centuries. The process continued till the last decade of the twentieth century, when several national minorities emerged in the wake of the collapse of socialism and the transition in Eastern Europe. Once again wars followed, and then new minorities emerged everywhere in form of the itinerant communities, indigenous population groups, immigrants, indicating at times a return of the minority question. Yet we must also remember that this history has been marked by several attempts to innovate conflict resolution mechanisms (such as partition, different autonomous arrangements, international and regional guarantee mechanisms, treaties, inspection, standard-setting exercises by the European Union, courts of human rights, charters of rights, Organization of Security and Co-operation in Europe, functions such as commiserating on the observance of human rights norms, particularly minority rights, punitive provisions, Council of Europe mechanisms, and so on). Treaties to protect minorities have marked the last two centuries. In many cases new constitutionalism also has set norms and mechanisms for minority protection. In terms of relevance of this history, we can say that *(a)* the European experiences of the simultaneous expansion of nationalism and democracy, *(b)* recognition and protection of minority rights in the wake of this double expansion, *(c)* regionalization of the issue and mechanisms, and *(d)* the emergence of a body of laws present for the post-colonial world a likely scenario towards which the minority question may evolve in countries like India. Yet, in spite of all these developments, the nationalist legacy and the colonial residues have remained strong in Europe. Added to these two factors now there is a renewed concern with security often affecting minority communities. Multiculturalism as a consequence is now regarded as having mixed success. No wonder, studies on minorities, concerned policies, definitional quibbles, constitutional-juridical readings, legal commentaries, sociological researches, economic studies, analyses of cultural institutions, linguistic studies, and finally the security scenario—all these studies propelled inter-governmental programmes, inter-university researches, various foundations, research grant schemes, human rights bodies—bear the marks of the ways the minority question has emerged in Europe in the last two hundred years, and re-emerges today. We can also see how these studies bear the mark of the shifting locus of rationality—from reason of state to governmental reason (a transformation we have briefly portrayed just now), also an increasing mix of the two. As a consequence we have also new lights on issues of sovereignty, rights, welfare doctrine, and rule of law, for after all the minority issue hurts most the established ideas and notions on all these four.

We can see the same shift taking place in India: how imperial and state reasons have gradually given way here also to governmental considerations, how the two considerations have overlapped, and how knowledge of minorities produced out of scholarly investigations, administrative inquiries, government policies, funding strategies for beneficiaries and mega research programmes have followed the trail of power in the form of state and governmental rationalities. But we must equally appreciate that not all knowledges are primarily marked by considerations of policies and governmental reasons; there are minor knowledges on what is conventionally termed as the minority question: knowledges that break the boundaries of the historical liberal project of 'knowing the minorities' and can give us rare glimpses into possible solutions to the most vexing question of democratic deficit, namely, how to redress the inadequacy of democracy, which tries to solve the minority problematic through the governmental mode. But this further means that we cannot make a neat typology of these encoded forms of knowledge. Such a classificatory exercise while serving some heuristic purpose should not be taken very formally, because research policies and the resultant knowledges may reflect the same state of mixed reasons and legitimacies.

The mix of rationality we are referring to was evident from the first well-known tract or report in India on 'the minorities'. Lord Mayo, who on assuming the post of the Viceroy of India (1868) had expressed his determination to 'put down Wahabeeism in India as [he] had put down Fenianism in Ireland', had engaged W. W. Hunter to conduct an inquiry into whether Muslims were bound by their religion to rebel against the Queen. Mayo's brief to Hunter was clearly around the 'vexed question of loyalty' in those transitional times of post-Mutiny India. Yet Hunter cautioned against war-like measures adopted by a civilian administration against a section of subject population. But as town after town on the frontier on the West in the last decade of the nineteenth century was razed to the ground and the frontier was ablaze in those closing years, of the colonial officials Sir William Hunter was one of the first to realize this when he wrote of the 'chronic conspiracy within our territory'. Any inquiry into the dynamics of knowledge and power in the colonial project of knowing the minorities must therefore begin with W. W. Hunter, the Director General of Statistics, who had written on being commissioned by Lord Mayo, *Our Indian Mussulmans: Are They Bound in Conscience to Rebel against the Queen?* (1876, reprint 2002). Hunter's work was quickly followed, in fact in little over 30 years, by the Morley-Minto Report and the reforms the Report suggested in terms of instituting separate electorate for religious communities. After the Morley-Minto Reforms came other reports, commissions (notably the Simon Commission, 1927), recommendations, awards, and when the Constituent Assembly finally met in the backdrop of the Great Partition, the situation was marked by several competing discourses each backed by enormous scholarly outputs.

Researches on aspects such as multi-cultural existence, presence of multi-faith communities, norms of protection, fundamental rights, rule of law, uniformity of civil code, linguistic minorities, indigenous population groups, high values of the nation, representational modes, violence on minorities, riots, virtues of majority strength, protection strategies such as reservation were already on. The Constituent Assembly proceedings show the clash of various discourses and provide us with clues regarding ways in which subsequent researches would develop, including those propelled by considerations of national unity, national integration, secularism, or regulated autonomy, as well as those propelled by liberal societal considerations of augmenting social capital and trust networks, enlightenment, managing political behaviours of communities, and improving modes of governance. Awareness in various forms remains: awareness of rights including women's rights, right to autonomy, fundamental liberties, of the need to democratize administration and, most importantly, the need to persist with rights-based arguments in face of an overwhelming atmosphere of national (in)security, and finally an awareness of social justice, most recently illustrated by the debates on the provisions for positive discrimination. All this is indicated by a still evolving juridical discourse (based on case laws, judicial interpretation, legislations, commentaries, constitutional provisions, and international human rights laws).

Yet this juridical discourse is as much legal, administrative, and political discourse, also reflecting the continuing clashes over norms, resources, social and material spaces, and political opportunities. These clashes (particularly the accounts of the riots) are also biographies of political entrepreneurs who have risen through the ranks of community mobilizations; these are also testimonies of what is called, 'opportunity hoarding' (a situation, when members of a categorically bounded network acquire access to a resource that it considers valuable, renewable, supportive of the network, and enhanced by the network's modus operandi, and thus subject to monopolistic control), 'the root of persistent or durable inequality'. As readers go through this book, they will see the footprints of the political scene on the ways knowledge has been produced in form of various discourses. To say the least, this phenomenon continues till this day, and what is to be noted in the present context of discussion is that the knowledge produced in this way becomes subsequently a part of the problem. Finally, all these also demonstrate how governmental imperatives and rationality (as examples we can refer to all the issues mentioned in the preceding and this paragraph) that began with a specific raison d'état (recall how Hunter was commissioned and what he finally wrote), now overwhelm researches and research policies. Our political imagination as a consequence is today severely constricted.

Readers will appreciate this point if they take particular notice of the institutional locations of these researches. The institutional story is significant in any comprehensive mapping exercise on the production of knowledge on minorities, and the formation of various discourses. The various governmental institutions in India on studies in social sciences, Indian Council of Historical Research (ICHR), Indian Council of Social Science Research (ICSSR), Indian Council of Philosophical Research (ICPR), social sciences associations (IHC, IPSA, ISC) have promoted a distinct type of research, marked by social science discourses. National human rights institutions (NHRC, NMC, and NCSC and ST and various state counterparts) have produced their distinctive type of knowledge, emphasizing socio-economic inquiries. There are some minority bodies, which have produced a distinct rights-centric narrative of minorities.[1] People have produced resource handbooks. Foreign academia has also been a prominent actor in this field, bringing in research paradigms that bear the mark of different liberal and neo-liberal thinking. Finally human rights organizations (PUCL, PUDR, APCLC, APDR, and so on) foundations, particularly human rights foundations, have encouraged rights-sensitive writings. These institutionalized knowledges reflect on property relations, state of legality and legitimacy, possibilities of autonomy, state of the rights' discourse, anthropological views of communities, and their past and current histories. It is important to keep this map in mind because it brings out the contradictory nature of the situation: These institutionalized researches, almost all or at least the majority of them, begin with the assumption that India is a democracy, that *rule of law* exists; only the quality of governance is low. And then faced with the starkly physical nature of violence, dispossession, attrition, and social war, they end with emphasizing the need to strengthen the rule of law, while certainly suggesting some new governmental measures. In their attempt to comprehend the new social rationality (new in the sense of being post-colonial, independent, free, democratic, and encouraging the ethos of what is conceived of as civil society) that tolerates and reproduces discrimination, often pushing discrimination to dispossession, their tools are all old, marked by conventional governmental ideas. The ideal of governance, which can make up for the democratic deficit, remains the unreachable, always deferred, goal inspiring these researches. By the same logic, therefore, they remain caught up in the mix of raison d'état and governmentality, producing in the process a sense of what the sociologist Chetan Bhatt calls 'hyper-governmentality'.[2]

While the anxiety concerning the minorities, particularly the Muslims, marked British colonial policy towards India since the late nineteenth century, the year 2008 marks the hundredth anniversary of the policy of reservation for the minorities in government-run educational institutions and offices. This chapter proposes to *(a)* make an assessment of the research policies and resources on the minorities of South Asia and argues that the current research boom in the field under review is seldom associated with any coherent research policy being followed in the region, and *(b)* raise a few questions and issues that remain un-addressed in the existing body of researches. It seeks to draw the outline of a new research agenda that might guide future researches in South Asia with a view to provide them with better constitutional, legal and political protection. Although this chapter proposes to take stock of research policies and practices concerning the minorities of South Asia, it is mostly and certainly not exclusively centred on India. For a good part of these hundred years, India remained undivided and her geopolitical centrality in South Asia even after Partition and subsequent reorganization of international borders, as we will see, has played a great role in shaping and influencing research policies and practices towards the minorities in the rest of South Asia.

CONTEMPORARY RESEARCH BOOM SANS CENTRAL RESEARCH POLICY

Compared to earlier researches, institutionally conducted researches on the minorities of contemporary India do not speak of any centrally coordinated research policy. Researches on minorities in South Asia are conducted at various levels. While the state continues to play an important role in encouraging and sponsoring higher education in most of the South Asian countries, various statutory agencies like the University Grants Commission, Indian Council of Social Science Research (ICSSR) in India enjoy varying forms of autonomy vis-à-vis the state. Although funded in a very substantial way, universities are seldom directly controlled by the state. But it is true that most of the institutions of higher education have to function within the state's broad policy framework and researches on minorities constitute one of the top priority areas in the list maintained by University Grants Commission in India. Besides, researches in certain minority-concentrated areas receive special grants-in-aid as in the case of India's Northeast. All the ministries including that of Human Resource Development directly under the jurisdiction of the Government of India have to keep 10 per cent of their budgetary allocation for the Northeast and the money gets accumulated in the non-lapsable pool of the central exchequer. The availability of funds has given a new, albeit unsustainable, fillip to researches on India's Northeast. While it has triggered off a new spate of researches on the minorities in South Asia, the state or for that matter its statutory agencies have very little control over the findings and outputs of such research. Researches driven by the imperative necessity of fund utilization have very little shelf life and do not reflect that any consistent policy has been followed in the field under review. In a country like India the state has very little control, if at all, for example, over the kind of Ph.D. dissertations being done from different university schools and research institutes. The states of South Asia may have a policy towards the minorities, but not on researches conducted on them.

A good deal of researches on the minorities roll out of the research institutes and centres of higher education beyond the established institutional framework. International Centre for Ethnic Studies (Sri Lanka), Lokayan of the Centre for the Study of Developing Societies and Calcutta Research Group (CRG), both in India, provide some examples. While most of the senior members of the faculty and researchers (along with some activists) happen to be associated with various universities and research centres, insofar as they work under institutional auspices, they are not obliged to follow the state's rules and regulations. Research centres like CRG enjoy comparatively greater autonomy than the established universities and research centres. It evidently follows a research policy that *(a)* provides its researches a collective and coherent focus, *(b)* breaks new directions and coordinates researches conducted under their aegis, and *(c)* serves as centre of policy advocacy. The spate of violence that followed the 'demolition' of the historic Babri mosque in Ayodhya (1992) and the Gujarat riots (2002) in India, post-election violence against the religious minorities in Bangladesh in 1996 and subsequently in 2001 have been instrumental in producing a number of investigative reports and researches. Most of them have been done beyond the state auspices and are very critical of the state policies towards the minorities. Of late, countries of South Asia have witnessed a steady growth of this variety of centres and institutions.[3] Moreover, there is another genre of researches, which is commissioned by a proliferating body of state institutions such as National Human Rights Commissions, National Women's Commissions, National Commission for Scheduled Castes and Scheduled Tribes, National Commission for Minorities, and so on, and their state equivalents. Besides, researches based on individual initiatives are by no means rare, particularly in a country like India. Such researches are made known to us only by their publications.

Researches on the minorities, in other words, are conducted at various levels, sometimes acting at cross-purposes with one another. In the absence of a clearly laid out, central and coherent research policy on minorities, we find considerable difficulties in assessing it. We propose to compare the present researches with a state in which researches are conducted without any central policy guiding, directing or administering them. Strange but true, the current research boom on the minorities does not seem to coincide with the presence of any central and commanding research policy. As we argue in this fashion, we need to add a couple of caveats lest we should be misunderstood: First, this should not give us the impression that what we call the current research boom has resulted in only haphazard and scattered researches on the minorities. Quite the contrary, it is possible to trace the sources of the current boom to discourses on the minorities circulating within the larger society. The discourse makes it possible to raise only a given body of issues and questions and not others. The point is: researches on minorities today are guided more by the reasons of government than by those of the state. The dominant discourses prevailing and circulating within the society and contributing in no small measure to its government have acquired a measure of autonomy from the state. Second and complementary to the first, while the current research boom is still in this state, this does not mean that framing a research policy is either impossible or unwarranted. In fact, we need to raise some issues and questions from within the mandate of our project so that we can change the terms of our present discourses. Research policy in that sense can serve as a catalyst for changing the terms of our ongoing discourses.

This chapter proposes to *(a)* raise a few issues and questions that have hitherto remained un-addressed in the existing stock of researches by way of assessing the research policies and practices, and *(b)* accordingly call for designing our research policy in a way that will prepare us for a discourse shift. The discourse shift envisaged in our project intends to *(a)* study country-specific constitutional and legal experiences within a comparative framework;[4] *(b)* take stock of the regional and supra-national sources of standards-setting initiatives in South Asia; and *(c)* probe into the best practices and model cases of minority protection and resolution of minority problems and explore the possibility of disseminating them.

A BRIEF ASSESSMENT OF RESEARCH POLICIES

Researches on the minorities in South Asia in general and in India in particular have been highly uneven in character and there is reason to think that these have primarily built on the general institutional practices and discourses circulating within the larger society. British administrative writings seemed keen on tracing the essentially divergent nature of Indian society and its innate inability to form a homogeneous nation. Since many of the groups do not form parts of any single nation, the term 'majority' or 'minority' becomes irrelevant unless their nationhood is recognized. More than branding a group as a majority or a minority, it was interested in discovering how they could be held together without interrupting the colonial rule. Colonial policy for a considerable length of time was guided by reasons of state. Thus with the initiation of the Morley-Minto reforms of 1909 referred to earlier, began an era of reserving seats and posts in government establishments and decision-making bodies so that minorities did not feel threatened by the political institutions oriented to serve the majorities. British ethnographic writings are replete with racial and ethnic stereotypes (like 'martial races', 'criminal tribes') that in their combination refuse to make India a nation. Besides, the colonial rulers also made an implicit distinction between the 'primitives' and the 'savages' residing in India's Northeast who did not deserve to be 'ruled' and 'civilized' and the 'subjects' who had 'submitted to our authority' and for whom 'white men had a burden'. Parts of the Northeast never constituted parts of British India and were administered as a 'frontier' by them. Given that Indians do not form a nation, the mediation of the British, as this genre of writings would have us believe, in holding the society together can never be doubted. This discourse gradually gave birth to the idea that the Hindus and the Muslims form 'two nations' who are entitled to two 'sovereign' states to be carved out by partitioning the subcontinent once the colonial rulers stage their exit.

The first batch of historians who became interested in studies in the minorities is also known as the Cambridge School (for their association with Cambridge University) represented by such eminent scholars as Anil Seal, James Gallaghar, John W. Broomfield and Rajat Ray, and others. Starting from the assumption that India is a land of minorities where numerous majorities are distributed at various layers and levels of society and polity—in their favourite phrase 'locality-province-nation'—thereby preventing them from forming one homogeneous entity, the school draws our attention to the extremely strategic and contingent nature of the political alliances that are designed and brought into existence by different elite groups claiming to represent diverse ethnic groups in relation to power: whether to acquire it or to dislodge others who have been successful in already acquiring it. The contestation over power determines the dynamics of diverse alliances between elite groups. The essentially minority nature of the components of these alliances confers on the alliances certain flexibility and temporality that also serve as an antidote to their homogenization, entrenchment and durability. Besides, the shifting nature of the alliances also provides scope for new leaderships and elites to emerge and further contest any form of political entrenchment by the already established elites. These alliances have a two-fold impact of democratizing the power base by constantly extending and making power available to newer claimants and de-ethnicizing and secularizing the claims of ethnic groups and minorities. By virtue of entering into alliances with others, ethnic groups are called upon to shed their exclusivist and ethnic character and discover issues that are common with those of others. The Neo-Cambridge school, a contemporary version of the early Cambridge school, points to the constantly expanding nature of the power base in South Asia. The writings on factional politics in Bengal, Uttar Pradesh and South India are a case in point. The involvement of castes in politics in India in the famous words of a very eminent political scientist resulted not in 'casteization of politics', but 'politicization of castes'.

It seems that the Cambridge School has run a full circle. While at one level it is now widely recognized that the dispersal of political layers and levels has become almost complete with the advent of globalization and loosening control of the states over their populations, including the minorities, the imperatives of elite alliances have started working in reverse. Emma Tarlow's study on the Sikh minorities who have been victims of the anti-Sikh pogroms organized across India in the wake of Indira Gandhi's assassination in 1984 in the hands of her Sikh bodyguards speaks of the new compulsions of local politics over which the regional and national politicians have little or no control. Hansen's study on the street politics of Bombay/Mumbai bears testimony to the complex nature of processes that have helped sever the connection between the national and the local and contribute to the latter's emergence as an autonomous terrain. They are, as it were, forced to come to terms with the new realities, and minority politics today refuses to be subsumed under the elitist models. Minority politics is also visited by the sudden torrents of mass politics that the Cambridge historians fail to appreciate.

The state's policy towards the minorities is best exemplified by the Constituent Assembly debates in India: one of the most prolonged debates in history on the question of minorities in any country. The philosophy of the state has attracted some scholarly attention in recent years. Partition, according to Bishnu Mohapatra, represented a traumatic event to the Indian elite and paradigmatic shift in the state's vision of minorities insofar as it sparked off paranoic fears about the Muslim minorities.[5] Thus, when the issue of reservation of seats and jobs for the Muslims was discussed on the floor and the subcommittee set up for the purpose recommended it, the framers of the Constitution scotched if off on the ground that 'they opted for Pakistan'. In simple terms, they were in favour of making a distinction between the minorities who declare them as nations like the Muslims and the national minorities like the Scheduled Castes and the Scheduled Tribes, often synonymously used as 'Hindu minorities'. The Constitution provided a template that also tamed and transformed the minorities declaring them as nations into national minorities and shunned any reservation or special provisions for them.[6] Summing up the whole debate as well as its record of minority protection during the last six decades, Samaddar observes that the Indian state looked upon the minorities as objects of 'government' rather than rights-bearing subjects.[7] While much has been written about the backwardness of the Muslims laid down in the recently released Sachar Committee report on them, the same tradition of viewing the minorities as objects of government and power continues since the late-colonial times.

The early Marxists were probably the first to have brought the phenomena of violence and riots to the centre-stage of social and political inquiry. Moin Shakir's pioneering study on *Politics of the Minorities* (1979)[8] shows how violence and riots between the communities serve no collective interest of any of the communities involved in them. Instead, they are organized by their respective elites who take advantage of the pre-existing religious differences and exploit them while pursuing their own narrow social and economic interests. The division between religious majority and religious minority, according to him, has no material basis and is intended to breach the growing 'revolutionary unity' amongst the masses.

Thus the more economic conditions worsen and revolutionary unity is in the process of coming into being, the more such divisive forces are played out in order to keep people's opposition divided and tide over the social and economic crisis. 'Communalism' and 'minority-ism' therefore constitute an ideology: a 'false consciousness' that stands in the way to the development of 'revolutionary unity' amongst the masses. People do participate in riots but they surely lack agency and fall prey to elitist machinations. A series of studies conducted on the riots having taken place in the 1970s and the early 1980s, particularly in Maharashtra, Uttar Pradesh and Bihar, point out in greater detail how the relative affluence and prosperity of the Muslim elite in brassware, stitching (particularly *zari, zardozi* and *chikankari*) and other such industries were sought to be contested and stalled by a rising Hindu elite by way of accentuating and widening the communal divide and mobilizing their respective communities against each other. The reverse has also been true.[9] A 'scientific' and revolutionary ideology that is capable of transcending the religious divide between the majority and the minority needs to be brought from outside in order to make a social revolution possible in the countries of South Asia. Not all Marxists however agree with Shakir on this issue. Asghar Ali Engineer's comparatively recent writings, for instance, question the very thesis of 'pre-existing religious differences'. While at one level religions in India including Islam have been 'syncretic', 'plural' and 'tolerant' unlike in other parts—thanks to the specificity of Indian culture that has made them so—at another, any 'revolutionary ideology' that makes the claim of becoming popular cannot be completely divorced from the cultural context within which it operates and must draw on its 'progressive elements' in order to remain rooted to it. The otherwise 'secular' cultural tradition of Kashmir, according to him, is in jeopardy insofar as the 'fundamentalists' take over and a composite and syncretic Islam of Kashmir (*Kashmiriyat*) undergoes radical transformation.[10]

While the exact nature of Indian culture has been a source of conflicting interpretations amongst the Marxists as we have just pointed out, it is now widely believed that violence and riots cannot be attributed to the diversity of religions per se in South Asia. The transformation of loose and composite 'faith' that existed in history into 'organized religion' with its inviolably sacred text and a determinate ecclesiastical authority under conditions of modernity, as suggested by Ashis Nandy, is said to lie at the root of violence and riots. In other words, interfaith differences did not necessarily push their adherents into conflicts and riots. It is only with the advent of modernity and the modern state's 'statistical' enumeration of populations through census operations into neat and precise categories that such populations started differentiating themselves from one another. There are communities across countries of South Asia (like the nomadic snake-charmers) whose religious identities are not definable, at least not clearly so. It is only with the introduction of modern census operations that such people are obliged to state their religious identities in contradistinction with what they consider as their other. Violence and riots according to this streak of sociological writings are catalyzed not so much by cultural traditions of South Asia but very much by the advent of modernity and most importantly by the introduction of modern governmental technologies by the modern secular state.[11] A more or less similar view was reiterated by Madan:

> The religious, traditional view of life has not really been the source of conflict between peoples, that it is the perversion which has been so. The scope of interreligious understanding is . . . immense, and it is in no way contradicted by the holism of religious traditions of mankind. And yet one surely may not turn a blind eye to the conflicts between religious communities which have for so long caused untold suffering to innocent people everywhere. The historicity of such conflicts does not however, constitute an argument against religion or signify its

> irrelevance; it only points to the unrealized promise of cultural pluralism.[12]

While the debate is continuing and shows no sign of subsiding in the near future, it took a slightly different turn with the intervention of the multiculturalists and social capital theorists. The project is more or less the same for both these streams of scholars. What they basically intend to achieve is convert the minorities from a political category of powerlessness into a simple numerical statement so much so that as a category, it loses all political salience. Both, in other words, seem interested in depoliticizing the category. The importance of some 'basic values' (like popular sovereignty, individual rights and human dignity) in holding the mutually hostile communities together under one social and political fabric can never be denied. But on the one hand, a group of multiculturalists express their doubt over whether such values are already existent in the prevalent religious traditions of South Asia. In this respect, the state as a secular and external agency can serve as a harbinger of social reform and transformation. As Rajeev Bhargava argues: 'The removal of oppression and subordination has been a function of a successful and democratic state. The state has had to democratically intervene in religious and cultural practices to get rid of oppressive practices'.[13] On the other hand, there are others amongst the multiculturalists who in fact emphasize on the important role that non-state agencies, particularly strong social networks, play in building strong 'civic ties'. Varshney's study on as many as six riot-affected cities of contemporary India, for example, shows how the existence of such strong 'civic ties' cutting across communities and often facilitated by the state and quite ironically its security agencies (as in the case of Bhiwandi), serves as an effective antidote to the occurrence of communal and ethnic riots.[14] His study (true to Putnam's writings on social capital) treats communal and civic ties as two clearly separate and separable categories. A few studies on the other hand point out how civic ties at times have a 'regressive effect' on structures of conflict resolution and peacemaking.[15] Moreover, Varshney's analysis does not seem to take into account the role of heterodoxies within Hinduism and Islam in India and the role they play in mitigating Hindu-Muslim conflicts. Similarly, in all these writings there is seldom any reference to civic ties that cut across the existing international borders. The writings of both these streams of multiculturalists aptly show how democratic state and civil society complement each other in depoliticizing the minorities and contribute to the overall governmental operations.

With the introduction of the Subaltern School to history since the late 1970s by Ranajit Guha and his associates, researches on the minorities have changed substantially over the years. The School critiques the earlier schools of having denied agency and subjectivity to the subalterns including the minorities of indigenous peoples, the ex-untouchables, the dalits (the 'ground down') and the tribal[16] communities, women and children, linguistic and sexual minorities and minority religious cults and so on and so forth. Even if agency and subjectivity are extended to them, they encompass only the elites that have slowly grown amongst them and not the common people. The Subaltern School brings their agency and subjectivity to the centre-stage of history by making at least two very significant departures: One, the agency and subjectivity of the subalterns consisting of a motley group of people, mentioned above, are expressed through everyday resistance in ways specific to them. The culturally defined means of minority resistance are highlighted in their writings. Minorities instead of becoming objects of protection become the agents and makers of history. Two, and this follows from the above, minority resistance does not necessarily hold society together. Nor does it abide by the requirements of networking and strategic resistance. The School tends to write history in its ruptures and fissures. Minorities do not write the same history inhabited by the majorities; their histories run parallel to those of others. Historical narratives are separate and separable. Their separation is a precondition of unearthing the significance of minority politics. Minority history is not a history that is added to it as a minor appendix, but a history by its own right with its own archive that can be made sense of only by deploying critical reading strategies. Subaltern consciousness has its paradigmatic features outlined in Guha's epoch-making work *Elementary Aspects of Peasant Insurgency in Colonial India.*

A comparatively recent stream of writings led by such scholars as Paul R. Brass, Philip Oldenburg, Lloyd and Susanne Rudolph and others, based mainly in the US schools and universities, emphasizes the 'embedded' nature of minority politics and the riots and pogroms in South Asia that take a toll on these countries, particularly during the last one and half decades. Riots are seldom, according to them, one-shot events, whose impact gets exhausted with their happening, but are deeply embedded in narratives and discourses that lend different meanings to them at different times of history. The circulation of and contest over these narratives and discourses make the reality of riots and pogroms not only unknown but also unknowable so much so that these are as it were 'produced' through them. Viewed in that sense, understanding riots and pogroms in South Asia is a cent percent political act. As Brass argues:

> The struggle to control the representation of riots is . . . one to cast and divert blame. If the people are responsible, the government is not to blame. If the government is not to blame, the argument can also be made that its powers and authority need strengthening in order to prevent further such events. If the police are blamed, then the politicians are saved. If the politicians are blamed, then the police may be freed from blame and their hands and those of their supporters strengthened in state and society. It is, in fact, one of the most astonishing features of riots that the very process of casting blame widely, of justifying,

> explaining, and interpreting riots contributes to the failure to prosecute the perpetrators of violence even when their identities are well known.[17]

These narratives and discourses are used in structuring the relations: 'to define the majority and minority, to differentiate the loyal from the disloyal, the weak and the strong, those that are privileged and the disprivileged, and to distribute rewards and punishments'. Thus, our notions of the minorities (like 'Muslims are headstrong and intolerant' and that they are 'out and out disloyal to India', and so on) are deeply embedded in these widely shared narratives and discourses. Accordingly, the state discourse too is not neutral to the majority Hindus and the minority Muslims by way of offering to mediate between them, but is based on 'an imagined nation which defines those who are not part of the 'nation' as 'minorities' who must accept a secondary position within the state.'[18]

It seems that minorities have become a hot topic of researches in South Asia, thanks to the initiatives taken by some of the leading civil society groups like SAFHR, Calcutta Research Group and Lokayan and others. At one level, they too emphasize on the dispersal of levels and layers in the body politic that have made the functioning of the established democratic dispensation in India based predominantly on the majoritarian principle problematic. Both systematic exclusion of the minorities and active discrimination have severely impaired the democratic framework. At another level, the state continues to proceed with the old principles and institutions. States are slow in thinking about institutional reforms to accommodate this situation. Political parties based on the principle of interest aggregation for gathering popular support are becoming increasingly incapable of representing the emerging minority interests that refuse to be aggregated into the larger wholes. Lokayan in particular has been flagging these issues for a long time and drawing our attention to the cases of emerging mediating institutions that are at the forefront of the new social movements.

ISSUES AND QUESTIONS

While most of the studies in South Asia focus on minorities within their respective countries, there have been very little, if at all, in the existing literature either by way of comparing them or discovering their continuities and linkages. The researches on the minorities in South Asia reflect little pan-regional awareness. Historical and cultural continuities provide as it were an ideal case for comparing the minorities across the countries of the region. This practice of studying the minorities within their national frontiers in isolated ways speaks of the persisting impact that the framework of nation-states makes on the research agenda and the typical nationalist fear ('cartographic anxiety') that any cross-border linkages and continuities between minorities are a potential or actual threat to the sovereignty and integrity of the states of South Asia. Minorities are held by the nation-states first of all as 'national minorities' and therefore fall under their sovereign domain. Governing the minorities in this context has turned into a problem of 'emplacing' them within a national body. After all, minorities as a category of powerlessness can wither away only by being governmentalized (variously termed as 'domesticated', 'institutionalized' and 'routinized' in the literature) into 'national minorities'. 'National minorities' may be numerically smaller groups but certainly not disempowered groups as long as they form part of a nation. Entry into the nation is the means of empowering the minorities.

Besides, any comparison between minorities across the countries of South Asia is likely to reflect on the relative performances of the states vis-à-vis the minorities within their respective countries and has the potential of being used and exploited by others. States of South Asia not quite known for being friendly to one another have the record of humiliating their rivals in diplomatic, regional and international forums on the count of discriminatorily treating their minorities. Any comparison reflecting on the state performances in this regard is likely to be politically volatile, if not inflammable. One can therefore say that the practice of studying the minorities within their respective 'national' settings is as old as the evolution of nation-states around the world. It is for this reason that comparisons (as in one case between the minorities of India and Malaysia) considered as politically benign and safe are attempted.

By all accounts, migration across nation-states has increased multifold over the recent years. Although an early attempt to study some of these population flows was made by Myron Weiner, it certainly requires to be revisited in the changed context of globalization in South Asia.[19] The 'mixed and massive' population flow has not only created new minorities but also triggered off schisms between the locals and the migrants and many of the societies of South Asia seem to be bursting at their seams. While the host country may have its reasons to feel unhappy with the massive immigration from across its borders, the sending country conveniently 'dumps its excess population' and refuses to acknowledge it. This has sometimes caused diplomatic standoffs between the countries of South Asia. It is true that such 'Alice-in Wonderland' policy is unhelpful, for, a solution will always elude us if the problem is not recognized in the first place. On the other hand, there cannot be any unilateral solution to such issues. A platform like this is ideally placed to first of all recognize minority-producing cross-border migration as a problem and then to evolve possible strategies of addressing it. Researches on scenarios of individual countries can at best be partial in their understanding of the magnitude and impact of such immigration and the interruption it causes to governmental operations.

While comparisons across the countries of the region are welcome and discovering their historical and cultural continuities and linkages are an important step to any project of evolving regional instruments of minority protection, the role of comparison and continuities and linkages can hardly be blown out of proportions. The presence of historical continuities and linkages should not lead us to bundle the minorities of the same ethnic origin but scattered into diverse cultural and political contexts into one category—homogeneous and indivisible—agitating for and demanding the same charter of rights. The same minority gets differently configured, culturally and politically, in many different ways. The importance of studying the 'minorities within minorities', therefore, can hardly be doubted. Both the processes of regional and contextual articulation are operative in South Asia and one has to find out when one acquires political salience over the other. In the existing literature, minorities of South Asia are generally never viewed with all these ramifications. Let us now formulate in more positive terms some of the issues that may form part of a research agenda necessary for a possible discourse shift.

Minorities across States

Many countries of South Asia formed parts of a politically unified landmass called India for most of their history. Empires of pre-colonial times occasionally stretched from Herat and Kandahar in Afghanistan to the island of Sri Lanka. While such instances of political unification have only been intermittent and occasional, there is no denying that the cracking and splitting of empires and kingdoms would take place along a culturally continuous scale so much so that these events did not trigger off mass exodus from one region to another. Indeed, one or two attempts at making political boundaries coincide with cultural ones by way of ordering population transfers produced grotesque results. The colonial rulers sought to transform the vast tracts of undemarcated and loosely administered frontiers of the Northwest and the Northeast into sharply drawn 'lines' towards the end of the nineteenth century. Thus, the Durand Line in the Northwest, separating India from Afghanistan, and the Macmahon Line in the Northeast, separating India from Tibet, were drawn in 1893 and 1903 respectively. But it was only with the Partition of India in 1947 and consequent reorganization of international borders that the masses of people felt the necessity of adjusting themselves to the 'right' side of the border through migration. As a result, an estimated one million people lost their lives due to communal riots that broke out on the eve of Partition and in its wake and a few millions shifted themselves from one part to the other while drawing new and hitherto unknown cultural boundaries and making them coincide with the newly reorganized political borders. In simple terms, the emergence of modern states in the region has enjoined on them the obligation of making them coincide with each other. As 'lines' are drawn on maps as the Commission led by Sir Cyril Radcliffe had done it in the east and most importantly lines are plotted on the ground, these bring into existence what Joya Chatterjee calls 'a new way of life'[20] and people are called upon to constantly adjust themselves to it. The region is caught between two diametrically opposed pulls of historically shared social, cultural and economic commonalities and linkages that otherwise cut across the newly reorganized international borders on one hand and the legal and political obligation of observing and remaining confined to them. The challenge of governing the post-Partition nations in South Asia lay precisely in converting this new reality into 'a way of life'.

By all accounts, this essentially statist dream of creating culturally homogeneous nations by encouraging mass migrations and population transfers was indeed shared by a good number of people who thought it 'unethical' to remain left in countries that was not theirs.[21] The metaphor of Partition continues to live on and shapes much of the so-called post-Partition politics. Partition is not an event, but a process and a process that does not exhaust itself with the event of the formation of nation-states. The same dream gets reenacted rather climactically and at great human cost in Gujarat, India (2002), Bangladesh (1996, 2001), Sri Lanka (1983) and Bhutan (1988) where violence is organized systematically more often than not at the state's instance to exterminate the minorities whether by indiscriminately killing them or through expulsion. Many of the reports prepared by even the statutory agencies of the state like the National Human Rights Commission accuse the politicians and security forces of having done such acts of commission and omission, which heavily discriminate against the minorities. The dream continues to inspire and elude the states of the region. The mixed and complex demography of the region and the historically shared nature of the continuities amongst different people make it absolutely impossible for the states of the region to create culturally homogeneous nations. Minorities are bound to remain caught on the 'wrong' side of the border for time to come. Viewed from this perspective, an in-depth study of some of these yet under-researched or even one-sidedly researched (for, they have been studied with inputs from only one side of the border) cases of bilateral minorities is suggested here. Our project is ideally suited to study these bilateral or as even in some cases multilateral minorities strewn across borders.

The case of southern Bhutan is one of trilateral minority subjected to discriminatory cultural policies informed by Partition albeit in a metaphorical sense. For, Bhutan was outside the massive surgical operation that accompanied Partition. Yet, the same metaphor of Partition also lives on in this case. Until 1985, there was hardly any hostility reported in the 'land of peace' notwithstanding its ethnic diversity. Crisis is said to begin with the passing of Citizenship Act in 1985. The Lhotshampas of South Bhutan, most of whom are of ethnic Nepali origin, have been branded by this Act as 'stateless people'. The subsequent Census of 1988 carried out only in the predominantly Nepali-speaking southern districts revoked their right to nationality in large numbers. The Royal Government of Bhutan encouraged a policy of 'one state, one nation' with the effect that the Lhotshampas were subjected to political and cultural discrimination. They were forced to wear the 'national dress', speak the 'national language' and deprived of their rights including that of landownership. Nepalese was replaced by the 'national language' in primary schools and other educational institutions. According to an early estimate, about 120,000 Bhutanese have been forced into exile in India and Nepal. Over 90,000 people were reported to have been living in UNHCR-supervised camps in Jhapa and Morong in eastern Nepal. Approximately 30,000 have been living outside the camps in Nepal and India. Their presence in the Dooars and Siliguri subdivisions of northern West Bengal seems to have changed the demographic composition of the area. While the new leadership of the Gorkhaland movement lays claim to this area and demands its inclusion in the proposed Gorkha ('Indian citizens of Nepali origin')-dominated state of Gorkhaland within the Indian union, this has unleashed newer currents of tension and schism between them and the majority of local Bengalis.

Although a living testimony to the impossibility of carrying forth the logic of Partition based on ethnic and religious divide beyond a certain point (for its inability to take note of the divisions that are implicit in each of the entities thus partitioned), Bangladesh seems to reenact Partition insofar as the predominantly Buddhist and non-Bengali-speaking tribal communities of Chittagong Hill Tracts (CHT) were subjected to discriminatory policies and forcibly ejected from their habitat. About 40,000 persons migrated to Arunachal Pradesh, India, and an estimated 20,000 went over to the Arakan region of the then Burma. Those who migrated to India and their children born on Indian soil continue to remain stateless. A movement was organized by the All-Arunachal Pradesh Students' Union (AAPSU) in the late-1980s with the demand of their expulsion to other parts of India, if not Bangladesh. While an investigation report commissioned by the National Human Rights Commission drew the nation's attention to the gross violation of human rights in Arunachal Pradesh, the Supreme Court of India in an epoch-making verdict upheld their right to life even for the non-citizens—and in this case the right to 'decent' life—guaranteed by the Constitution and asked the Government of Arunachal Pradesh for their protection. Although forced migration occurred during the conflict between the mid-1970s and 1997—the year when an accord was signed with the Jana Sangram Samiti (JSS), the roots of conflict and discrimination may be traced to the construction of the Kaptai dam between 1957 and 1963. The construction led to the submergence of 54,000 acres of cultivable land and about 100,000 tribals were displaced from their homes. A Bangladesh Government Task Force estimated in July 2000 that 128,000 families were displaced due to conflicts in this region.

In 1987 as Burma erupted against military rule, many of the leaders and activists of the pro-democracy movement were forced to leave the country and take shelter in neighbouring India. India publicly extended her moral support to the movement. In 1988 alone, Burmese migrants came to India in three waves. In 1997 the scenario changed and India decided to develop a working relationship with the Burmese military junta. Burmese migrants considered India's decision of 'doing business' with the military rulers of Burma a great blow to their movement, and as a result their freedom was severely curtailed. Much of the pro-democracy movement was inspired by ethnic Burmans consisting of such groups as the Kachins, the Karens, the Chins and the Arakanese, targeted largely by the military rulers and their policy of nationalization and forced labour for 'national' development. In 1990, the junta extended its control over the Sagaing Division of the Chin state, inhabited mostly by the ethnic Chins numbering between 1.5 and 2.5 millions. Chins are known to have migrated in trickles over the years from the Division, one of the poorest in Myanmar, again one of the poorest countries of the world. In 1988 when persecution against the Chins reached its peak, it is difficult to say how many of them were evicted as a result of political compulsions and how many due to economic reasons. A good many Chins are settled in the Indian state of Mizoram. By all accounts, a distinct change in attitude of the Mizos towards the Chins has been noticeable. While they were initially very hospitable towards these migrants because of the ethnic affinity they share with them, the early bonhomie seems to have been ruptured with too many people chasing after the limited pot of resources and growing cases of human rights violations reported against them.

The minority Tamils of Sri Lanka concentrated mainly in the north and the east are said to have shared their ethnic and cultural affinities with those of South India throughout history. The proliferation of Tamil political organizations in the 1970s was in many ways a response to 'the policy of nationalization' followed by the Sri Lankan state. Tamil representation in political and decision-making institutions, in bureaucracy and security forces has been incomparably low, much lower than their percentage vis-à-vis the total population. The Citizenship Act passed way back in 1948 made a distinction between the 'Ceylon Tamils' and the 'Indian Tamils' and the former were regarded as people of indigenous origin and therefore granted citizenship while the second category instantly became 'stateless'. In 1956 Sinhalese was declared the official language of Sri Lanka, including in the Tamil-majority north and the east. But the matters came to a head when on 23 July 1983 a convoy of army jeeps and trucks was attacked a few kilometers away from Jaffna. The rest is part of the region's widely known history. The changing attitude of various Tamil groups and political parties towards the Tamils in general and the Tamil refugees migrating to South India in particular speaks of the bilateral nature of the Tamil minority in the region. Some of these Tamil groups including of course the Liberation Tigers of Tamil Eelam had released maps of Eelam or free Tamil land, consisting of the Tamil-dominated parts of not only Sri Lanka but of South India.

The bilateral or multilateral nature of the minorities just mentioned above sensitizes us to the essentially supranational nature of the minority question in South Asia. During the civil war in the then East Pakistan during 1971, about 10,000 Garos of Modhupur in Bangladesh crossed over to neighbouring Indian state of Meghalaya in order to escape violence and persecution in the hands of the Pakistani forces. Many of them went back as the dust storm of war gradually settled down. Going by the available researches, the Indo-Pak war of 1971 resulting in the formation of Bangladesh as a separate state in South Asia was triggered off by the imperative necessity of sending back about 9.8 millions of Pakistanis who had taken shelter in the bordering states of India. While bilateral nature generally expresses itself through such mutual acts of seeking refuge and shelter as in the cases of the Garos, the Tamils, the Chakmas, the Hajongs and the Chins, it more often than not is underlined by reflexive violence, acts of vendetta and revenge killings. The persecution of minorities in one country has its obvious repercussion in another where they are not necessarily in a minority. The demolition of the Babri Masjid by a section of fundamentalist and rightwing Hindu forces in 1992 left its almost instant impact on the minorities of both Pakistan and Bangladesh. Temples and places of worship of the minorities were systematically destroyed much in the same manner as the Taliban busted the ancient relics of Buddhism in the Bamian mountain of Afghanistan during its reign. Policy-oriented researches are called for so that early warning systems can be put in place and the mass violence resulting from unchecked communal pogroms organized at times with full state connivance does not take its toll on the societies of South Asia.

Linguistic Rights in Europe and India

The use, preservation and enhancement of minority languages represent one of the principal means by which minorities can assert and preserve their identity. Language is paramount to the protection of minorities and this issue is a cornerstone of the right of minorities to preserve their identity and characteristics. But which measures are applied by states to implement those fundamental rights in daily life? In most South Asian and European state constitutions different cultural and linguistic identities are recognized or the state is even constituted as a multinational and multicultural reality like India. But what are state authorities and legislatures doing to actively ensure their existence and promoting their development? Which is the situation of smaller or 'lesser used' languages, which in no state and perhaps not even on regional or district level are used as an official language?

In the framework of minority rights, language is probably the issue which in Europe has got major attention in both the legislation and implementation and also in research regarding its impact on social and cultural reality. Consequently the two major international covenants today in force in Europe (the Framework Convention on National Minorities and the European Charter for Regional and Minority Languages) attach utmost importance to the language rights. In many countries there is a certain record of application of linguistic rights of ethnic groups or national minorities. The Framework Convention on National Minorities (FCNM) State reports are listing out extensively the measures and efforts of public institutions and state agencies to promote minority languages and the results of those interventions. On the other hand, independent research and comments point out many critical situations of endangered languages and thus still very much has to be done.

The Constitution of India has recognized the rights of minorities to use their own language (Article 29). Article 344 of the Constitution lists the officially recognized languages of single states with regard to the Union. Article 345 grants the freedom of any state of India to adopt any or more of the languages in use in that state as the language to be used for all or any official purposes of that state (Article 347). The states of the Indian Union, and this is an interesting similarity with most of the European states, are constituted on a linguistic basis, though other factors (economic, political and social) were also kept in consideration. Those states are free to adopt their own language of administration and educational instruction from the 22 languages officially recognized, though it does not stipulate how the objective is to be achieved. Article 350 A enunciates that it 'shall be the endeavour of every state and of every local authority within the state to provide adequate facilities for instruction in mother tongues at the primary stage of education to children belonging to minority groups, and the President may issue such directives to any state'. This is of particular relevance for the Scheduled Tribes-dominated areas of India, but the application is far from meeting their cultural needs and rights. According to Article 350 the linguistic minorities have the right to be taught and have instruction in their languages, but again this is a discretionary provision, not mandatory for the state. From a European viewpoint it could be useful to compare Europe's and India's linguistic reality with the legal arrangements adopted so far. But how are those rights applied in reality? Which is the social and political reality of 50 years of application of linguistic rights? Which results have some State Acts in minority language matters produced? Which political tools and legal provisions on the contrary have failed? Finally, Article 350 B provides for the appointment of a Special Officer for Linguistic Minorities. This Commissioner of Linguistic Minorities operating since 1957, in pursuance of Article 350 B of the Constitution is endowed with controlling the implementation of the rights deriving from that article for linguistic minorities. He has submitted 38 annual reports so far. Again this institution finds a counterpart in Europe's international institutions with the OSCE High Commissioner for National Minorities who monitors and reports on the situation of many smaller ethnic and linguistic groups.

The proposal is to work out a comparative study in linguistic rights of ethnic minorities of South Asia and Europe. This kind of comparison between Europe (the signatory states of the Framework Convention of the National Minorities: FCNM) and India in particular could be done focusing on some basic linguistic rights: the right of the public use of its language, the right to use the language in the public sphere in contact with public authorities and bodies, the right to be taught in its mother tongue, the right to information in minority languages. The comparison must analyse the legal provisions adopted in various states and evaluate the progress and in different case studies too. In some cases, the evaluation of linguistic policy is well established. What has been done so far in India and in South Asia so far? Which are the grievances and proposals of the concerned ethnic minorities? What about the 'threatened languages and peoples' in Europe, India and other South Asian countries due to discrimination and denial of basic rights? This kind of research on a methodological level could also lead to a useful scholarly exchange with regard to methods of investigating and empirical measuring of the 'comprehensive situation of a language'.

Minorities within Minorities

In a region like South Asia and perhaps elsewhere, minorities can seldom be treated as a homogeneous category. There are individuals and minorities within minorities. As minority groups have become more vocal in demanding some form of accommodation, few have paid attention to the different types of 'minorities within' including women,[22] children, gay men and lesbians, religious dissenters and linguistic minorities within religious minorities. The crucial question is: What happens to individuals or minorities who find that their community discriminates against them?

Even Muslim women in India like all minority women elsewhere in South Asia do not constitute a homogeneous category. If the Muslim women constitute a minority within minority, Muslim lesbians, let us say, constitute, yet another layer of minority, a minority within a minority within a minority. The regression of the minorities as a category seems infinite and as one sets out to deconstruct it, one literally peels an onion. The condition of the Muslim lesbians, as a recent report prepared by the Peoples' Union for Civil Liberties, Karnataka, puts it, amounts to 'a double bind'. The lesbians and the transgender amongst the Muslims are to be considered a special minority particularly in South Asia. As Amena Ali, an Indian living in Canada and a bisexual by confession, admits that she has to face far less social stigma than the kind of cruel social isolation that Rehan—the first Muslim woman to have changed her gender in West Bengal, India—does. Such cases are by no means rare.

Where do we go from here? The recent debates on minority women in South Asia seem to have taken a three-way normative course: One, it is argued that the rights claims of the minorities should not be stretched beyond a critical point where they become detrimental to those of the women belonging to these groups. The minority claims, it is argued, may be conceded provided they are not incompatible with the 'basic values'. There are some problems with this line of argument. Even if we choose to ignore the standard denunciation coming from the extreme cultural relativists questioning the existence of such universal 'basic values' in the governance of our moral lives, we cannot ignore the strong statist traces implicit in the argument. While the state is made the protector and defender of 'basic values', the states in South Asia seem to have refused to bring about radical transformation in the society at the risk of causing instability and violence. This is a point where the reasons of state intersect with those of government. Two, argumentation is often cited as a means to the 'advancement of the cause of equality in different spheres of life'. While in the first case, the rightfulness of rights claims emanates from their compatibility or lack of it with the 'basic values', the second does not seem to set forth any given and unalterable set of universal values but subjects all values to the processes of deliberation and argumentation. Three, there is assumed to be an inevitable correlation between minority assertion and subjection of women. Under such circumstances, women must be able to assert their rights claims independently of the minority groups they belong to. Their alliance with the women of the majority groups is likely to be more enduring and beneficial than the men of their own minority groups. The feminists of this genre call for an autonomous women's movement that will transcend all the divisions internal to their identity as a gender group, including the one between the majority and the minority.

The Minority Accords

Minority accords of South Asia signed between two states of the region constitute yet another almost untouched area of research. While ethnic accords signed between organizations claiming to represent ethnic groups, especially minorities, and the state have been one of the favourite subjects of research, thanks primarily though not exclusively to CRG,[23] accords between two nation-states focusing on the question of bilateral or multilateral minorities are yet to attract the attention of scholars and researchers. The accords signed between India and Sri Lanka on one hand and those between India and Pakistan/Bangladesh on the other may provide excellent case studies, illustrating at the same time how the minority problem has been one issue that has brought the otherwise rival nation-states of the region together. It shows yet another side of our story of how the states of South Asia eventually submit to the reasons of government. A close study of select accords may provide us with clues to supranational bases of cooperation for minority protection in the region.

We have already briefly mentioned the Citizenship Act passed by the Sri Lankan Parliament in 1948. According to government estimates, the act rendered 800,000 Tamils stateless on the ground that they were 'Indian Tamils'. In order to overcome the impasse, an accord, popularly known as Shastri-Bandarnaike Pact, was signed between the two Prime Ministers of India and Sri Lanka on 30 October 1964. According to the terms of this accord, Sri Lanka agreed to accept some 375,000 Tamils and regularize them as Sri Lankan citizens, India acknowledged her responsibility towards the rest and agreed to take them back to India. Afterwards, on 29 July 1987, Sri Lanka and the Liberation Tigers of Tamil Eelam signed a tripartite agreement with India in the capacity of a third party vested with the special responsibility of monitoring and enforcing it. The subsequent course of events however tells us a different story. The Accord converted what was essentially a war between LTTE and the Sri Lankan state into one between LTTE and India, resulting in the assassination of Rajib Gandhi, then the prime minister of India. Sri Lanka, as it were, was watching the conflict from the sidelines. There were initial hiccups as the ruling United Nationalist Party showed its reluctance to ratify the Accord in Sri Lankan Parliament. But as the prime minister threatened to dissolve Parliament and seek fresh mandate from the electorate, the United Nationalist Party did not take much time to ratify an Accord that was crafted not by Premadasa but by his predecessor, Junius Jayewardene.

We have already made a reference to the massive population movements that took place both immediately before and after Partition. The fear of being reduced to a minority propelled the Muslims of the East to migrate to East Pakistan as much as many Hindus living there did not feel any longer safe to remain there and migrated to India, although according to Amalendu De the flow from the East to the West was disproportionately more than that from the West to the East.[24] The population flow seemed unstoppable so much so that much of the population flow that takes place now has its roots in the history of Partition. The leaders of both India and Pakistan appeared to be interested in stopping the flow of minorities and in ensuring safety and security in their own countries, although for very different reasons. While Nehru, India's first prime minister, considered protection of minorities the key to India's professed ideal of secularism, Liaquat Ali Khan, his counterpart in Pakistan, regarded it as central to Islam. One has to keep in mind that Pakistan was born as an Islamic state. Both prime ministers signed what is known as the Nehru-Liaquat Pact in 1950 that entrusted the respective states with the responsibility of ensuring safety and security of the minorities and provide for their protection in their own countries. While Bangladesh maintains that not a single Bangladeshi migrates to India, the now-dysfunctional 'Treaty of Friendship, Cooperation and Peace between India and Bangladesh'—popularly known as Indira-Mujib agreement, named after the two signatories—vowed to settle all major international problems 'through meetings and exchanges of views at all levels'. The Treaty may not have made it in black and white; but Indira Gandhi, then the prime minister of India, is understood to have given the assurance to Sheikh Mujibur Rahman, the prime minister of Bangladesh widely called 'Bangabandhu' (friend of Bengal), that the immigrants settled in India before the civil war broke out in 1971 would be accepted by India and would not be sent back.

In 1950, the Indo-Nepal Treaty was signed between Chandreswar Prasad Narayan Singh and Mohan Shamshere Jung Bahadur Rana on behalf of the two governments. Although not a treaty exclusively focusing on the minorities, it contains provisions for their protection and imposes on both the governments the reciprocal obligation of protecting them in their respective countries. Due to the porous nature of the Indo-Nepal border and the landlocked nature of the Himalayan state, Nepali immigration to India has been historical by nature. Article 7 of the Treaty is designed to grant reciprocal rights to live and own properties, participate in trade and commerce and move without papers from one country to another to the citizens of another country. The Treaty, however controversial it is for having obliterated the distinction between the Nepalis and the Indians, is meant for protecting rights of immigrants/migrants in the alien country and should be regarded as a landmark treaty in the sphere of minority protection between the two contracting states.

An analysis of the minority accords is likely to give us an idea of the possible bases of governmentally induced cooperation on some of the outstanding issues like their mass exodus and reflexive violence. While states in the region are not going to wither away, at least in the short term, the 'metaphysic of the nation-state' may not be an appropriate framework for understanding and analysing the problems of minorities. Can such bilateral experiments provide the basis for a South Asian Treaty for the protection of minority rights including the right to protection of places of worship, in the signing countries? We also call for some of the intermediate policy regimes that may be placed between either of the two extremes mentioned above. We will discuss the highlights of this policy debate in one of the subsequent sections. Suffice it to say here, an analysis of the minority accords will lend to us a template within which the possible sources of international and supranational cooperation may be deciphered.

EXPERIMENTS WITH REGIONAL AUTONOMY

Regional territorial autonomy, sometimes in combination with cultural or personal autonomy, in both concerned areas, Europe and South Asia, has been a major issue when it came to develop instruments for ethnic minority protection and self-governance. Regional autonomy as a specific power sharing arrangement between the central and regional government levels has a proven potential of conflict-solving when addressing the needs of a homogeneously settling minority population or smaller peoples in a given limited territory. Whereas Europe since 1921 has experienced the establishment of some 36 autonomous regions in 11 states (9 of whose are members of the EU plus Moldova and Ukraine), in South Asia regional autonomy so far has been adopted only in India. India has decades-old experience with territorial autonomies especially on the sub-state district level. Jammu and Kashmir, after a first period with fully autonomous status, in the 1950s lost its special autonomy status (according to article 370 of the Indian Constitution), which contributed to the ongoing conflict and unrest in the area. Apart from creating new states, a range of accords and unilateral measures on several regions has been created either as autonomous areas or district councils under the Fifth and Sixth Schedules of the Constitution. Nepal with its new constitution, to be forged in the coming months, will probably transform into a federal republic in order to cope with its ethnic and cultural diversity. In Sri Lanka the efforts of federalizing the state's structure as a compromise with the Tamil minority dramatically failed, re-igniting the civil war and 'defeating' the Liberation Tigers of Tamil Eelam. In Bangladesh the long struggle of the Chittagong Hill indigenous peoples for their fundamental rights and territorial autonomy did not yet lead to any lasting and stable solution: the first treaty on which the central government in Dhaka and the concerned minority peoples convened, did not match their expectations and needs. In Pakistan, besides the general requirement to reform the federal structure, the issue of regional territorial autonomy concerns especially the northern areas of Gilgit-Baltistan, a huge region trapped in the Indo-Pakistani conflict, deprived not only of the right to self-governance, but also of the fundamental rights to democratic participation.

Europe, from a perspective of the concerned minority peoples and national minorities, shows most positive experiences with regard to territorial autonomy and other forms of autonomy (e.g., cultural autonomy). Most of the existing regional autonomies are developing towards a more complete range of autonomous competencies, thus obtaining a higher degree of self-governance. This tool of solution of ethnic conflict is slowly emanating to other countries, particularly in Eastern Europe (e.g. in Romania with the Szeklerland, inhabited by a majority of ethnic Hungarians), although still several state parties are looking with suspicion at such proposals. Not only is regional autonomy a consolidated experience on the ground but also, step by step, it is approaching a stage of codification on the level of international conventions. In 1994 the FUEN (the Federal Union of European Nationalities) launched the 'Draft Convention on Autonomy Rights of Ethnic Groups in Europe', and other examples are the Council of Europe with its resolution no. 1334 of 24 June 2003, the Lund-Recommendations on the Effective Participation of National Minorities in Public Life, and recently the recommendations of the Council of European Regions and Local Authorities in the same matter. Many of Europe's national minorities and ethnic groups (out of more than 300 existing groups) have hopes of the further development of this juridical concept and its codification in international soft law.

Starting from this situation, autonomy applications in South Asia and Europe in a comparative perspective could be an interesting issue for further research efforts, also oriented to policy consultancy, taking into account the diverse historical, political and juridical context and based on empirical evidence. First, there should be an empirical assessment of the results that the territorial autonomies in India and Europe have produced so far; second, an analysis on which are the major factors which have still prevented autonomy to unfold its positive potential for conflict solving and self-government could be presented, integrating other means of minority protection; and third, which new proposals could be developed in the face of ongoing conflict in various areas. In this context, regional autonomy should neither be considered a magic recipe for all times and all places, nor just a specific European form of territorial power sharing, but as a concept of state organization which with due adaptations can be and is applied in all continents.

In this framework we may elaborate three case studies for South Asia:

1. Pakistan and Gilgit-Baltistan: elaboration of a proposal of a procedure to start and run a negotiation process aimed to draft an autonomy statute by a platform of locally based scholars and activists.
2. Bangladesh and the Chittagong Hill Tracts: in-depth-analysis of the major flaws of the currently adopted self-administration of the CHT and elaboration of a proposal of an authentic and stable autonomy solution for the whole region.
3. Autonomy on district level in India: experiences, achievements and future requirements, starting from an assessment based on some examples like Darjeeling, Bodoland, Assam, Tripura and Mizoram Tribal Areas.

As for the cases of regional autonomy adopted in Central Europe, first of all, South Tyrol could be chosen as one example, also for practical reasons; Corsica would be a good example as well, being a case of 'uncompleted regional autonomy' that is still highly disputed and not meeting given minimum standards of political autonomy. Further examples could be selected based on criteria of geographical distance in order to limit travel costs.

As for the methodology, there should be a close collaboration of one or more European researchers with one or more South Asian fellow researchers, based on the existing resources within the various participating academic institutions. Some field research in both areas (autonomous regions in Central Europe and regions with autonomy conflicts in South Asia) should be carried out, keeping in mind the mutual exchange of experiences and research output. Besides the results of the research, this team of scholars could also elaborate new concepts and proposals as useful inputs for the political debate in the concerned areas along with some media-oriented documents and materials for broader dissemination and didactical activities. In this context also the related issues of local autonomy (self-administration) and cultural autonomy have to be discussed. Finally, which conditions have to be created in order to introduce a 'right to autonomy' in the framework of an international convention of fundamental minority rights within international (regional) soft law in both areas of Europe and South Asia could also be analysed.

The Model Cases

The claim of a few cases of South Asia to serve as 'models' to be followed elsewhere for the resolution of minority problems should also be closely examined. For instance, the Indian state of Mizoram in the Northeast is showcased in official circles as a success story. The Mizo Accord (1986) has been described as the 'only accord that has not fallen apart or spawned violent breakaway groups'. But empirical researches conducted albeit sporadically in the region tend to show how the Accord that did not result in any fatal split and factious conflict within insurgent ranks has slowly produced an 'illiberal' society in which individual dissent is more or less throttled and dissenters are forced to give way to the commands of the ex-insurgents or even Mizo civil society organizations. The so-called success story of the Accord will have to be read together with many other stories that compel us to read it against its grain. The Hmars fell apart from the Mizos the moment the separate state of Mizoram had come into existence in 1986. The demand for 'Hmar Ram' to be carved out from the newly formed state of Mizoram made by Hmar Peoples' convention (HPC) symbolizes a deep ethnic divide between the two hitherto friendly communities of the Mizos and the Hmars. Interestingly, the Hmars had joined the Mizos in their struggle for the statehood of Mizoram.

Reangs constitute the second largest population group in Tripura, spreading across several northern and southern subdivisions of Dharmanagar, Kailasahar, Kamalpur, Udaipur,

Amarpur, Belonia, and the bordering states of Assam and Mizoram and, of course, Bangladesh. Insofar as they are scattered over a number of territorial and administrative units, they face the problem of being reduced to a minority everywhere. The general perception of the Reangs that transpires from the interviews with their political leaders is that their culture cannot flourish 'because of the dominance of other majority groups within the recognized territorial spaces in Mizoram, Tripura or in Assam'. Mizo society's intolerance to dissent was exemplified when Vanramchhaunvy, a leading Mizo woman activist, was threatened in May 2005 by the Young Mizo Association (YMA) while protesting against the deaths of four persons and cruelty towards many others for their alleged involvement in peddling drugs and liquor. The YMA had launched a programme of curbing drugs and liquor and the victims who had died or had to suffer other forms of cruelty were 'punished' by the organization as part of its campaign for meting out instant justice to the deviants and offenders in the society. When she saw two women on the roadside apparently accused of some offence and made to wear large placards around their neck, she pleaded for turning them to the appropriate authorities and trying them according to the constitution and the law of the land. She was summoned the next day by the YMA and nine local YMA leaders descended on her place as per the orders of the Central Committee and threatened her. However, tensions are brewing within the ranks of the ex-insurgents. Today when the Peace Accord MNF (Mizo National Front, the rebel body that led the insurgency struggle) Returnees' Association (PAMNFRA) accuses the government for not implementing the provisions of the accord, it blames itself for having signed it in good faith and not any of its rival factions.[25] In simple terms, the so-called model cases of governing the minorities in South Asia need to be investigated further as the interstices and fissures involved in the process become increasingly pronounced.

DEBATE ON STATE POLICIES

South Asia as a region has generated a rich and growing body of literature, particularly since the late 1980s. Yet it is important to note that much of this literature is not focused on any exploration into possible policy alternatives in order to address the issues and questions underlined above. The region is still a long way from evolving what may be called a policy culture where concerned people can continuously debate on minority problems and possible policy alternatives. An attempt will be made in this section to review some of the hitherto suggested alternatives and briefly discuss their successes and limitations. A thoroughgoing research into the debates on policy alternatives will go a long way in ensuring and guaranteeing better protection of the minorities in future.

There are very few policy advocates in the region (excepting perhaps the official sources), who continue to recommend a *pure* 'law and order' solution to the ethnic and minority problems. The measures suggested in this connection range from overhauling security structures in order to secure and protect the nation's interests and greater deployment of security forces to legislation and implementation of 'emergency' laws (like the controversial Armed Forces Special Powers Act of 1958, presently in force in many parts of the India's Northeast) often involving temporary suspension and abrogation of rights and liberties that are otherwise enshrined in and guaranteed by the constitution and laws of the land. The efficacy of 'multi-force operations' (popularly known as 'unified command') in Assam has already become a frequently referred topic of discussion. While the law and order solution may be both desperately necessary and effective in the short run, it cannot be an answer to the region's ethnic and minority conflicts. The paradox that democracies all over the world face today is how to respond to the problems of minorities and insurgencies without reneging on its commitment to rights and liberties of the citizens including those of the minorities.

But there are others who advocate a change in policy regime in the countries of South Asia while addressing the problems facing the region. The change, according to them, will have to be brought about predominantly, though not exclusively, by the state and an entire series of measures is suggested to make the state move in this direction. A change in policy regime is possible through 'an alternative institutional imagination' that calls for salvaging ethnic identity from any notion of fixed and territorially rooted collectivity and encourages constant experimentation with diverse institutional arrangements till the disentanglement of identity from territoriality can be completed. It is indeed argued that the emphasis in policy interventions will have to give up granting some form of politically enclosed and exclusive units or ethnic homelands (state, Autonomous District Councils, government by traditional institutions and in accordance with the customary laws, and so on). It should instead move to the minority communities in recognition of their particularistic identities to 'good neighbourliness and development'. How do we bring about such a transformation? Being deeply powered by the same state-building imagination intent on throwing its weight in favour of demands of the minorities for ethnic homelands, do most of the 'actually existing civil societies' in South Asia provide a solution? Being deeply powered by homeland imagination, actually existing civil societies can hardly be regarded as the site where any 'flexibilization' of homeland regime will be possible. Civil societies in the region too require an alternative imagination so that these can provide the normative ground for the initiation of such a change in policy regime. Groups like Women in Security, Conflict Management and Peace (WISCOMP), Kali for Women, Pakistan-India Peoples' Forum for Peace and Democracy and CRG and others have been involved in civil society activism across borders. But there are not many of their ilk that are involved in similar work across South Asia. This by no means undermines their activism within the territorial confines of their respective countries.

The debate on institutions has already begun. Efforts are being made to break free from the paradox inherent in the early framework of state-building in which the consolidation of a particular community within a geopolitical space necessarily creates its minorities. For example, the vicious circle in which a minority becomes a majority by way of getting the borders redrawn and thereby creates its own minority and the circle continues to roll with alarming regularity is inherent in India's established federal setup. Attempts are now being made to explore newer institutional alternatives. We may refer to at least three interesting strands, not necessarily mutually exclusive, of this debate: First, reform-minded scholars and activists recommend a Scandinavian SAMI-like multi-layered parliamentary system in which ethnic communities will have the right to represent themselves instead of being bound by the majoritarian commands of the existing parliamentary system. Second, some have argued that the 'first-come-first-served' electoral system in which the minorities dispersed over a large space are constantly under the subjection of the numerical, and therefore political, majority is incompatible with the pluralistic nature of South Asian societies; reservation of seats for them would not help the situation. Introducing proportional representation is considered as a means of protecting these groups from majority rule and retaining their autonomy. Third, a case has been made for widening the consociational (power sharing) base of our democratic system. Lijphart (1996), for example, shows how the basic preconditions of a consociational democracy were met during the first few decades of India's independence and how that base has been weakened as a combined result of 'centralization of the Congress Party and the federal system' in the 1980s and growing 'attack on minority rights' in different parts of India.[26] He in fact pleads for resuscitating the institutions and practices of consociational democracy that, according to him, protected India reasonably well in the first few decades against inter-group violence and communal riots.

While suggesting the possible policy alternatives, one has also to explore how such non-territorial forms of minority representation might spill over the international borders and include more than one nation-state for consideration. For example, a 'Work Permit' regime that is believed to be situated between the formal principle of territorial sovereignty and complete impenetrability of international borders and the popular practice of disregarding them by way of immigrating across the borders. The regime implies a certain blurring of the distinction between citizens and foreigners considered as central to the identity of any nation-state. A person working in the host country with a permit is not considered a citizen and is obliged to leave it as soon as the tenure of permit expires. But such a regime is expected to address the problem of rising demand for cheap and inexpensive labour currently filled up by the 'illegal' immigrants for all practical purposes. The regime can operate provided both the sender and the host countries agree to introduce it. South Asia provides a vast and hitherto un-researched field of all such experiments with various institutions and such an exercise may be initiated under the aegis of this project.

REGIONAL INSTRUMENTS

South Asia, by all accounts, has been slow in evolving supranational and pan-regional instruments for the protection of minorities. A few of these attempts made in recent years mostly outside the scope of state initiatives, however, merit attention. It was South Asian Forum for Human Rights based in Kathmandu (Nepal) that made one of the earliest attempts in August 1998 towards this direction. While expressing their concern that 'during the five decades South Asian states have drifted to a hegemonic and majoritarian political culture', the participants of the consultation meeting felt 'worried by the failure of the governments to protect the minorities against the violations by the members of the majority community'. The participants preferred to define 'minority' not as a simple numerical statement but as groups with 'ethnic, religious and linguistic features' because of which they are actively discriminated against in the society.[27] The presence of constitutional and legal provisions do not mean much to the minorities unless, as they argued, there is proper accountability in all cases of rights violations. Perhaps for the first time in South Asia, it raised the demand for the constitution of an independent National Minorities Commission as a constitutional body with adequate powers to intervene in all instances of infringement of minority rights. At a supranational level, they urged on the SAARC to create the office of a Special Rapporteuer, who should be empowered to review and report every year to the heads of the states of South Asia on the status of minorities in the countries of the region. They also called on SAFHR to create in collaboration with other non-governmental and civil society actors a forum for the preparation of an annual People's Report on the status of Minority Rights in South Asia. They appreciated the importance of reforms in the educational institutions so that they play a role in promoting the values of tolerance, amity, respect for language, culture and religion of different communities. The meeting also underlined the need for 'impartial and independent mechanisms for monitoring minority rights' and ensuring easy access and speedy redress to all cases arising out of violation of minority rights.[28]

SAARC Social Charter signed by the 7 states of South Asia on 4 January 2004 is considered as a remarkable advancement in the field of protection of minority and group rights including those of the elderly, the women and the children. Although the term 'minority' has never been explicitly used, the idea, as Clause 2 (XI) of Article II explains, is to secure for 'the disadvantaged, marginalized and vulnerable persons and groups' legal rights and make 'physical and social environment' accessible. While legalization of their rights is an effective first step, the Charter also puts emphasis on obtaining enabling conditions for their observance and protection. The immediately following sub-clause calls for 'observance and protection of human rights and fundamental freedoms for all'. In simple terms, the Charter aims at protecting the rights of these groups as part of the larger project of investing each one of South Asia with rights and freedoms irrespective of their religion, race, caste, sex and place of birth and promoting 'effective exercise of rights in a balanced manner at all levels of society' and 'social integration'. Much in the same vein, Clause 1 of Article VI declares that 'discrimination against women is incompatible with human rights and dignity'. The Charter clearly rules out any exclusivist path to be pursued while protecting their rights and freedoms.

At the instance of the International Centre for Ethnic Studies (Colombo), a Statement of Principles on Minority and Group Rights in South Asia was drawn up and revised in April 2006. A South Asian Charter on Minority and Group Rights was elaborated on the basis of the Statement by a group of voluntary organizations across South Asia including International Centre for Ethnic Studies (Colombo), Centre for Alternatives (Dhaka), Human Rights and Democratic Forum (Kathmandu), Mahanirban Calcutta Research Group (Kolkata) and Human Rights Commission (Karachi).[29] The main aim of the Charter published in May 2008 is to effectively address minority issues and concerns, which cut across countries in South Asia and enhance regional responses to some of the current weaknesses in constitutional and legislative protection and promotion of minority and group rights. More specifically, the Charter may be used 'as a reference tool for governments, non-state actors, human rights institutions, NGOs and human rights advocates and policy makers to draft national legislation, promote legislative reform, undertake advocacy, influence decisions, policies and programmes to ensure that they focus on the promotion and protection of minority and group rights'. The Charter, instead of formulating new norms for the protection of minority and group rights, builds on existing instruments like SAARC Social Charter, International Covenant on Civil and Political Rights, Covenant on Economic, Social and Cultural Rights,

Convention on the Elimination of All Forms of Discrimination against Women and International Convention on the Elimination of All Forms of Racial Discrimination and adapts them to the specific context of South Asia. It not only urges the States Parties to 'reaffirm and adopt' the Charter but also provides for 'effective remedies', should violations of these rights ever take place, 'for the purpose of promoting general welfare in a democratic society, without discrimination of the life and well-being of people'. The Charter views the question of protection of minority and group rights as part of the larger problem of inculcating some basic democratic values in the states of South Asia, rather than isolating their cause and ghettoizing them in the process. As a tribute to this principle, Article 5 of the Charter clearly lays down:

> The States Parties to the present Charter guarantee the exercise and enjoyment of the rights recognized in the present Charter without discrimination of any kind as to race, colour, language, religion, caste, gender, political or other opinion, national or social origin, property, birth or other status, and protection against any acts of such discrimination, and any incitement to such discrimination.

But nothing in this Article prevents any state from 'protecting the existence and the identity of the minorities within their respective territories' and providing for 'affirmative action'.

On the one hand, the Charter entitles the minorities to the 'right to freedom of association' including that of establishing and maintaining 'free and peaceful contacts' with the other minorities as well as 'contacts across frontiers with citizens of other states to whom they are related by national or ethnic, religious or linguistic ties'. On the other hand, Article 7B recognizes the connection between ethnic minority and ethnic homeland and provides for their protection 'within their respective territories'. Besides, the Charter serves as one of the unusually detailed documents for the recognition and protection of linguistic rights of the minorities. It envisages the establishment of a South Asian Human Rights Committee composed of nationals of the States Parties serving in their personal capacity in a bid to enforce its various provisions. Each State Party is empowered to nominate not more than two persons from its nationals for the membership. The Committee is empowered to receive and handle 'communications to the effect that a State Party claims that another State Party is not fulfilling its obligations under this Charter' provided it is submitted by a State Party that has made the declaration 'recognizing in regard to itself the competence of the Committee': 'No communication shall be received by the Committee if it concerns a State Party which has not made such a declaration.' The provision is likely to reduce the otherwise widely prevalent diplomatic abuse of such a sensitive issue as minority and group rights and their subordination to 'national interest'. The issue proves to be critical insofar as the assertion of these rights is sought to be understood beyond the realms of national interest and governmentality. The same declaration from the allegedly 'violating' State Party is necessary for receiving communications from individuals accusing it of having violated the minority and group rights recognized by the Charter.

As a follow-up to this Charter, Sabyasachi Basu Ray Chaudhury on behalf of Calcutta Research Group drafted another Charter on Minority Rights in India, which was subsequently published in August 2007.[30] While taking off from the assumption that 'the Constitution has not always been able to reflect the realities of majoritarian basis of the Indian polity, the poor state of the protection available in the country, and the low level of the constitutionally acknowledged minority rights', it lays down a set of 11 Principles on the basis of which constitutional and legal provisions are likely to function. In simple terms, the Principles do not seek to introduce any new principle to the Constitution or the legal system but aim precisely at reinforcing them and most importantly the secular ideal embodied in them. While the South Asian Charter is expected to be 'reaffirmed and adopted' by the States Parties, the Principles are laid down in the form of some moral imperatives to be followed by the Indian state because they are in consonance with the legal and constitutional provisions. The Principles per se are not enforceable, but only facilitate the enforcement of the already enforceable provisions. Besides, the Indian Charter envisages synergy between 'the State, authorities, public and private organizations, institutions, corporations, NGOs, groups or persons, public officials and private individuals, whether state or non-state actors and irrespective of their legal status' that, according to it, is absolutely essential for ensuring their enforceability.

Researches on minorities of South Asia, otherwise rich and growing, fail, albeit with notable exceptions, in lending a pan-regional and supranational focus to them. By contrast, South Asia provides the example of a region where both minorities and majorities are caught in a complex web of social, economic and cultural relations across the state borders reorganized particularly in the wake of Partition. The reality of supranational and cross-border linkages is completely incompatible with the current research boom that mostly focuses on minorities insofar as they are confined to state territories and thereby become victims of discrimination. Solutions interestingly are sought at the national level by way of subjecting them to the reasons of government, by firmly emplacing them within the national body and converting the minorities as a category of powerlessness into a merely numerical category. A research policy that probes into these linkages and connections can throw light on the possible policy options of how we can provide for better and more effective protection of minority rights particularly at a time when minorities have increasingly become the object of active discrimination by various social forces including the states of South Asia within their borders.

NOTES

We thank Guenther Rautz for his inputs to the preparation of the chapter. In addition, the paper is the product of a joint research exercise conducted in dialogical mode by the members and researchers of CRG and an earlier draft of it was discussed in the Eurasia-Net Project Steering Group meeting held in Bolzano on 29 and 30 August 2008.

1. For details one can access CRG website — http://mcrg.ac.in/inst1.htm and http://mcrg.ac.in/ad.htm
2. Chetan Bhatt, Frontline and Interstices in the Global War on Terror', *Development and Change,* 38, 6 (2007).
3. A Directory was compiled by International Centre for Ethnic Studies in collaboration with Calcutta Research Group and others. See ICES et al. *A Directory of Minority Rights and Institutions (*Colombo: ICES, 2008).
4. Since the exercise has already been done elsewhere, we refrain from repeating it here. See, for example, Nepal Institute of Peace, Guide to Minority Rights, *Directory, Personnel and Publications* (Kathmandu: Nepal Institute of Peace, 2004); Rita Manchanda, *The No-Nonsense Guide to Minority Rights in South Asia* (New Delhi: Impulsive Publications, 2006); Ananda Wanasundera, ed. *Protection of Minority Rights and Diversity* (Colombo: International Centre for Ethnic Studies, 2004); Sumanta Banerjee, *Shrinking Space: Minority Rights in South Asia* (Kathmandu: SAFHR, 1999).
5. Bishnu Mohapatra, 'Understanding the Discourse on Minority Rights in Contemporary India' (2001), mimeo.
6. Samir Kumar Das, 'Social Justice in the Constitutional Mirror', in *State of Social Justice in India,* vol.2: *Social Justice and the Limits of Deliverables of Law* edited by Ashok Aggarwal and Bharat Bhusan (New Delhi: Sage, 2009).
7. Ranabir Samaddar, *The Materiality of Politics: The Technology of Rule* (London: Anthem, 2007): 133-88.
8. Moin Shakir, *Politics of the Minorities* (Delhi: Ajanta, 1979).
9. See Asghar Ali Engineer and Moin Shakir, eds, *Communal Riots in Post-Independence India* (Delhi: Ajanta, 1984); Asghar Ali Engineer, *Bhiwandi-Bombay Riots: Analysis and Documentation* (Bombay: Institute of Islamic Studies, 1984).
10. Asghar Ali Engineer, ed., *Secular Crown on Fire: The Kashmir Problem* (Delhi: Ajanta, 1991).
11. Ashis Nandy, 'The Politics of Secularism and the Recovery of Religious Tolerance', *Alternative* 13 (1988).
12. T. N. Madan, 'Religion in India', *Daedalus* 118, 4 (Fall 1989):117.
13. Rajeev Bhargava, 'Introducing Multiculturalism', in *Multiculturalism,*

Liberalism and Democracy, edited by Rajeev Bhargava, Amiya Kumar Bagchi and R. Sudarshan (New Delhi: Oxford University Press, 1999).

14. Ashutosh Varshney, *Ethnic Conflict and Civic Life: Hindus and Muslims in India* (New Delhi: Oxford University Press, 2001).
15. Dwaipayan Bhattacharyya, Niraja Gopal Jayal et al, eds. *Interrogating Social Capital: The Indian Experience* (New Delhi: Sage 2004).
16. Used widely in official and popular circles in South Asia without any necessarily pejorative sense.
17. Paul R. Brass, 'Introduction', in *Riots and Pogroms* edited by Parl R. Brass (London: Macmillan, 1996): 5.
18. Ibid: 37.
19. Myron Weiner, 'Rejected Peoples and Unwanted Migrants', *Economic and Political Weekly* 28, 34 (21 August 1991).
20. Joya Chatterji, 'The Fashioning of a Frontier: The Radcliffe Line and Bengal's Border Landscape 1947-52'. *Modern Asian Studies,* 33 (1) (February 1999).
21. See Samir Kumar Das, 'Governing Minority Rights?' in *Political Governance and Minority Rights: The South and South East Asian Scenario,* edited by Lipi Ghosh (New Delhi; Routledge, 2009).
22. See Paula Banerjee, 'Mapping Minority Rights and Protection in India', in *Towards a New Consideration: Justice for the Minorities.* Policies and Practices 14 (Kolkata; Calcutta Research Group, 2007); Paula Banerjee, ed, *Women in Peace Politics,* South Asian Peace Studies 3 (New Delhi: Sage, 2008).
23. See Samir Kumar Das, ed. *Peace Accords and Peace Processes,* South Asian Peace Studies 2 (New Delhi: Sage, 2005).
24. Amalendu De, '*Bangladeshe Dharmiya Sankhalaghu Janabinyas: Manchitra Paribartan'* (The Demographic Composition of the Religious Minorities in Bangladesh: The Changing Contours) *Parichay* (May-July 1992).
25. For a more critical understanding of the Mizo accord, see Samir Kumar Das, *Conflict and Peace in India's Northeast: Role of Civil Society,* Policy Studies 42 (Washington DC: East-West Center, 2008).
26. Arénd Lijphart, 'The Puzzle of Indian Democracy: A Consociational Interpretation', *American Political Science Review* 90, 2 (June 1996).
27. By contrast, Myron Weiner refuses to view them as victims of active discrimination. His argument looks upon minorities as victims without as it were victimizers. See Myron Weiner, 'India's Minorities: Who are they? What Do They Want?' in Myron Weiner, T*he Indian Paradox: Essays in Indian Politics* (New Delhi: Sage, 1989).
28. For details see Sumanta Banerjee, ed, *Shrinking Space: Minority Rights in South Asia* (Kathmandu, SAFHR. New Delhi: Manohar, 1999): 211-13.
29. International Centre for Ethnic Studies, Centre for Alternatives, Human Rights and Democratic Forum, Mahanirban Calcutta Re-

search Group and Human Rights Commission, *A South Asian Regional Charter on Minority and Group Rights* (Colombo: International Centre for Ethnic Studies, 2008).
30. Sabyasachi Basu Ray Chaudhury, 'An Indian Charter for Minority Rights' in *Towards a New Consideration; Justice for the Minorities,* Policies and Practices 14 (Kolkata: Calcutta Research Group, 2007)

2

MAPPING THE MINORITIES IN INDIA

PAULA BANERJEE

THE QUESTION OF minority rights and protection in India acquired particular urgency after the genocide of Muslims in Gujarat in March-April 2002. As India is the largest democracy in the world and since elections in the Gujarat State Assembly were due within a year, human rights communities in most of South Asia waited to see how Indian democracy would respond to such horrific violence against its largest religious minority. Elections in Gujarat the same year portrayed the fallacy in thinking that democracies have a better track record in providing protection to minorities. The people's mandate brought back Narendra Modi, who is said to be the chief architect of violence in Gujarat, and his cronies in huge numbers, portraying 'the dark side of democracy', once again.[1] Although Narendra Modi did not perform as well in 2009, he still came back to power. Attacks on Muslims and other minorities are nothing new in India or even in Gujarat. But the Gujarat riots of 2002 are of significance because of their magnitude and because of the large-scale involvement of state machinery in designing and carrying out the attacks.

India is a multi-ethnic, multi-religious, multi-cultural and multi-linguistic country like all the other countries of South

Asia. India is perhaps the most diverse of all the countries in the region. Muslims form 13.4 per cent, Christians 2.3 per cent, Sikhs 1 per cent and other religious communities about 2 per cent of the total population.[2] These numbers do little to portray the magnitude of complexity regarding protection of minority rights. There are minority pockets in large parts of India and so the targeting of minorities is a recurrent phenomenon. For example, Northeast India houses Christian minorities who are also ethnic and linguistic minorities. As Christians they are often afraid of attacks from the Hindus. Also the ethnic and linguistic diversity among the Christians means that they are not unified in their responses. In fact the numbers game is so pervasive that local ethnic or linguistic majorities target the minorities in their own region. So in Assam the Ahoms and Bodos try to marginalize each other but also target the Muslims and the Santhals sometimes in tandem. Such a situation makes a mapping exercise of particular significance so that policies for protection of rights of minorities can be envisioned. This is meant to be such an exercise.

SITUATION OF RELIGIOUS MINORITIES

The expression 'minorities based on religion means that the only or the main basis of a minority should be its adherence to one of the many religions and not a part or sect of the religion and that other characteristics of the minority are subordinate to the main feature, namely, its separateness because of its religion.'[3] In India Hinduism is the religious faith of the majority and by the 2001 Census, Hindus form 80.5 per cent of the total population. Their numbers are about 827,578,868 in a total population of approximately 1,028,610,328 persons. The total population of Muslims in India is approximately 138,188,240.[4] They are the largest religious minority in India. As just mentioned, there are other religious minorities such as Christians and Sikhs but none as important as the Muslims in India.

MUSLIMS IN INDIA

The partition of the Indian subcontinent is considered by most Indian intellectuals to be a direct result of the Muslim claim that they form a separate nation. Interestingly, however, there are historians today who claim that the call for Partition came originally from Hindu leaders such as Bhai Parmanand, who were living in Muslim majority areas.[5] For our purposes this is not a crucial question. What is important is that even after Partition there were 35 million Muslims remaining in India. By the 1951 Census Muslims formed 9.8 per cent of the total population.

Thus the growth of communal feelings is attributed to representative politics in India. It is often said that the leadership or the elite of the communities in an effort to maintain its positions of power deliberately creates an atmosphere of confrontation. The Census then becomes a tool for this artificial exacerbation of tensions leading to conflict. Therefore, to understand such conflicts an analysis of Census reports over the past 50 years assumes importance.

By the 1941 Census it was ascertained that the Muslims were 23.7 per cent of the total population. In the 1951 Census their percentage was reduced to 9.8 per cent. In 1961 it went up to 10.7 per cent of the total population and by 1981 they were 11.4 per cent of the total population. In the 1981 Census their numbers in Assam were not counted as no Census could be taken in Assam. In 1991 the Census in Jammu and Kashmir could not be taken. In the present Census, as has been stated before, the Muslims formed 13.4 per cent of the total population. The decadal growth rate of Muslims between 1951 and 1961 was 32.5 per cent, between 1961 and 1971 was 30.9 per cent and between 1971 and 1981 was 30.6 per cent. This is an artificial lowering of decadal growth rate because in Assam, where Muslims form over 30 per cent of the population, the Census could not be taken. On the other hand, between 1991 and 2001 their decadal growth rate was figured at 36 per cent. This is also an artificial high. In 1991, as has been stated earlier, the Census of Jammu and Kashmir could not be taken due to political tumult in the state. It is only in Jammu and Kashmir that the Muslims are a majority. In the 2001 Census they formed 67 per cent of the total population of that state with a population figure of 6,793,240. Therefore, since this number was not factored in ten years back, their growth rate seemed unusually high by the 2001 Census and all hell broke loose.

The Census data that were released on 6 September 2004 stating that the Muslim decadal growth rate has increased from 1991 raised a storm. The Bharatiya Janata Party (BJP), which is the Hindu nationalist party and the main opposition in Parliament, took it up as an issue for further agitation. Their then President, M. Venkaiah Naidu, expressed 'concern' at this apparent demographic shift. Their party spokesman, Arun Jaitley, said that the figures have raised some concern and was worrying because of the national target to reach population stabilization by 2026. He further said, 'It is regrettable that instead of being concerned and alarmed at the population explosion, pseudo secular political parties are concerned at those who are expressing concern at this.'[6] All attention turned to Assam and West Bengal, the two states where Muslims although in minority, were 30 per cent and 25.2 per cent of the total population respectively. Percentage-wise after Jammu and Kashmir these were the two states with the highest per cent of Muslim population. Also these are border states and Hindu nationalist concerns that illegal immigrants are swamping border regions were given credibility.

That illegal Muslims hordes are entering through the India-Bangladesh border was an old concern of the people of Northeast India. Newspapers from the region have been reflecting such concerns for the last few years. Typically, news on illegal migrants in Northeast India often runs like this: 'BSF has apprehended 298 smugglers, including 206 Bangladeshis, along the international border with Bangladesh in the North-east during the first seven months this year.'[7] That the Bangladeshis mentioned in these reports are largely Muslims is stressed by stereotyping their dress. Often these reports say that: 'A group of about 15-20 Bangladeshi dacoits clad in lungis and armed with country made guns raided the houses,' of villages in the border areas.[8] The lungi is a dress typically worn by Bangladeshi Muslim peasants. Thus a negative attitude towards Muslims and their harassment is nothing new in Northeast India, particularly in Assam.

Apathy towards Muslims, particularly Bangladeshi Muslims, led to the anti-foreigner movement in Assam in the late 1970s and early 1980s. The movement was ideologically aimed at preserving the socio-economic, cultural, lingual and political identity of the Assamese nationality. The leaders of the movement demanded a stop to the participation of foreign nationals in the democratic political process, and their identification and deportation from Assam/India. As a result of this movement, however, not just Bangladeshis but even Indian Muslims were persecuted. For example, in Nellie in 1983 thousands of Muslims were massacred. According to one observer, the massacre of Nellie, 'by a conservative count, took more than 1200 lives—mostly of women and children. An eminent Assamese journalist has estimated the death toll of the Nellie massacre to be 3,000 dead. All the victims belonged to the Na-Asamiya (Neo-Assamese) Muslim community. I have pointed out elsewhere that the Muslims of Assam are an inseparable part of contemporary Assamese society. Not a single victim of the Nellie massacre belonged to the category of foreigners as defined by the existing laws of the country.'[9] The Nellie massacre is without doubt one of the worst pogroms faced by Muslims in India, surpassed probably only by the events in Gujarat in 2002. It was clear that the police and the civil administration had prior information that such an attack against the Muslims was impending yet no one took any steps to avert it.[10] Even after the massacre almost no one was brought to justice. Nellie portrays how secular and social movements can suddenly become communal and how the minorities bear the brunt of such movements.

It would perhaps be unwise to make gross generalizations about the situation of Muslims in India. There is a great diversity noticeable among Muslim populations in India on the basis of their lifestyle, work participation, and pattern of work. Today Muslims in India form the second largest Muslim population in the world after Indonesia. One observer points out that, 'The Indian Muslims are by no means a monolithic, homogeneous community but are culturally and ethnically diversified group bound together by their common belief in Islam.'[11] In terms of the work participation rate of Muslims in India there are 31.3 per cent Muslims who are working. For Hindus, the work participation rate is 40.4 per cent. In 1981 the share of Muslims in the Indian Administrative Service was 116 out of 3883, which is only 2.99 per cent. Regarding Indian Public Service, in 1981 again there were 50 Muslims out of 1753 persons making their percentage only 2.85. Summarizing the findings on socio-economic indicators, such as occupation, ownership of land and standard of living, and by religion, Abusaleh Shariff of National Sample Survey Organization (NSSO) states:

> Muslims are mostly self-employed and their share in regular paid jobs is low. The Hindu population is relatively better employed in regular salary-paying jobs in urban areas. The work participation of Muslim females is extremely low. The landholding is better among Hindus than Muslims, and Muslims work on non-agricultural occupation in substantial proportions in rural part of India. Muslims, are, by far, the least educated when compared with Hindus and Christian populations in India.[12]

By the NSSO figures of 1987-88 again there are 53.4 per cent Muslims who are self-employed, 28.9 per cent are regular wage earners and 13.4 per cent are casual labourers in urban areas in India. Although the work participation rate by the present Census have gone up by about 2 per cent, according to one observer 95 per cent of Muslims in India are, 'estimated to belong to the categories of peasant, craftsmen, semi-skilled and unskilled labourer. In rural areas most of them are agricultural labourers.'[13]

Muslims are extremely under-represented in all government services where their percentage is far below their total population. In a study on the composition of the armed forces and the paramilitary forces in the six states of Uttar Pradesh, Bihar, Andhra Pradesh, Karnataka, Maharashtra and Gujarat, he comments on the lack of Muslims in these forces. The Indian Army had 30-36 per cent Muslims at the time of Partition. The Armed Forces Reconstitution Committee, which divided the forces at the time of Partition, assumed that all Muslims would join Pakistan. But they were wrong in their assumptions. As many as 215 Muslim commissioned officers and 339 Viceroy's Commissioned Officers opted to remain in India and refused to go to Pakistan. But in the post-Partition years the number of Muslims in the armed forces was reduced to 2 per cent. Often Muslims' allegiance to India is doubted, particularly when the adversary is Pakistan. Yet the Rajput regiment consisting of largely Muslim soldiers performed with much distinction in the 1965 war with Pakistan. In a letter to the Chief Ministers dated 20 September 1953, Prime Minister Nehru had noted, 'In our Defence Services, there are hardly any Muslims left. In the vast Central Secretariat of Delhi, there are very few Muslims. Probably the position is somewhat better in the province, but not much more so. What concerns me most is that there is no effort being made to improve this situation, which is likely to grow worse unless checked.'[14] The previous government in India might have made a concerted effort to garner the support of the security forces on the basis of religion if the Gujarat riots are any indicators. According to Aftab Ahmad Ali, the former Director of SVPN Police Academy, the situation of minorities in riots depends to a large extent on the political party in power in that state. The police chief often has to work according to the dictates of the chief minister who can otherwise instantly remove or transfer police personnel. No wonder then in Gujarat the police often supported genocidal acts of the Modi government. Perhaps keeping an eye on events in Gujarat, veteran journalist A. G. Noorani has commented, 'In this there is a lesson for Muslims. Improvement of their lot is part of a wider secular agenda for reform.'[15]

According to a National Minorities Commission Report it is not just in the security services but also in the field of education that Muslims are grossly underrepresented. The report says that the percentage of Muslim students in state aided or majority-managed schools is disproportionately low.[16] Less than 4 per cent of the total populations of engineering schools are Muslims. Government spending on minority education is also disproportionately low and even in a state such as West Bengal it is about 2 per cent of the total spending on education. *Khariji Madrasas* are the educational institutions that most Muslim children go to. These institutions double-up as orphanages and there is a popular opinion that these are the breeding grounds for fundamentalism. Attitude towards Muslims thanks to the rise of Hindutva is at low ebb in most of India today. According to a social scientist this has been happening from 1990 onwards from when there is a noticeable increase in communal rioting against Muslims whereby Muslim peasantry and working classes are getting displaced in large numbers.[17] The riots of 2002 in Gujarat could be considered as a result of such growing communal polarization in India.

CHRISTIANS IN INDIA

In 1981 the Christian population in India was 16,165,447 and they formed 2.43 per cent of the total population. In 1991 the Christian population rose to 19,640,284 but their percentage dropped a little, to 2.34. In 2001 their numbers rose to 24,080,016 and their percentage dropped again a little and currently they form 2.3 per cent of the total population. Hence the decadal growth rate of Christians is on the decline. Most of the Christian population in India is found either in South India or in Northeast India. In Nagaland, Mizoram and Meghalaya the Christians form overwhelmingly the majority of the population, being 90 per cent, 87 per cent and 70.3 per cent respectively. The sex ratio of Christians in India is much above the national average and it is 1009 women to a thousand men. In India only among Christians does one find women more in number than men; although in the sex ratio of 0-6 years, girls are much less in number, being only 964, but even that is higher than the national average. Education is a priority for Christians in India. The literacy rate of Christians in India is 80.3 per cent, which is considerably higher than the national average. Even female literacy rate among Christians is as high as 76.2 per cent by the latest Census. By 1995 there were 226 colleges in India run by Christians with a total enrolment of 343,378. There are three medical and two engineering colleges run by Christians. Christians are pioneers in the field of women's education. Among the 950 women's colleges in India Christians run 87 of them.[18]

However, education does not reflect the only reality of the lives of Indian Christians. Their work participation rate is as low as 39.7 per cent. In urban sectors their work participation rate is as high as 56 per cent but in rural areas it is much lower. Over 75 per cent of Christians live in rural areas. In urban sectors most of the jobs taken by Christians are those of secretaries, nurses, teachers, salesmen, and so on. There are very few Christians in the higher administration of the government and there are equally few Christian CEOs. Also very few of them are doctors and engineers and there are practically no big Christian entrepreneurs.[19]

Most Christians in India are converts from backward communities. This has been one of the main reasons for pro-Hindutva governments such as the BJP-led government to start virulent campaigns against missionary preaching because these political parties consider it a camouflage for religious conversions. Since 1954 missionaries are required to obtain entry visas before coming to India. Although Article 25 guarantees to every person the right to profess, practice and propagate any religion that they might want, the Indian state is extremely cautious about missionaries. Way back in 1956 the Niyogi Committee report had condemned Christian missionaries by alleging that they have exploited uneducated people. In 1960 there was an effort to introduce a bill to save SC and ST from forced religious conversion. In 1978 Morarji Desai had to withdraw a bill to ban conversions. When the BJP came to power in 1999, it embarked on a policy of terrorizing minorities in the name of alleged conversions. According to a social scientist, 'Minorities were made to suffer in the name of conversions as it happened to the Christians during the years from 1998 to 2001,' coinciding with the arrival of BJP to power.[20] Many of the states such as Tamil Nadu banned conversions. In 1998 attacks on Christians began in six districts of Gujarat and even a girls school was attacked in Rajkot. In a meeting on displacement in Bangalore in 2002, representatives of Christian Church groups from Gujarat spoke to the author about the great insecurity that they were facing after the Gujarat riots.

Since over 90 per cent Christians in North India belong to the Scheduled Castes (SC) and Scheduled Tribes (ST), Christians often share the disabilities of ethnic minorities such as the tribal people. Hence any mapping exercise remains incomplete if one does not look at the situation of ethnic minorities such as the tribal people of India.

SITUATION OF ETHNIC MINORITIES

In 1981 more than 7.8 per cent of the total population belonged to the Scheduled Tribes. Today their population is about 8 per cent. These tribes are often called Adivasis or original inhabitants of the land. Article 366 (25) of the

Indian Constitution has defined Scheduled Tribes as 'such tribes or tribal communities as are deemed under Article 342 to be Scheduled Tribes for the purpose of this Constitution.' By the Constitutional Order of 1950 the President of India made 212 Scheduled Tribes. Later by Acts of Parliament some other groups were included. Today the number of Scheduled Tribes is 698. From 1999 India has a separate ministry on tribal affairs. Tribals are also ethnic groups and so they form the largest part of ethnic minority groups in India. Most tribes have their distinct social structures, dialects, rituals and lifestyles. Many of the tribes are demanding recognition as peoples and nations. For example, the Indian government and the Naga tribal people are engaged in the longest State versus Community conflict in South Asia. Although Nagaland became a separate state in 1963, that was too little too late. The Naga demand by then had become a demand for self-determination and no longer a demand for autonomy. All through the late 1980s and early 1990s the GOI tried to douse the flame of independence among the Naga people through draconian acts. The Oinam massacre, the Mokokchung killings, the Kohima firings, and others have become legendary as repressive acts of the state. From 1997 there is a ceasefire between the GOI and two major Naga rebel groups and violence has slightly abated in that region.

From the 1980s there are other tribal groups who are demanding some form of autonomy. The GOI imposed the Armed Forces Special Powers Act (AFSPA) of 1958 on the frontier tribes as a response to such demands. Although this dreadful Act was supposed to be operational only for 6 months, it has continued to be in operation even now. Today civil society of Manipur has created a huge protest against this Act. The Manipur government was forced to withdraw this Act from certain parts of Imphal, the capital city. The AFSPA has been imposed on almost all frontier tribes' peoples from the late 1970s. Still the tribal people have continued their fight for autonomy, resulting in demands for

Gorkhaland or Boroland, and so on. In the late 1990s the GOI started exploring possibilities for a political solution. Three new tribal majority states, namely, Uttaranchal (renamed Uttarakhand), Chattisgarh and Jharkhand were created in 2000. But this did not solve the ethnic problem. There are many more demands for autonomy among tribal people. The tribal people have a grievance that the mainstream has never considered them as equal participants in Indian democracy.

TRIBAL PEOPLE AND DEVELOPMENTAL DISPLACEMENT IN INDIA

In India alone one study testifies that 3.6 million Adivasis have been displaced and only about one-third have been rehabilitated.[21] If one looks at World Bank reports after 1993 on the construction of dams one gets this picture even more clearly.[22] The Sardar Sarovar Project, often described as one of the most flawed projects, displaced largely the Tadvis, Vasavas, Bhils and the Bhilalas but very few Hindus who were not dalits. In a recent survey it was again stated that tribal population has been disproportionally affected by developmental projects in India. An estimated 2 per cent of the total Indian population has been displaced by development projects. Of these, 40 per cent are tribal people, although they constitute only 8 per cent of the total population today.[23] During the last fifty years, some 3.300 big dams have been constructed in India and another 1,000 are under construction. Many of them have led to large-scale forced eviction of vulnerable groups. The situation of the Adivasis is of special concern as they are reported to constitute between 40 per cent and 50 per cent of the displaced population. In 1994 even the GOI came up with an estimate that over 15 million people have been displaced and over 11 million were still awaiting rehabilitation. Although non-governmental agencies give a much larger figure of displaced people in India, the government figures are important because they reflect that most of the displaced have not been rehabilitated.

One of the most controversial development projects in India is the Narmada Valley Development Project. It envisages building 3,200 dams that will reconstitute the Narmada and her 419 tributaries into a series of step-reservoirs and become easy sources of water for irrigation. The first dam on the Narmada River, the Bargi Dam that was completed in 1990, reportedly displaced 1,14,000 people from 162 villages and today irrigates only 5 per cent of the land it was said to benefit. Most of the evicted did not get any compensation.[24] The people who are evicted are largely tribals and the dams are meant to benefit landowners who are largely Hindus. Although the Census marks most of the tribal people as Hindus, their situation is very different from that of upper-caste Hindus. Human Rights activists say that the construction of more than 3,000 dams will flood thousands of acres of forestland largely populated by tribal people, striking a devastating blow to human lives and biodiversity. Furthermore, the displacement of the Narmada Valley residents from their lands threatens their rights to livelihood and self-determination. Since 1985, the Narmada Bachao Andolan (NBA) has been organizing massive rallies and peaceful demonstrations to protest the destruction of the Narmada Valley. Despite the non-violent nature of the protests, NBA activists have been arrested and beaten on countless occasions. In 1993 the World Bank withdrew from the project and this was deemed a victory for the rights movement in India but in 2000 a ruling by the Supreme Court authorized renewed construction of the dam. Those who oppose the project place themselves in danger of rising floodwaters and of arrest and detention.

The new forest laws and orders on encroachments have led to further displacement of tribal people. On 1 April 2002, the following order was passed by the Supreme Court, 'The Union of India has received responses from various states with regard to the problem of encroachment in forests. The said responses are being attended to and a final decision will be taken and directions issued by the Union of India within six weeks.' Following this, on 3 May 2002, a letter from Inspector General of Forests called for eviction of encroachers. As a result of this order thousands of tribals were evicted. Yet they have been living in these lands for generations. But because they did not have the pattas or legal documents to these lands they are now being evicted from them.[25]

In most of South Asia tribal people are a persecuted lot. Just because the frontier tribes are largely in conflict with the state it does not mean that the non-frontier tribes are any better off. Development projects and forest laws work against them. Recently we visited a region called Sonbhadra in Uttar Pradesh, bordering Madhya Pradesh. The situation of the tribal people here portrays the seriousness of their situation in most of India. This region on account of its natural barriers, rough terrain and extensive forests became the abode of different tribal groups. In the post 1950s it was the site of massive developmental projects such as dams. Also big industries such as Kanoria chemicals and Hindalco were set up. This was followed by coal and limestone mining, leading to a massive influx of non-tribal people in the region. Colossal industrialization projects led to soil erosion, deforestation and growing pollution. Many acres of tribal land were soon submerged due to the construction of reservoirs of the Rihand dam. Due to the construction of this dam more than 2,20,000 tribal people from 140 villages were displaced. Of them the majority were displaced multiple times, not only due to building of dams but also because of coal mining and the establishment of a thermal power plant. Then by declaring tribal land as forest land the government made many more homeless.

The local people who had already suffered because of massive environmental degradation and deforestation now lost almost 80 per cent of their common property resources. This resulted in their increasing pauperization. Most of them were reduced to subsistence living. Today these people are faced with near starvation. Located close to the infamous Kalahandi, where people still starve to death despite greater prosperity elsewhere, the people of Sonbhadra face a similar situation of starvation today. Their children are dying of a disease called hunger. In December 2003, when I visited the area, at last 18 children belonging to the Ghasia tribe died of hunger and the number keeps increasing. Numerous civil liberties organizations are working in this area including People's Voices for Civil and Human Rights (PVCHR) and Fellows for Reconstruction, Initiative, Education, Nourishment and Development of the Society (FRIENDS).

If one looks at highway-building projects in metropolitan cities in India one sees how tribals are displaced from the vicinity of these cities. As yet there are only very few protests against such displacements. Tribals are facing persecution in most parts of India. They are now being forced to move away from natural resources such as forests on which their lives depend. Since most of them practised *jhum* cultivation (slash and burn) and since there is a state policy against jhum cultivation, their lands are being taken away from them. In the process their children are dying of starvation and yet there is very little effort by the state to address this problem. It has to be realized that without substantial help from the state and Adivasi friendly policy the situation will not change.

OTHER MINORITIES

There are a number of other minorities in India. Among religious minorities the Sikhs form 1.9 per cent of the population today. However, most of the Sikhs are located in one state within India and that state is Punjab. In a total Sikh population of 19,215,730 people, 14,592,387 live in Punjab. Sikhism and Hinduism have coexisted for many years. But in the 1980s the Sikhs came up with a demand for homeland that was symbolized in their movement for Khalistan. That movement was contained through military and political initiatives and today the Sikhs are participating in the political processes once again. However, what needs to be realized is that the Sikh demands have been contained and not solved.

There are a number of linguistic minorities in India. Language came to be recognized as a legitimate basis for state formation in India from the 1950s. Many Indian states were organized on linguistic lines. As a result, most of these states have what may be called a home language. According to the 1981 Census, India has over 700 languages of which only 15 are recorded in the Eighth Schedule and which are spoken by 95.6 per cent of the population. That linguistic minorities or speakers of minority languages can have major problems was revealed by discrimination faced by Bengalis in Assam during the anti-foreigner movement. However, today language is an add-on issue and can become problematic when it is mixed with other issues such as religion and ethnicity.

DALITS AND THE ISSUE OF PROTECTIVE DISCRIMINATION

According to a number of social scientists there are 'special types of minorities mentioned in the Constitution,' and they are the backward classes or the dalits.[26] The situation of caste minorities or dalits is much more serious than that of many other minority groups in India. There might have been some controversy in accepting dalits as a minority but the United Nations Committee on the Elimination of Racial Discrimination at its sixty-first session in Durban, 2001, recognized discrimination against dalits as racial discrimination. The dalits, officially called the Scheduled Castes (SC), were victims of the inhuman practice of untouchability. As late as in 1997 there were 1157 untouchability-related crimes registered in Indian courts.[27]

It is not as if reservation of seats and posts in government-run or government-aided educational institutions and government posts for SC/ST and Other Backward Classes

(OBC) was accepted without protest. In the late 1980s the Mandal Commission identified 3743 caste groups as OBCs. The Commission recommended that 27 per cent jobs be reserved for the OBCs in addition to the already accepted reservation of 15 per cent for SCs and 7.5 per cent for STs. The decision of the United Front Government to implement the Mandal Commission led to massive protest culminating in 'a number of cases of soul-searing self-immolation attempted by students.'[28] This was not the first or the only protest by upper caste Hindus against reservation for minorities. In Gujarat there were attacks against SC, ST and OBCs in 1980 and 1985. Cases for reservation have come up before the Supreme Court a number of times. In 1997, 504 dalits were murdered, 3462 were grievously hurt, 1002 dalit women were raped and 12149 faced other atrocities.[29] This was in no way an exceptional year but rather a typical year in terms of atrocities towards dalits.

The National Campaign on Dalit Human Rights (NCDHR) reports that although there are legislations against bonded labour between 1976, when the Act against bonded labour was passed, and 31 March 1999, the Indian government identified 280,340 bonded labourers largely from dalit community. Almost half of the rural dalit population (49 per cent) are agricultural labourers, while only 25 per cent are cultivators. Even the Ceiling Land, or surplus land, which has been distributed is not being enjoyed by dalits. In 1996, a door-to-door survey of 250 villages in Surendranagar District, in the state of Gujarat, found that 1087 dalit landholders possessing title to Ceiling Land are unable to enjoy cultivation of the land. The main reasons for this were that: those who had title to land had no possession; those who had possession had not had their land measured or faced illegal encroachments from upper castes.[30] Activists working on the issue of dalit rights, however, state that whatever improvement there is in the situations of dalits today is largely due to state policies.

MINORITY WOMEN IN INDIA

A mapping exercise on minority rights and protection needs to give special attention to the question of women. The Indian state has traditionally viewed women less as individuals and more as members of their communities. Often neither the secular judiciary nor the state has helped women to fight discrimination enforced by their own communities as in the Shah Bano and the Ameena Cases. Although a lot has already been written by social scientists on such cases, it would still be of significance to revisit them, especially within the context of autonomy of minorities. Also it would be of particular significance to bring on board the debate on the Uniform Civil Code and reflect on how the state and the minority communities have responded to it.

Among the tribal people who are giving up jhum cultivation, women are the poorest. We find differing opinions regarding the relative position of women in tribal India. Some say that women here enjoy much higher status in this region while others call them 'primitive'. Population movements and pressure on lands have impacted heavily in areas where people practised jhum cultivation before. Now that the tribal people are forced to give up jhum cultivation the situation of women who were the majority among the cultivators is becoming worse, as is the case of Naga women or Reang women in Tripura. Their social and economic positions are affected by this transition yet there are hardly any programmes to retrain them for income generation, thus leading to further pauperization of tribal women.

Even in displacements of tribal people due to developmental projects, women are at the receiving end of the spectrum and can hardly ever access resources for their sustenance. As has been pointed out earlier, although the beneficiaries of the dam are meant to be large landowners, tribal people are paying the price. In such situations it is common that women from these communities will be the worst affected. As one observer points out, relief programmes tend to overlook women's crucial roles as producers, providers, and organizers, and have delivered assistance directly to male heads of households, whether it is food, seeds and tools, or training. This reduces women's influence over areas previously controlled by them, such as the production and provision of food, undermining their position within the household and the community.[31] Therefore, tribal women face problems both for being tribal people as well as for being women.

Among dalits, women face increased atrocities. An NCDHR report states that: 'Women are the worst victims,' of violence against dalits.[32] It says that 'Dalit women are the most discriminated and exploited persons in a society dominated by caste hierarchy and patriarchy. For them, the intersection of caste and gender means that they are subject to the most extreme forms of violence, discrimination and exploitation, even at the hands of women from upper-castes.'[33] In 1984 there were 692 rape cases against dalit women and in 1994 the number had risen to 991. Literacy among dalit women is just 23.76 per cent, that is, about half the literacy rate of non-dalit women. Such low levels of literacy have profound consequences for their lives and the rest of the dalit community. Illiteracy makes them susceptible to superstitious beliefs and misinformation regarding their bodies, reproduction and health, due to which their fertility rates continue to be higher than those of non-dalit women. The representation of dalit women in the job market is very low. Dalit women are perhaps the most economically deprived section of society. According to one commentator the 'workforce structure of dalit women is such that they rarely own land.'[34] In 1991, dalit women workers numbering about 71 per cent were agricultural labourers in rural areas. Only 19 per cent were cultivators. The new economic policies of opening public sectors to private companies have reduced jobs for women, particularly dalit women. Some of these women as in Andhra Pradesh are forced to become jogins (similar to devdasis). These girls are married to village gods and are then sexually exploited by the upper castes. Among 15,000 jogins in twelve districts of Andhra Pradesh 80 per cent are dalit women.[35] Also because these women are considered polluting they do not get jobs in people's homes. All these things taken together drive these women towards prostitution and further sexual exploitation. The state seems oblivious to the condition of these women and positive discrimination does not seem to have touched these women to any great extent.

CONCLUSION

In a mapping exercise such as this it needs to be remembered that the category of minorities is not fixed, but rather time-specific. The composition of minorities changes on the basis of state policies and today's tentative majority can become a minority tomorrow. In India every day new minorities are created. Speaking of the Indian situation, eminent sociologist Dipankar Gupta has commented, 'minoritization can be so indiscriminate and disrespectful of previous consensus, then no matter how exhaustive the listing of minorities, the exercise will always be both incomplete and futile.'[36] The determinant for the creation of minorities is not number but powerlessness. In a majoritarian and patriarchal state system such as found in India, old cleavages on the basis of class, caste, gender, race, ethnicity, and so on, get accentuated within societies. Added to that the New Economic Policies of globalization and a new world order drives us further away from a just world. In such a situation new minorities emerge and the older ones get even more marginalized. It is not as if within those communities there is no space for accessing power. The ascendancy of the Bahujan Samaj Party (BSP) portrays that there is such scope. But for that powerless groups need to play the majoritarian game whereby a few of them are able to access greater resources while the rest remains marginalized. This is the state of material politics of minorities in India.

This mapping exercise of minorities in India is not intended to be a summary of the situation of all minorities in India as that is an impossible project. Rather, the effort has been to look at the issue of autonomy of minorities by examining some cases that reflect on the ability of different communities to access resources and to negotiate with the state and other communities as a group. Such a mapping exercise amply portrays that a great deal needs to be done before minorities of today can be called equal participants in Indian democratic processes.

NOTES

1. Michael Mann, 'The Dark Side of Democracy: The Modern Tradition of Ethnic and Political Cleansing,' *The New Left Review* 235 (May/June 1999): 18-45.
2. 'The First Report on Religion,' *Census of India,* 2001. All data in this mapping exercise unless otherwise mentioned are taken from 1991 and 2001 Census.
3. Rajendra Pandey, *Minorities in India: Protection and Welfare* (New Delhi: APH Publishing Corporation, 1997): 72.
4. All population figures are taken from 'The First Report on Religion,' *Census of India 2001.*
5. Christophe Jaffrelot, '*The Relationship between Democracy and Communalism in India,*' Lecture in CERI, Paris, 28 January 2004.
6. 'Census Relook at Muslim data,' *Times of India* 9 September 2004.
7. '206 B'deshis held in 7 months: BSF,' *The Sentinel* 17 August 2003.
8. 'B'deshi dacoits penetrate security cover in Khowai,' *Tripura Observer* 21 August 2003.
9. Monirul Hussain, 'The Muslim Question in India,' in *Religious Minorities in South Asia: Selected Essays on Post-Colonial Situations,* vol 2, edited by Monirul Hussain and Lipi Ghosh (New Delhi: Manak Publications, 2002): 130.
10. M. J. Akbar, 'The Children of Nellie,' *Sunday* 3 March 1984: 15-18.
11. Muthaharunnisa Omar, quoted in *The Social Structure of Indian Muslims,* edited by F.R. Faridi and M. M. Siddiqi (New Delhi: Institute of Objective Studies, 1992): 65.

12. Shariff Abusaleh, National Sample Survey Organization (NSSO), 43rd round, 1987-88, quoted in Sebastian Vempeny, *Minorities in Contemporary India* (New Delhi: Kanishka, 2003): 92.
13. Ibid: 90.
14. Jawaharlal Nehru, *Letter to the Chief Ministers* quoted in A.G. Noorani, 'Muslims in the Forces,' *Counter Currents.Org* 13 October 2003, http://www.countercurrents.org , p.3 of 7.
15. Ibid: 6 of 7.
16. GOI, *National Minorities Commission Annual Report*, 1996-97: 41. http://nhre.nic.in/ar96-97.htm
17. Ajazuddin Ahmad, *Muslims in India 1990-1993*, vol.2 (New Delhi: Inter India Publications, 1994): 14-15.
18. Figures given by All India Association for Christian Higher Education (AIACHE) Publication, http://www.aiache.org.documentationcentre.
19. Sebastian Vempeny, *Minorities in Contemporary India* (New Delhi: Kanishka, 2003): 104-05.
20. Ibid: 210.
21. Stan Swamy, 'New State, Dying Hopes', *Combat Law: The Human Rights Magazine* 2, 1 (April-May 2003:) 83.
22. Lyla Mehta and Bina Srinivasan, 'Balancing Pains and Gains: A Perspective Paper on Gender and Large Dams', Working Paper of the World Commission on Dams (unpublished), prepared for *Thematic Review*, Cape Town, South Africa, http://www.dams.org/p.2.
23. Courtland Robinson, *Risks and Rights: Causes, Consequences, and Challenges of Development-Induced Displacement* (Washington DC: Brookings-SAIS Project, May 2003): 10-11.
24. Report by Global IDP Project, http://www.db.idpproject.org/Sites/idpSurvey.nsf/wViewCountries/9E49C4B9CFA1B344C1256A940028BDDD
25. Pradip Prabhu, 'Tribals Face Genocide', *Combat Law: The Human Rights Magazine* 1, 4 (October-November 2002): 73.
26. Vempeny, *Minorities in Contemporary India:* 184. Many other social scientists such as Imtiaz Ahmad also prescribe to this view.
27. Annual Report of Commissioner for SC/ST in *Combat Law: The Human Rights Magazine*, 1, 4 (October-November 2002): 5.
28. Rajendra Pandey, *Minorities in India – Protection and Welfare* (New Delhi: APH Publishing Corporation, 1997): 205. cited in full earlier
29. Annual Report of Commission for the Scheduled Caste and Tribe, Delhi, 1997, in *Combat Law: The Human Rights Magazine* 1, 4 (October-November 2002): 6.
30. Ibid.
31. Tehmina Rehman, 'Internal Displacement: Atrocities on Women in India,' *Gender Issues*, http://www.punjabilok.com/india_disaster_rep/

issue_significance/gender_issues.htm

32. 'National Campaign on Dalit Human Rights,' www.dalits.org/CERDSubmissionNCDHR.htm p.2.
33. 'Broken Promises and Dalits Betrayed: Black Paper on The Status of Dalit Human Rights,' NCDHR, http://www.dalits.org/Blackpaper.html
34. Vimal Thorat, 'The Least of the Oppressed,' in *Combat Law: The Human Rights Magazine* 1, 4 (October-November 2002): 24.
35. Ibid: 25.
36. Dipankar Gupta, 'Secularization and Minoritization,' in *Minority Identities and the Nation-State,* edited by D. L. Seth and Gurpreet Mahajan (New Delhi: Oxford University Press, 1999): 54.

3

'MINORITIES-IN-MINORITIES' IN SOUTH ASIAN SOCIETIES:
Between Politics of Diversity and Politics of Difference

JOANNA PFAFF-CZARNECKA

CRITICAL POSITIONS ON multiculturalism are caught in the dilemma between affirming the obvious urgency of minority protection in states and societies while simultaneously paying attention to the constraints that any such collective accommodation brings about. At the beginning of the third millennium, the majorities' 'fear of small numbers' (Appadurai 2006) persists, and blatant human rights' abuses experienced by minority members continue to characterize late modernity. Simultaneously, the scope of minority assertion, the growing sensitivity to minority grievances and demands as well as the expansion of regimes aimed at diversity accommodation form an important feature of politics around the globe. Collective provisions appear as appropriate instruments of protection and recognition under these circumstances. And yet internal differentiation and dynamics of change occurring 'outside' and 'inside' the minority 'groups' put collectivizing practices to test, in particular those that pose restrictions to individual freedom and that act against the norm of equality.

At the beginning of the third millennium, the tensions entailed in endeavours to accommodate diversity in contemporary societies are located between constellations of governance and governmentality. The present-day governance structures open up spaces of opportunity for minority activism that increasingly draws upon global connectivity. Global dissemination of ideas and transnational networking have significantly buttressed minority aspirations and their politics of identity and belonging. With the 'third wave of democratization', human rights' protection and diversity accommodation acquire a growing importance in most of the architectures of national governance (Reynolds 2002), and will be discussed, here, by drawing upon South Asian examples. Among the central demands in the postcolonial era are cultural rights: comprising protection and recognition of 'cultural units', devolution of power (up to territorial autonomy) as well as power sharing.

Today, governance is understood as a complex formation of societal steering; where continuous negotiations between the state and the civil society (under conditions of globality) play a crucial role. Among the state guarantees, the right to participate is an important prerequisite for community leaders to raise their voice, to engage in mobilization pursuing collective goals, and to make sure that rights are realized in practice. Under the conditions of majoritarian control, state-society accommodations evolve around designs for a 'proper system through which all [the] aspirations can be channelized' (Ghosh 2009: xxx). These negotiations have had substantial effects upon the internal dynamics within minorities because 'groups operate in a social field of pressures' (Weinstock 2005: 239). They tend to act in reaction to majoritarian practices, for instance, by drawing sharp collective boundary-lines between the 'outside' and the 'inside' (Wimmer 2008). Also in organizing their internal affairs, they respond strategically 'to the political, legal and cultural environments in which they find themselves' (ibid: 239; also Shachar 2001: 37-38).

While representing collective identities and seeking to match governmental criteria for collective accommodations entailed in multicultural politics, community leaders have frequently embarked upon communitarianism that reinforces ethnic boundary-closure, internal homogenization as well as subjugation under collective norms. These practices often endorse internal hierarchies and highlight patriarchal values. In the ongoing negotiations of democratic models for minority accommodation, the challenge of governmentality is vital. According to Foucault, governmentality is a technology of self-government and population control that conditions all actors within a given social field. This model envisages that those who govern and those who are governed adopt a common set of rules through their entanglements. This normative rapprochement results in reinforcing particular norms—that, for instance, buttress identitarian positionings—'no matter whether these actors intend to contain conflicts' (Thies and Kaltmeier 2009) or whether they are entangled in strategies of rebellion and resistance. Normative convergences result from jointly putting value stress on communitarian ideals, on the importance of maintaining collective boundaries as well as on according special value to collective identity (often considered perennial) and to the quest for its preservation. This often poses restrictions upon individuals as well as upon internal collectives, who are exposed to hardships in a double way: by suffering discriminatory practices directed against their minority and by enduring 'internal' pressures.

The problem of 'minorities-in-minorities' has already been extensively discussed in the field of political theory (Kymlicka 1995; Shachar 2001; Eisenberg and Spinner-Halev 2005; Benhabib 2002; in South Asian context by Mahajan 2005, in particular). The main thrust of these preoccupations has so far been on the complexities entailed in the normative foundations of minority protection—that is, the values of freedom, equality, autonomy and principles of recognition—that inform state policies dealing with diversity. These debates have centred upon these values that conflict in multicultural societies, and especially on the collision between inter-group and intra-group equality. Mahajan (2005) has thematized this tension, suggesting that the quest for the former is likely to impede the latter, given the differentiated and hierarchical nature of 'traditional communities'. Of special importance here are three sets of issues: first, the problem of tolerance vis-à-vis internal pressures limiting individual freedom (including the freedom of exit) and equality; second, the (im)possibilities of state interference into a minority's internal affairs, and third, the tensions entailed in legal pluralism, in particular those resulting from the priority given to religious personal law within secular legal frameworks.

This essay adopts an evaluative rather than a normative perspective, and seeks to address this problem from the point of view of 'internal' dynamics and the hardships suffered by the 'minorities-in-minorities'. The emphasis will be on the differentiated character of minorities and on external and internal pressures endured by collectivities and individuals 'inside' minorities. The discussion concentrates upon diverse South Asian examples, particularly drawing upon empirical data from India, Sri Lanka, and Nepal, also revealing the national diversity in political cultures, laws, and institutions of their enforcement that evolve in the very diverse postcolonial constellations. The aim is to highlight the scope and the depth of problems 'minorities-in-minorities' face in contemporary South Asian societies. In particular, this inquiry reveals that lacking social and economic rights by vulnerable persons within minorities results in greater hardships than are usually acknowledged in multicultural discourses.

'MINORITIES' AND 'MINORITIES IN MINORITIES': CONCEPTUAL PROBLEMS

It is impossible to discuss the predicaments of 'minorities-in-minorities' without formulating two major disclaimers. First, the notion of 'minority' is academically unclear and often contested in political communication. Second, the notion of 'minorities-in-minorities' can consequently be used only as a problematic 'short-cut' term.

Scholars disagree upon the definition of what minorities are. The most widely disseminated approach, formulated by Capotorti (1991), defines a minority group as one 'which is numerically inferior' and in a 'non-dominant position', 'whose members possess ethnic, religious or linguistic characteristics which differ from those of the rest of the population' and who 'if only implicitly, maintain a sense of solidarity, directed towards preserving their culture, traditions, religion or language'. Deschene (1985) provided a similar definition, based on the former one, but instead of stressing the quest for preserving culture, he highlighted the 'collective will to survive' and the aim 'to achieve equality with the majority in fact and in law'. Activists recently found the first definition as 'inadequate as it did not accommodate groups who did not wish to preserve the basis of their difference, for example the Dalits'[1] (Manchanda 2009: 5). Deschene's emphasis on minorities' desire for assimilation or integration was also criticized on the ground that it does not apply to all kinds of minorities (ibid).

The criterion of numbers is problematic as majorities do not necessarily form the establishment, while minorities are not necessarily subordinate (for South Asian examples, see Das and Samaddar 2009, passim; Manchanda 2009, passim). Also, individual members of minorities can acquire dominant positions while the majority of a minority population remains disadvantaged. Another important problem lies in representing minorities as corporate units. Whether all persons identified as members of a minority feel solidarity vis-à-vis a given minority is an empirical question. Ghosh (2009: xviiff.) rightly embarks on the problematic nature of equating the terms 'community', 'ethnicity', and 'minority' with homogeneous groups (for a critique of 'groupism' prevailing in minority discourses, see Brubaker 2004). At the same time, it is easy to understand that this equation well serves communitarian positions.

Communitarian positions—that are very influential in minority activism—put high value-stress upon self-preservation, seen as going hand-in-hand with the interest to protect internal cohesion by maintaining strong ethnic boundary-drawing mechanisms (Wimmer 2008). In this figure, both the aim of protecting collective identity and the quest for survival as a cultural unit, legitimize the subordination of members under particularist norms. In addition, ethnic boundary-maintaining mechanisms prevent members from leaving ('exit'). How far communitarian pressure can go is illustrated by the case of the Nepalese ethnic group of Dhimals who recently introduced fines on their members who perform wedding rituals that are at odds with the group's tradition (personal communication with M. Lawoti, September 2009).

Critique of the notion of 'minority' comes also from persons addressed by this term. Indigenous activists have recently argued that the term 'minority' wrongly denotes the subordinate position of their constituencies in relation to the mainstream. The status of 'native people' who strive for autonomy is neglected through the discursive figure of a minority. This critique was recently also embraced by the Dalit activists in India and Nepal, who increasingly draw upon ethnic discourses. At a different level, the notion 'minority' and its collectivizing connotations cover up the significant internal differentiation of persons belonging to a 'minority' as will become apparent throughout this essay.

Yet another problematic is given by the fact that the status of 'minority' in any given national context is the result of prolonged accommodations in the framework of societal negotiations and institutional arrangements. Consequently, the legal status of 'minority' is granted to some 'collectivities' while it is denied to others. In India, the Muslims enjoy this status that allows for a far-reaching autonomy when it comes to internal arrangements, in particular in the realm of Personal Law. Other minority categories such as the 'Scheduled Tribes' do not have this status, while at the same time enjoying entitlements to collective provisions.

The concept of 'minorities-in-minorities' suffers therefore from a double shortcoming: when the notion of 'minority' as such proves problematic, so does its multiplication. Who is meant here? Eisenberg and Spinner-Halev (2005) identify the major dimensions of predicaments denoted by the term 'minorities-in-minorities': 'Traditional family law systems often discriminate against women. Indigenous groups have been criticized for discriminating against women and, in some cases, Christians. Religious groups, too, have been accused of discriminating against women and homosexuals and mistreating children'. It is problematic, of course, to treat women as a 'minority' alone because of the criterion of numbers (see Das and Samaddar 2009 and see below). Also, persons enduring predicaments coming about with their precarious status within a 'minority' can hardly be treated as a collective *a priori.* For this reason, the notion of 'minorities-in-minorities' will be used within quotation marks, for want of a more adequate term.

Through the lens of intersectionality approach, the importance and also the ambivalence of the 'minorities-in-minorities'—problem come probably best to light. 'Intersectionality argues that it is important to look at the way in which different social divisions inter-relate in terms of the production of social relations and in terms of people's lives . . . classes are always gendered and racialized and gender is always classed and racialized' (Anthias 2009: 10)—and we can add: ethnicized. This approach sees prioritizing ethnicity over other social markers as problematic. 'People connect and engage not only in ethnic ways (indeed the saliency of ethnicity will vary contextually and situationally) but also in terms of other social categories and social relations, for example those of class, gender, age, stage in the life-cycle and political beliefs and values as well as trans-ethnicity' (ibid: 7). Members of minority groups such as women, adherents to minority religions and persons of homosexual orientation, or indeed, persons combining a number of minority characteristics (i.e. female-homosexual-Christian in India) are prone to be in a significantly more disadvantageous position than the male Hindus of high caste-status. But since entire minorities often feel at a disadvantage within the Hindu 'mainstream' in India, this can result in collective pressures to subsume 'sub-collective' (female) or individual (homosexual) orientations and grievances under the imperative of the 'minority mainstream'. An obvious rationalization of such claims consists in highlighting the necessity of community preservation that relies on coherent images of internal solidarity and positive representation, consisting above all in adhering to collective traditions. Given the internal differentiation, minority politics privileging religious and ethnic markers reveals a problematic of frontstage/backstage hierarchies entailed in multicultural orderings. Are internal measures of silencing grievances cross-cutting ethnic and religious commonalities the price for minority protection?

ACCOMMODATING DIVERSITY IN SOUTH ASIA'S DIVERSE POLITICAL CULTURES

The 'minorities-in-minorities'-problem closely relates to the (im)possibilities of minority self-assertion and adequate representations in the age of late modernity. These (im)possibilities have roots in the genesis of minorities and in their subsequent struggles in majoritarian societies for recognition and against discrimination. Minorities and their collective claims came into existence under the conditions of modernity (Anderson 1996; Gellner 1983; Wimmer 2002), while ethnicity formation and ethnic boundary-making is a significantly older phenomenon. Former political formations, such as the Ottoman Empire, ranked collectivities within hierarchical orders, by drawing between them clear-cut lines of distinction, and differentiating collective rights and duties. In this political logic, 'nationalities' were subject to hierarchical ranking, while numbers mattered little. Imperial orders, including the colonial (throughout the South Asian subcontinent, but for Nepal) and semi-colonial regimes (as was the case in Nepal) thrived on cultural diacritics that were used to legitimize inequalities. Imperial orders therefore highlighted difference and established inequalities based on cultural boundaries.

It was only under conditions of modern nation-building that numerical considerations which created the figure of 'minority' acquired a crucial importance. In many countries, notably in most modernizing postcolonial societies, nation-building provoked cultural homogenization, using formerly established cultural hierarchies. Cultural characterizations of national societies drew upon markers of societal majorities while minority cultures were relegated to subordinate status. In most national self-representations, cultural difference did not have a space. In the nation-building process on which a number of countries embarked since the beginning of the nineteenth century, minority ethnic traditions were shunned in the name of modernity. Minority populations were often subjected to cultural practices that encouraged assimilation. Most of the nation-builders considered preservation of traditional cultures as interfering with the quest for national progress, and impeding communication. Also, minority practices cultivating 'traditional' custom were often portrayed as disloyal vis-à-vis the national collective. By contrast, in India, the multi-religious, multi-linguistic and multi-ethnic character of society was recognized through constitutional provisions, but cultural hierarchies have also been at work here.

Paradoxically (or not), forging nations as culturally homogeneous entities, with state practices—like communication, representations, and so on—being linked to majority cultures, divided the populations in many countries. Exclusion from public representative bodies, pejorative portrayals of minority cultures, reinforced by obstacles to participation in politics and administration for members of minorities lacking the necessary cultural, social or economic capital turned in many countries into a negative integration matrix against which increasing resistance started to build up. Previous experiences of ordering, counting and classifying in imperial hierarchies matched with subordination and silencing in nation-building regimes enforcing assimilation have provided a powerful template on the basis of which current governmental policies *as well as* their minority contestations evolve. Previous measures at societal ordering are challenged by minority activists, often striving at normative inversions (Wimmer 2008), reacting to negative depictions of their collectivities in the past, and engaging in pressure politics. Under these conditions, 'minorities-in-minorities' become subject to governmentality.

In the current epoch of minority self-assertion, majorities and minorities are caught in struggles that are often antagonistic, but that are nevertheless mutually accommodative. In course of mutual negotiations and contestations, readjustments of discourses take place that often have solidifying effects in governmentality constellations. Collective categories are created along which collective identities are endorsed and from which collective claims to rights ensue. These dynamics buttress often reviving traditional practices. 'Traditional' positionings tend to privilege internal hierarchies and discourage dissidence by 'minorities-within-minorities', that is, challenging established gender-roles, sexual norms, or shunning religious conversion. Strategic essentializing and collective victimization voiced in public representations referring to past regimes form an important element of political communication in which minority activists engage.

Viewed from the vantage point of state practices, who qualifies as 'minority' and which minority-parameters are (more) recognized (than others) is the result of accommodations within postcolonial political orders as well as of political constellations underlying contemporary struggles for recognition. In consequence, state parties differ in their readiness to acknowledge difference. They often resist attempts of political conceptualization and legal codification that would put state practices (or their neglect to deal with minorities' objectives) into question. International law mirrors the diversity of national accommodations and national 'subtleties' in dealing with minority objectives by failing to define what is understood by the term 'minority'. This notion is so contested and so multifaceted that the international bodies refrain from providing an overarching definition, leaving this task to governments dealing with diversity within state borders.

The diversity of accommodation processes in three South Asian countries is indicated here.[2] For instance, India acknowledges 18 languages (out of 145 registered in the census of 1981) as official state languages. It recognizes four religious minorities (Muslims, Hindus, Christians and Parsis) allowing them the practice of Personal Law while subsuming others within the mainstream categories (the Sikhs and the Buddhists falling under the rubric of the 'Hindus'). Hindu-Muslim accommodations and their problems remain a very important feature of India's politics today (see below). India very early adopted collective provisions for special categories such as the Scheduled Castes, the Scheduled Tribes, the Backwards Classes as well as the Other Backward Classes and many hundreds of applications for acquiring these statuses are pending (personal communication with Sara Shneiderman in October 2009). Over the last two decades, federal states were built that correspond to territorial identities. It is impossible, of course, to do justice here to India's tremendous diversity and to the on-going measures to govern it.[3]

Sri Lanka's postcolonial politics tied modern nation-building to the politics of numbers in a particularly pronounced way. The post-independence '*Singhala-only*' doctrine adopted in 1956 resulted in discrimination against the Tamil population that had detrimental effects for Hindu Tamils (differentiated among themselves by caste, origin and rights) as well as for the non-Hindus among the Tamils (especially for

Muslim and Christian communities). In the aftermath of the coming into existence of the Liberation Tigers of Tamil Eelam (LTTE), violent ethnic conflict proved to be the outcome of an exclusivist nation-building process that by putting numerical considerations in the forefront gave way to powerful ethnic bi-polarity (see Rajasingham-Senanayke 1999), resulting in ethnic un-mixing, a practice of making sections of populations move to their 'original' regions so that regional compositions of population homogenize.

Since Nepal embarked on the process of modern nation-building by the mid-twentieth-century, it initially was oriented to modernization coupled with measures of cultural assimilation. Since the beginning of the 1990s, Nepal reversed its policies.[4] It constitutionally recognized ethnic and linguistic diversity and currently engages in a constitutional process of 'state-restructuring'. Since ethnic grievances were incorporated into the Maoist agendas in the late 1990s, cultural representation and equity, popular participation, gender justice, along with economic and social rights have simultaneously become the key issues in political mobilization. Yet it remains to be seen which political and judicial measures Nepal will adopt in order to combine this broad agenda, and how successful the new constitutional designs will prove in practice. From the 'minority-in-minorities' perspective, it is intriguing to observe a process that overtly subscribes to diverse sets of rights in an equal measure.[5]

Numerous hardships, discrimination and exclusions that minorities face in contemporary South Asian societies come particularly to light while concentrating on the 'minorities-in-minorities'. Individuals and collectivities falling under this 'rubrique' are not a quantité negligible. Rather the contrary.

EVERYDAY DISCRIMINATIONS AND THEIR CONTESTATIONS: SOUTH ASIAN EXPERIENCES

The 'minorities-in-minorities'-perspective analyses minority predicaments being viewed from the 'margins', that is, from the perspective of those individuals and collectivities who do not fit into a minority's self-representations and social arrangements. It is not coincidental that the following discussion centres on women, in particular. In their case, gender-difference, ethnicity, socio-economic status as well as, in select cases, the sexual orientation come to intersect. It is problematic to consider women as a 'minority', of course, but this term will be used here as an indicator of the severity of the numerous predicaments experienced by women. It is in no way implied here that all women face the same problems. The heterogeneity of women's 'social locations', that is, the very diverse positions in societal hierarchies, the heterogeneity of interests and capabilities as well as the differing scope of female agency and 'rooms-for-manoeuvre' —horizons have already been demonstrated for women within the realm of Islam (see e.g. Hasan and Menon 2004; Sarkar 2008). Discussing large sections of female populations under the rubrique of 'minorities-in-minorities' may also wrongly create an image of collective victimization that is by no means intended here.

'External' Threads: Violence against Minority Women

The problematic of female minority existence shows drastically in the vulnerability of their bodies. Minority women endure the same forms of suffering as women belonging to majorities: marital rape, abuses by in-laws, the killing of the girl child, forced marriage at a young age, prostitution as well as the vital problematic of widows' existence have been reported for all 'communities'. Together with male members of their communities, minority women often suffer hatred and discrimination. In addition, they suffer special forms of violence. When minorities are under attack, minority women are likely to turn into 'privileged' targets.[6] This came prominently to light during the Gujarat riots in 2002, following the BJP's 'manipulating communal violence as a political weapon to polarize an already divided society for the consolidation of the Hindu vote' (Basu Roy Chaudhury 2009: 47) in the Legislative Assembly Elections of 2002. In these riots more than 1000 men and women of Muslim faith lost their lives,[7] health, protection by relatives, and belongings[8] through immeasurable acts of cruelty.[9] Women and children were under a double attack on numerous instances: killings, torture and rape executed on women and children have been directed at themselves as well as at their entire communities. Symbolic pollution of women performed through rape and mutilation constitutes a powerful 'statement' denigrating minorities expressed in patriarchal language. As Basu Roy Chaudhury (2009: 55) puts it:

> Rapes, especially gang-rapes were used as a means of humiliating the minority community. After all sexual violence against women signifies a simultaneous humiliation of the patriarchy of the attacked community, by dishonouring their women . . . sexualized torture of women is particularly destructive to patriarchal notions of female honour.

These mechanisms were observed in other parts of South Asia as well. Pakistan is another example for minority women's vulnerability. According to Tikekar (2009: 129), 'minorities in Pakistan suffer from physical attacks, social stigmatization, psychological insecurity and economic marginalization'. Female members of particular minority categories, especially dalit women, are often gang-raped, murdered or are forced to convert to Islam, 'but no action is taken against the perpetrators of such heinous crimes' (ibid). A number of such incidents were also recorded for Christian women (ibid: 130).

These findings are matched by those from Sri Lanka where Tamil women, whether Hindus, Muslims or Christians have not only been targeted in the violent periods of conflict. They also face particular risks under the conditions of displacement (see Banerjee 2009: 65ff.). According to reports produced by Amnesty International,[10] many displaced women have fallen victims of rape also to the security forces. Many reports confirmed that the risk of sexual violence for displaced women dramatically increases in the conditions immediately prior to, during and after their flight. Simultaneously, rape has repeatedly been used to displace women. This condition was facilitated by the fact that conflict in Sri Lanka—as in other parts of South Asia—has often resulted in a collapse of community and family structures. Having to leave their homes without family and community support has rendered women particularly vulnerable to sexual violence (ibid). Physical vulnerability is reinforced through the lack of opportunities of employment,[11] lacking access to health facilities as well as the extremely hard living conditions in camps where displaced people from Sri Lanka live, which usually turn into 'homes' for very long periods of time. Often left behind without husbands and their extended family members, as in the aftermath of Gujarat riots, women were suddenly stepping out from life in seclusion, forced into self-dependence, under the conditions of displacement, dispossession and—if at all—usually very meagre compensation (Basu Ray Chaudhury 2009: 44ff.). Their former subordination, lack of education and professional skills, bear particularly heavy upon women under these circumstances.

States and their representatives, in particular the policemen, often appear as taking sides. States are often perceived as acting on behalf of societal majorities and the experiences described here confirm this view. Instead of protecting minority members, security forces have often refrained from curtailing power, or even overtly supported the perpetrators, as has been reported for the Gujarat riots. The state's neglect to curtail violence, to punish abuses, to provide for symbolic compensation though fact-finding missions and trials and the state's neglect to create decent living conditions for the victims bear witness to its partisanship.

International law increasingly denounces violence directed against minority women, interpreting it increasingly in structural terms. Acts performed upon individual female bodies in the course of collective violence are seen as expressions of abominable values nurtured within institutional frameworks. States and their authorities are increasingly taken to task for tolerating, often supporting, normative standards resulting in violence against women, targeted against whole communities and in particular against their male representatives (see Coomaraswamy 1999 b).

Two inferences are of particular importance here. First, women and children from minority groups become targets in actions directed against their entire communities because patriarchal gender norms within minorities as well as among the 'majority' perpetrators match with one another ('normative rapprochement'). Women's vulnerability is therefore the outcome of accommodations finding a common denominator in communitarian 'purity' norms. Second, this mutual accommodation of values linking 'purity' of women to collective preservation results in women's seclusion and marginalization. Their low level of education and the inability to care for themselves render women all the more vulnerable in situations of conflict. This is particularly noticeable when their traditional constellations of belonging come under attack.

'Internal' Predicaments: Subordination of Women through Religious Personal Law

Communitarian norms clash with gender justice in numerous circumstances, and these clashes reveal the social and economic vulnerability of women all the more. Indian audiences were especially made aware of the magnitude of this problem through the Shah Bano controversy that raged through the Indian public sphere in 1985-1986 and that remains a widely debated case in academic literature, until today. After more than forty years of marriage, Ahmad Khan, Shah Bano's husband, of an affluent middle-class background, unilaterally terminated their partnership in 1978 by pronouncing the *talaq*-formula. Being married and divorced according to Islamic Personal Law that is officially recognized in India, Shah Bano was left without a divorce settlement going beyond an initial two-year period. Shah Bano opted—as a number of Muslim women before her, for a secular code in her quest for bettering her financial situation. Until 1986, it was possible to take recourse to the *Criminal Procedure Code* (§ 125) which forbids a man of adequate means to leave close relatives in a state of destitution.

Having been successful with her move, Shah Bano had subsequently to face another trial because her husband appealed before the Supreme Court of India in 1985, challenging the settlement. He argued that Shah Bano ceased being his partner in marriage after he took a second wife. Ahmad Khan questioned the applicability of § 125 of *Criminal Procedure Code* for the Muslims. The Supreme Court ruled that it was the case and compelled Khan to make divorce payments to his former wife, Shah Bano. This might have settled the married couple's controversy, but the judge Chandrachud used this opportunity to express his critique vis-à-vis Muslim religious practices. This evoked a storm of criticism voiced against Muslim practices in general and it rapidly opened doors for voicing mutual resentment. Under mounting political pressure, the Supreme Court passed in 1986 the Muslim Women (Protection of Rights on Divorce) Bill demanding that divorced Muslim women who cannot look after themselves financially be put under the care of their blood relatives. Should these be not able to provide a diverse financial support, then the religious communities would have to perform this duty.

Through this new law, the autonomy of Muslim institutions in India was confirmed and reinforced. The judges made a strong statement subjugating the Muslim citizens under the Muslim Personal Law, thus precluding 'forum shopping', that is, the possibility to select between laws and courts in individual cases. The judges ruled that the social and economic rights of Shah Bano were to be handled by the Muslim community that was made to provide her with a minimal pension. Benhabib comments:

> Clearly, the purpose of . . . this . . . reform bill was to anchor the dependency of women upon a male-dominated, hierarchical structure, either the natal family or the community board. The possibility of assuring the divorced woman's independence through integrating her into a larger civil society and making her to some extent financially autonomous was totally blocked (2002: 167).

In Shah Bano's case, the Supreme Court weighted the right to Muslim communal autonomy over the state guarantee to gender equality. It is therefore important to distinguish between legal guaranties, on one hand, as well as the potentials of their realization, on the other. Legal guarantees such as gender justice constitutionally recognized by all South Asian States can be jeopardized in the process of weighting by courts different sets of rights against each other. These processes are likely to be affected by political pressure, with judges more often succumbing to strongly voiced public opinion than usually is acknowledged.

Shah Bano's case cannot merely be interpreted as an individual example. It rather sheds light on the magnitude and complexity of 'minorities-in-minorities'-problems faced particularly by women. Bringing one's own relatives to court and challenging community norms is a particularly precarious option when one's well-being depends upon this community. The importance of this case lies especially in its transformative force. It sparked off a very high degree of politicization in the public realm and resulted in the legal endorsement of a particular (i.e. Muslim community's rights and liberties) above those of women, restricting women's room for manoeuvre all the more. Shah Bano's case brought diverse political camps to contest each other. Right-wing Hindu organizations found here an excellent opportunity to denigrate Islam by highlighting its patriarchal norms and oppression of women, as if these malpractices were confined only to Islam. The recognition of religious law was criticized by secularists. Conflicting notions of freedom were debated between 'communitarians' as well as feminists of diverse political convictions. Indeed, communitarian feminism came to oppose liberal feminist versions (see Pfaff-Czarnecka 2007: 286ff).

Under the circumstances of political cleavages coming more and more into the open, the Supreme Court of India opted for a political compromise at the expense of Shah Bano who capitulated under severe public pressure and at the expense of other Muslim women (see also Kumar 1998). Despite the fierce protest from the feminist camp, in the case of Shah Bano, gender justice was relegated to a lesser priority while communitarian ideals as well as the quest for depoliticization of communal tensions acquired the centre stage. The pronounced disagreements between diverse feminist groups certainly did not help Shah Bano's cause.

Cultural Rights in Collision with Social and Economic Rights

Shah Bano's case generally points towards the Muslim women's discrimination in the social and economic field.[12] Numerous ethnographic accounts as well as censuses and reports (see in particular the Sachar Report 2006) document the scope of dependence, poverty, and underemployment among this religious group. These are matched by lack of access to health facilities as well as by inequalities within the educational system. In all these fields Muslim women are reported as particularly disadvantaged, but these findings hold for women in other minorities as well. One among many cases in point is the situation among the Adivasi (indigenous) women in Bangladesh, though women's situation varies from community to community and from region to region. According to Rahman (2009: 113), most Adivasi women are quite marginalized, even among the matrilineal Khasi and Mandi groups. Notable exceptions exist in the case of the Mandi (Garo) people, and to a lesser extent, the Marmas. Compared to women from the majority Bengali community, Adivasi women face fewer social restrictions, though. Still, their inheritance laws tend to discriminate against women. 'The literacy rates for women are far lower than for men in all parts of the country. Although no separate estimates are available for the Adivasis, the 1991 Census suggests that literacy rates among women are lower even in areas with a significant Adivasi population' (ibid).

Children, another important 'minority-in-minority', cannot be forgotten here. Traditional family law systems can often have detrimental effects on their well-being. Patriarchal norms have frequently led to killing of female babies, to unequal treatment of boys and girls as well as to child marriage. In the educational field religious orientations can induce parents to send their children to special schools that later affect their chances in the labour market and consequently, the overall living conditions. This can particularly bear on girls who are denied the possibility to become economically independent when their educational course is restricted by their parents. Another very important field is the treatment of children born of 'mixed' partnerships. Minority communities often ostracize these children and deny them rights.

Socio-economic inequalities that often put entire minorities at disadvantage are therefore reinforced by internal inequalities. Multiculturalist positions vary significantly in their weighting the diverse sets of rights in relation to each other. Is the protection of particular sets of rights more urgent than that of other rights? Fierce proponents of cultural rights suggested *sequencing*, that is, giving priority to cultural rights vis-à-vis full enjoyment of other sets of rights. This position forgets to acknowledge the magnitude of oppression of persons denied chances in education, in employment and in exerting political will. Will Kymlicka argues that strong group-based protections should not be secured at the price of violating rights fundamental to individual well-being. According to him, the aim of multicultural citizenship and minority rights is to provide groups with *external protections* and not to protect minorities in imposing *internal restrictions* on their members (1995, Ch.3). The 'minorities-in-minorities'-perspective adopted in this essay brings the close relationship between the disadvantages in ownership relations, the lack of education and hence professional skills and the vulnerability of women to light. Minority women are precisely the ones in need of social and economic resources for the sake of self-protection, whereas a tension exists between cultural rights of collectivities and the social and economic rights of their members.

Internal Inequalities and Possibility of Reforms 'from Within'

Under these circumstances, a major question centres on the possibilities of how to strengthen rights of minorities within minorities. If the scope of state interference into the minorities' internal affairs is restricted, then reforms 'from within', paired with civil society assistance, remain the major option to reverse internal inequalities. 'Voice' appears so far a problematic option as communitarian value systems depend upon and reinforce internal hierarchies. Dissent is usually shunned. However, empirical cases document that internal reforms are possible, indeed occur within pronounced communitarian contexts. One recent example is provided by India's Catholic organizations.[13]

In the ongoing struggles within the Catholic Church in India, female activists have repeatedly denounced the persistence of patriarchal norms buttressing female subjugation and violence against women in public and private realms, inequalities in the field of social and economic rights as well as the lack of women's representation in organizational bodies. Catholic women's problems extend to a full range of issues, including abuses in intimate marital relations, power differentials within households and in communities as well as the lack of *voice* at the organizational level. Female activists from within the church have already scored success in reforming Christian Personal Laws after 20 years of struggles by the year 2000 (Mahajan 2005: 108).

According to official statements by the Catholic Bishops Conference of India (CBCI), at the end of 2009 the church has begun to undertake measures geared at 'redeeming a centuries-long injustice'.[14] It is to adopt a policy to grant equal representation within commissions that take decisions regarding all aspects of Catholic life: seminaries, parish and diocesan pastoral councils which take administrative decisions, finance committees, marriage tribunals and social service societies. It also promises to grant women the right to become pastoral assistants in all parishes and to take part in a common decision-making process. The CBCI also foresees sensitization courses and feminist theology as main subjects in seminaries where priests and nuns train and also call for biblical interpretations from women's perspective. Sensitization courses extend to highlighting equal partnership in marriage. Among CBCI's major stated objectives is boosting the self-confidence among women and working towards land and property rights for women as well as towards equal pay for equal work within parishes.

This ambitious plan is yet to be translated into an approved policy and it remains to be seen to what degree these policies will be put into practice. At present, this plan reveals above everything else the scope of women's subordination in one important South Asian minority (and similar findings are reported from other continents). Simultaneously, the CBCI's plan is a telling indication of the *possibility of change* within minorities that occur under the conditions of ongoing societal change, and is the result of prolonged contestation of Catholic female activists. CBCI's official statement identifying pronounced inequalities and discrimination within its patriarchal structure and envisaging far-reaching change that would challenge its basic normative orientations is an important step towards recognizing the problem within the organizational structure. Very importantly, the significant reversal of normative orientations and the promise that it holds out for women indicate that substantial revision of previous practices within minority communities—corresponding to the crucial changes in the societal mainstream—is possible. The organizational reform plan that is envisaged here points to the possibility of collective boundary-maintenance while engaging in normative reorientation and allowing for tearing down unjust structures. This example illustrates that social dynamics cannot be seen in the simplistic 'either your culture or your rights' dichotomy (Shachar 2001: 90).

Discrimination of Homosexual Practices: 'Exit' as Viable Alternative

A different dimension of 'minorities-in-minorities' problem opens up for persons with a special sexual orientation. Homosexuality that has been recently widely debated in Nepal's and India's public spheres has only sporadically been taken up as a topic relating to minorities. After Nepal actually acknowledged the validity of homosexuality in its interim constitution, the Delhi High Court 'read down' the aspect of Section 377 of the Indian Penal Code which hitherto criminalized 'carnal intercourse against the order of nature' (EPW, 11 July 2009).[15] The court was guided by the rationale of 'inclusion', granting 'everyone a role' within the Indian society. The core of the judgment was that criminalization of homosexuality contravened the right to liberty, equality and non-discrimination guaranteed by the Constitution.

Recent liberalization of sexual practices in Nepal and in India extends to all cultural groups, in theory. Communitarian norms tend to shun homosexuality, however. With regard to minorities, two issues concerning special sexual orientation are particularly important. First, a section of religious leaders in India—notably Christian, Hindu, Muslim, and Sikh—has expressed severe criticism against state measures ending discrimination against same sex relationships (ibid: 5). It therefore remains to be seen whether the recent judicial reforms will be endorsed within the confines of religious minorities. The second issue, raised by Jacob Levy (2005) in general, and not specifically with reference to the South Asian context, relates to the first one. Concerns of homosexuals within minorities are only sporadically taken up because persons with homosexual orientation *are expected* to disengage themselves from their natal community life. Same-sex relations are usually felt as so unorthodox that shifting the personal context of living seems to be a necessary solution. Such rationalization obtains for majority populations as well: communitarian projections see communal belonging as an alternative to lifestyles related to homosexuality. It goes without saying that 'exit', in the form of disentangling oneself from closeness with one's kith and kin and from the embeddedness of community life, is a severe demand put upon homosexuals. The problem with this option is pointedly described by G. Mahajan:

> Communities oppress, not only by denying individuals the right to exit, but by imposing a very heavy cost for differing from the accepted way of life. For people who value their community identity and see themselves as a part of that collectivity, ex-communication or forced exit from the community is often the hardest punishment. (. . .) It is, therefore, of the utmost importance that valuing a community identity must not become a way of closing options and choices for the members (2005).

Ostracizing Non-Conformist Marriage Practices Through Caste Panchayats

Transgressing community boundaries in the form of 'exit' can—as in the above example—provide a solution to minorities' quest for maintaining communal traditions. On the other hand, minorities often punish transgressions to rules organizing boundary-maintenance. Inter-caste-marriages, a case in point here, produce therefore yet another type of 'minority-in-minorities' situations. Inter-caste marriages, especially when the hierarchical distance between the castes is too wide and when the woman's caste ranges higher than the man's (*hypogamy*), continue to be shunned in many parts of South Asia. It is in particular the case in North Indian rural communities (Punjab, Haryana and Uttar Pradesh). In the same vein, breaches to village and to *gotra* exogamy-rule can result in severe punishment of the spouses as well as of their families. Caste Panchayats exerting pressure and meting out punishment and co-villagers expressing their anger have caused numerous deaths and injuries to persons whose marriage was not considered as *comme-il-faut*. On numerous occasions government authorities provided police protection to persons fearing physical assaults. The *Frontline* magazine (28 August 2009: 3-16) provides several accounts of spouses put to death, even in police presence. In Dharana village (Haryana) the government has dispatched 450 policemen in order to protect a family whose grandson married a woman breaching the rule of *gotra*-exogamy, according to the Kadyan khap (Caste Panchayat). Besides threats to life, persons accused of acting against their 'caste honour' have been excommunicated, isolated and made to face economic hardships. This occurs when fellow villagers refuse to accept their occupational services and mutual trade relations. Measures of isolation are not only imposed upon individual couples, but also on their extended families that are often asked to move out of the region.

CONCLUSION: ON THE (IM)POSSIBILITIES OF 'NAVIGATING' IN THE CONTESTED TERRAIN OF MULTICULTURAL POLITICS

What do we learn from our analysis of the 'minorities-in-minorities' problem? Above all, the internal heterogeneity of 'minority groups' comes to light. Relevant literature contains uncountable disclaimers stressing that minorities are internally differentiated, but the ensuing narratives tend to homogenize minority descriptions, by stressing unity and sameness that result in reinforcing strong collective boundary–drawing mechanisms (Wimmer 2008). Analyses of internal differences concentrating on the more disadvantaged and vulnerable sections of minorities provide therefore a fuller picture of minority existence than overtly collectivizing accounts do. Views 'from the margins' provide insights as to what extent state practices and civic enmities, often hatred, came to bear upon disadvantaged minority members. 'Fear of small numbers' has created time and again state-society alliances that put uncountable minority members to death and caused unbearable losses.

Acknowledgement of internal heterogeneities reveals numerous instances of exclusions and inequalities that are internally created, or at least reinforced through internal minority relations. 'Minorities-in-minorities' often experience tensions, inequalities and discrimination within their own communities. Internal heterogeneity often results in internal inequalities. Minority value systems often buttress internal hierarchies that find expression in reduced chances in social, economic and political spheres, as discussed in this essay. Patriarchal values, in particular, come to clash with women's claims to equal treatment. Individual freedom is often curtailed by communitarian values. Groups' positionings as strategic responses to practices of state governance tend to impose upon their members loyalty and subservience to collective goals. Given how contested minority politics are in contemporary South Asian societies (as in other regions around the globe), internal politics of difference are quickly denounced as dissidence. Simultaneously, external pressures can easily be used as an excuse to force members to embrace collective norms that the internal 'minorities' perceive as detrimental to their well-being and convictions, placing severe demands on them.

How do persons then 'navigate' in the contested terrain of multicultural politics? Three scenarios are possible. In the first scenario, individuals or small collectives can dissociate themselves from communitarian life. Intellectual positions denouncing communitarian ideals oscillate towards universalist-individualist values, highlighting cosmopolitanism and/or highlighting the value of non-communitarian orientations. These can entail political convictions based on class or environmental consciousness, priorities given to professional standards as well as conscious contestations vis-à-vis any form of communal boundary-making. Such positionings are usually connected to elite social locations that allow individuals to afford their autonomy. They often go with the price of giving up communal belonging.

The second option was termed as 'rooted cosmopolitanism' by Kwame Anthony Appiah (2005). Communal orientations can be paired with cosmopolitan orientations and tend simultaneously to stress mobility, the importance of broad (global) horizons of interconnectivity as well as the value lying in communal boundary-crossing. Ascriptive belonging, that is, the dense webs of togetherness forged though familial and communal ties, reciprocities and commitments, as well as cosmopolitan aspirations are not seen as exclusive in this position, though. Rather the contrary. Late modernity is characterized by multiple belonging. But it goes without saying that navigating within the multiple parameters of belonging depends upon availability of resources. While the first option meant 'exit' from ascriptive belonging, rooted cosmopolitanism is likely to strengthen 'voice'. Resourceful minority members are likely to be those moving across majority-minority boundaries, triggering reforms, engaging in 'democratic deliberations', and forging ties in activist arenas.

The third option is having very little choice. In particular, in rural societies, minority existence evolves within clear-cut community demarcations. Hierarchical paternalistic structures are embedded in dense social ties of mutuality and commitment. Under the conditions of scarcity, these ties largely decide upon the availability of food, help and protection. Subordination under collective norms is therefore an important prerequisite for enjoying the basic necessities of life. While the other two options envisage a complete or partial dissociation from communal life, should their norms become too oppressive, those persons confined to the third constellation can hardly afford to dissociate themselves from ties of belonging, which makes contesting collective norms particularly problematic. Given the differentials of power and wealth and the many risks involved in minority existence, leaving the confines of minority boundaries, as oppressive they may seem to weak members, is hardly a feasible option.

In her important contribution to 'minorities-in-minorities' research, Ayelet Shachar (2001) discusses the paradox of *multicultural vulnerability*. She refers to situations in which the rights of individuals inside the group are violated by the policies that are designed to promote their status as members of a cultural group. Aiming at striking the balance between accommodating diversity without sacrificing individual rights, she proposes a no-monopoly model envisaging a *transformative accommodation*. The basic assumption here is that since members of cultural groups are at the same time citizens of a larger political community, they always have multiple affiliations. Both the cultural group and the state have legitimate claims on citizens belonging to their jurisdictions. This is buttressed by the fact that both the group and the state are viable and mutable social entities that are constantly affecting each other through their ongoing interactions. There is therefore in the self-professed interest of the group and the state to compete for the support of their constituencies and no entity should acquire exclusive control over the interests of the individual (Shachar 2001: 117ff).

Given the manifold vulnerabilities faced by individuals within cultural groups who are exposed to negative sentiments of 'outsiders' as well as to internal group pressure, the state's guarantees in the field of social and economic rights, paired with far-reaching measures against discrimination and providing safety would help uncountable persons described here as 'minorities-in-minorities'. Yet, as necessary as they are, such protective mechanisms would not solve the manifold dilemmas of belonging that are a common feature of late modernity.

NOTES

1. Literally meaning ground down, thus the oppressed.
2. For a comprehensive overview, see Manchanda (2009).
3. For a short account on Indian 'minorities-in-minorities', see Mahajan (2005: 93).
4. Nepalese politics are since the first constitutional acknowledgment of diversity in 1990 increasingly dominated by minority assertion. One of the two dominant discourses, that of social inclusion, names four major categories of minority existence as Janjatis (indigenous people), Madheshis (the inhabitants of the Southern region of Nepal), women and Dalits (whose minority existence has not been acknowledged in India). The discourse of state restructuring foresees a federal model with autonomous regions delineated along territorial boundaries determined on ethnic basis.
5. See Gellner, D., J. Pfaff-Czarnecka and J. Whelpton (2008, passim).
6. According to M. Sarkar, the Gujarat violence draws attention to 'the liminality of certain women vis-à-vis the state and the law'.
7. The official number being stated as 762, but according to Basu Ray Chaudhury (2009: 49) ca. 2000 dead would be an appropriate figure.
8. With more than 100,000 people being displaced (Basu Ray Chaudhury 2009: 49
9. Vgl. 'Threatened Existence: A Feminist Analysis of the Genocide in Gujarat', Report by the International Initiative for Justice (IJI), Bombay, December 2003, pp. 33-45.
10. Quoted from Banerjee (2009: 71).
11. Despite displaying comparatively higher levels of education than in other parts of South Asia, 75% of Tamil women have enjoyed primary education as against 89% for all Sri Lankan women.
12. This is not a homogeneous category of course (Hassan and Menon 2004). Significant differences prevail according to socio-economic position, caste, ethnic affiliation and region.
13. For a thorough discussion of this option, see Mahajan (2005) who convincingly argues that it is on the one hand very difficult to impose internal reforms through democratic procedures upon minorities and that on the other hand the potentials of this option are restricted, given that vulnerable groups generally lack voice.

14. See *The Telegraph*, Calcutta, 20 September 2009: 6.
15. 'The result is that the Section remains to protect minors and guard against rape, but that mutual consented sexual acts between adults of the same sex are no longer criminal' (*EPW* 11 July 2009: 5).

REFERENCES

Anderson, Benedict, 1996. *Imagined Communities. Reflections on the Origins and Spread of Nationalism.* London: Verso.

Anthias, F. 2009. Translocational Belonging, Identity and Generation: Questions and Problems in Migration and Ethnic Studies. *Finnish J Ethnicity and Migration* 4(1): 6-15.

Appadurai, A. 2006. *Fear of Small Numbers: An Essay on the Geography of Anger.* Duke University Press.

Banerjee, Paula 2009. Negotiations with a Difference: Minority Women in the Borderlands of Sri Lanka and India. In *Political Governance and Minority Rights: The South and South-East Asian Scenario,* edited by L. Ghosh. London: Routledge: 65-82.

Appiah, Kwame A. 2005. *The Ethics of Identity.* Princeton: Princeton University Press.

Benhabib, S. 2002. *The Claims of Culture: Equality and Diversity in the Global Era.* Princeton: Princeton University Press.

Brubaker R. 2004. *Ethnicity Without Groups.* Cambridge Ma.: Harvard University Press.

Capotori, F. 1991. Study on the Rights of Persons Belonging to Ethnic, Religious and Linguistic Minorities. Geneva: UN Center for Human Rights, UN Doc E/CN.4/Sub.2/384/Add.1-7.

Chaudhury Basu Roy, Anasua, 2009. Violence, Victimhood and Minority Women: The Gujarat Violence of 2002. In: *Political Governance and Minority Rights: The South and South-East Asian Scenario.* edited by L. Ghosh. London: Routledge: 44-64.

Coomaraswamy, R. 1999a. A Question of Honour: Women, Ethnicity and Armed Conflict. Lecture delivered at the Third Minority Rights Lecture on 25 May 1999 at Hotel Intercontinental, Geneva. http://www.sacw.net/Wmov/RCoomaraswamyOnHonour.html (download 25th October 2009).

—, 1999b. Reinventing International Law. Women's Rights as Human Rights in the International Community. In *Debating Human Rights. Critical Essays from the United States and Asia,* edited Peter van Ness. London: Routledge: 167:83.

—, 1999c. Report of the Special Rapporteur on Violence Against Women, Its Causes and Consequences. Mission to Indonesia and East Timor on the Issue of Violence against Women. E/CN.4/1999/68/Add. 3, part 2, 21 January 1999.

Das, Samir Kumar, and Ranabir Samaddar. 2009. *Ways of Power, Minorities, and Knowledge of Minorities: An Assessment of Research Policies and Practices.* Kolkata: Mahanirban Calcutta Research Group.

Deschene, J. 1985. Proposal Concerning a Definition of the Term 'Minority'. UN Doc. E/CN.4/Sub.2/1985/31 § 181.

Eisenberg, Avigail, and Jeff Spinner-Halev, eds. 2005. *Minorities within Minorities. Equality, Rights and Diversity.* Cambridge: Cambridge University Press.

Gellner, D., J. Whelpton, and J. Pfaff-Czarnecka.2008: 'New Nepal, New Ethnicities: Changes sincc the mid-1990s' In: *Nationalism and Ethnicity in Nepal,* edited by D. Gellner and J. Whelpton. Kathmandu: Vajra Publishers: i-xxxiii.

Gellner, Ernest, 1983: *Nations and Nationalism.* Oxford: Blackwell.

Ghosh, L., ed. 2009a. *Political Governance and Minority Rights: The South and South-East Asian Scenario.* London: Routledge.

Ghosh, L. 2009b. Introduction: Alchemy of Community Divides: A Historical View. In *Political Governance and Minority Rights: The South and South-East Asian Scenario,* edited by L. Ghosh. London: Routledge: xvii-xlii

Hasan, Z., and Ritu Menon. 2004. *Unequal Citizens: A Study of Muslim Women in India,* New Delhi: Oxford University Press.

International Initiative for Justice (IJI). December 2003. Report 33-45: *Threatened Existence: A Feminist Analysis of the Genocide in Gujarat:* 33-45.

Kumar, Radha. 1998. Personal Law and Communal Law. In *The History of Doing. An Illustrated Account of Movement for Women's Rights and Feminism in India 1800-1990.* Delhi: Kali for Women: 169-71.

Kymlicka, W. 1995. *Multicultural Citizenship. A Liberal Theory of Minority Rights.* Oxford: Clarendon Press.

Levy, J. 2005. Sexual Orientation, Exit and Refuge. In *Minorities within Minorities. Equality, Rights and Diversit,* edited by A. Eisenberg and J. Spinner-Halev. Cambridge: Cambridge: University Press: 172-188.

Mahajan, G. 2005. Can Intra-Group Equality Co-Exist with Cultural Diversity? Re-Examining Multicultural Frameworks of Accommodation. In: *Minorities within Minorities. Equality, Rights and Diversity,* edited by A. Eisenberg and J. Spinner-Halev. Cambridge: Cambridge: University Press: Cambridge: 90-112.

Manchanda, Rita 2009. *The No Nonsense Guide to Minority Rights in South Asia.* New Delhi: Sage.

Pfaff-Czarnecka, Joanna 2007: Menschenrechte und kulturelle Positionierungen in asiatischen Frauennetzwerken: Zur Diffusion des Menschenrechtsdiskurses in der reflexiven Moderne. In *Transkulturelle*

Genderforschung – Ein Studienbuch zum Verhältnis von Kultur und Geschlecht. Edited by Mae Michiko and Britta Saal. Wiesbaden: VS Verlag, 271-301.

Rahman, Atiur 2009. 'Fighting Exclusion: Towards Understanding the Predicament of Adivasis in Bangladesh. In *Political Governance and Minority Rights: The South and South-East Asian Scenario,* edited by L. Ghosh. London: Routledge: 104-20.

Rajasingham-Senanayake, D. 1999. 'Democracy and the Problem of Representation: The Making of Bi-Polar Ethnic Identity in Post/Colonial Sri Lanka' In *Ethnic Futures: The State and Identity Politics in Asia,* edited by J. Pfaff-Czarnecka, D. Rajaningham-Senanayake, A. Nandy and T. Gomez. New Delhi: Sage: 99-134.

Reynolds, Andrew, 2002. *The Architecture of Democracy: Constitutional Design, Conflict Management, and Democracy.* New York: Oxford University Press.

Sarkar, M. 2008, *Visible Histories, Disappearing Women: Producing Muslim Womanhood in Late Colonial Bengal,* Durham: Duke University Press.

Sachar Committee Report 2006. http://minorityaffairs.gov.in/newsite/sachar/sachar.asp - (download 25 October 2009).

Shachar, Ayelet 2001. *Multicultural Jurisdictions: Cultural Differences and Women's Rights.* Cambridge: Cambridge University Press.

Spinner-Halev, J. 2005. Autonomy, Association and Pluralism. In Eisenberg, Avigail and Spinner-Halev, Jeff 2005. *Minorities within Minorities. Equality, Rights and Diversity,* edited by A. Eisenberg and J. Spinner-Halev. Cambridge: Cambridge University Press: 157-171.

Thies, S., and O. Kaltmeier. 2009. From the Flap of a Butterfly's Wing in Brazil to a Tornado in Texas? Approaching the Field of Identity Politics and Its Fractal Topography. In: *E Pluribus Unum?: National and Transnational Identities in the Americas/Identidades nacionales y transnationales en las Americas.* Münster: LIT Verlag and Tempe: 25-46.

Tikekar, Maneesha. 2009. Non-Muslims in an Islamic Republic: Religious Minorities in Pakistan. In: *Political Governance and Minority Rights: The South and South-East Asian Scenario,* edited by L. Ghosh. London: Routledge: 121-50.

Weinstock, Daniel M. 2005. Beyond Exit Rights: Reframing the Debate. In *Minorities within Minorities. Equality, Rights and Diversity,* edited by A. Eisenberg and J. Spinner-Halev. Cambridge: Cambridge University Press: 227-48.

Wimmer, Andreas, 2002: *Nationalist Exclusion and Ethnic Conflict. Shadows of Modernity.* Cambridge: Cambridge University Press.

Wimmer, A. 2008. Elementary Strategies of Ethnic Boundary Making, in *Ethnic and Racial Studies* 31(6): 1025-55.

4

THE PARADOX OF SOVEREIGNTY: The Indian Experience of Governing Minorities

RANABIR SAMADDAR

THERE IS A need to work on the familiar theme of the minorities in India, not from the usual angle of rights, but from the angle of rule, government, of governmental rationality. Much of what I shall describe in the simplest of terms is known. Why do we then need to discuss how governmental style has developed in India on the issue of controlling the minorities, that is, the minor groups in society?

There are several reasons: First, the government has to renegotiate the question of minorities at regular intervals to maintain sovereign power; Second, in the wake of globalization, this need to re-negotiate has become pressing, particularly in view of the changing circumstances of global capitalism in which the communities find themselves and the functions they have to serve. These circumstances include various movements of belonging, associated with increased intensity and extensity of connections enabled by global constellations, development initiatives and the new technologies, institutions such as the United Nations or the European Union, and above all migration. The formation of transnational connections now reinforces minor identities clamouring for autonomy. Finally, with globalization, ironically, place-belongingness has only become stronger: the process being reinforced by a variety of discursive constructions of the 'place'. One has only to take note of the political process when a territory is newly opened to a flood of mineral prospecting, and as a consequence the region is re-inserted into the global whole as a new resource frontier for capital. The place at the same time begins to be actively imagined as a 'community', built in the mundane and material acts of immediate daily life. These are all minor places such as the Chittagong Hill Tracts, or the Chattisgarh mines in South Asia. In short, modern capitalism and the effects of globalization have renewed the problematic of community as a question mark before the unlimited sway of sovereign power. Hence, governmental technologies are once again re-inventing to tackle the 'community' phenomenon. We have to see in this light the re-emergence of the minority problematic in the decolonized countries of Asia.

Simply speaking, the minority issue since its birth hangs between the markers of identity and development. If minor groups are strident about 'identity', and if governmental policies of cultural pluralism (mainly in the form of select cultural rights) fail, then the sovereign power must coerce them to fall in line. But lest that should result in rebellion, what is required is 'development' of these minor groups and places. This indicates policies for social legislation, social governance, and social jurisprudence. In short what we call policies of hegemony. The grammar of government in this way vacillates.

To develop the point further: The main weakness in this grammar of governing the minorities lies in the difficulty of finding adequate forms of coping with various reactions and responses of the minor groups in society, which are driven, as we all know, by the attraction of the ideas of complete independence and self-government as an exit route for the minor groups. Governmental reason oscillates between policies of domination and of producing consensus among the minorities based on policies of social governance. In this lies the persistence of the minority problematic. It will mean henceforth that the minorities must remain as an in-eradicable feature of society. They cannot be erased; they cannot be effaced. They must be trained henceforth in the art and restraints of representation and imitation. They must not be allowed to make insidious use of how they eat, speak, see, marry, lead family life, listen, read, write, get together, pray, make use of their faiths and beliefs, and confabulate: the simplest of the acts of existence, which now become concerns of the government. In the eyes of the government these become significant practices, potentially dangerous. Their *conduct* must be governed.

This was precisely the concern of one of the chief officials of colonial India, W. W. Hunter, who wrote *The Indian Musalmans* (1871)[1] in response to an inquiry mooted by Lord Mayo, 'Are the Indian Musalmans bound by their religion to rebel against the Queen?' The context was the Wahabi rebellion and the Great Mutiny of 1857. We should also have in mind the well-known context of the rebellion and the Mutiny to understand how a minor population group was born.

The first thing to note is Hunter's remark that the source of persistence of the rebellion and mass insubordination was a 'mystery'. This was a 'chronic conspiracy'.[2] He referred to the economic breakdown of areas in the Frontier region, the travels of Syed Ahmed to Mecca and other places, but significantly repeatedly mentioned the mystery of faith, to which Syed Ahmed, whom he mentioned as the 'Prophet', would successfully appeal to, so much so, that even if some recruits would die in the holy war, others would join or at least help with money and other resources. Therefore beneath the mystery of conduct remained the question of faith. But Hunter did not stop there, and this is the second point. He thought that he had found a way to break that mystery of conduct. He proceeded to first show how the style of congregation, and here he was referring to the Patna centre of the Wahabis, prevented the officials and outsiders to enter and know what was happening inside the seminary. He spoke of the 'labyrinth of walls and outhouses . . . and side doors, and little secret courts in out-of–way-corners'.[3] Secrecy led to conspiracy, which would become 'chronic'. As we know, the Patna centre was razed to ground by an order of the colonial administration after the Patna and Ambala trials. Third, Hunter undertook to analyse carefully how clerics and Islamic jurists had interpreted the duty and the call to *jihad*, and he argued at length that in India there were both moderate, sane-minded clerics and 'fanatic' clerics interpreting the faith. Hunter noted the impact of the punitive policies of the administration on the clerics, and pointed out the need to understand the significance of the division within the clerics. In anticipating a policy of division and playing on it in order to ensure loyalty of the subjects, he of course had to answer, namely, who were the 'fanatics'? Here he was not only indicating a governmental strategy, he was basing himself on a long tradition of the Enlightenment in calling a line of thought as 'un-reason', as 'fanaticism'. His entire prescription of what Her Majesty's Government should do depended on this fundamental diagnosis, his analysis of the 'decisions of the Muhammadan Law Doctors'.[4]

Fanaticism, Hunter found, was an emotion filled with excessive, uncritical zeal for one's faith; it emerged when in mindless pursuit of aims efforts were re-doubled, and the follower refused to change mind and subject. Therefore the fanatic displayed very strict standards and little tolerance for contrary ideas or opinions. Hunter noted among the Muslims high levels of intensity, enthusiasm, commitment and zeal shown for particular activities. Like today's psychological experts in the business of counter-terrorism, Hunter too used terms indicating attitudes, behavioural proclivities, at times indicating a kind of cultural syndrome or deep psychopathology only which could explain the resistance of the Wahabis, their 'Islamic' intolerance, and by inference, their 'illiberalism'. Wahabis therefore could not be subjects of the 'rule of law', their revolt had raised the spectacle of fanaticism. It was in the oriental mind, and appeared as an invariable in the colonial context. In understanding why Hunter had to take this line of reasoning, readers may if they like recall how in modern European thought faith played a big role in defining racism.

But Hunter did not end there. He opened the next chapter of his report by saying,

> The Indian Musalmans are therefore bound by their own law to live peaceably under our rule. But the obligation continues only so long as we perform our share of the contract and respect their rights and spiritual privileges. Once let us interfere with their civil and spiritual status so as to prevent the fulfilment of the ordinances of their Faith, and their duty to us ceases. We must enforce submission, but we can no longer claim obedience. It is the glory of the English in India, however, that they have substantiated for their military occupation of all former conquerors a Civil Government adapted to the wants and supported by the goodwill of the people.

Thus government would mean complementing military administration by civilian efforts at administration, moving away from the tactics of occupation, listening carefully to complaints and grievances, because persistence of even 'minor grievances' could attain the 'gravity of political blunders'. He said that the colonial government must realize that it had already committed such blunders and in no small measure, while it was true that the full force of arms must be brought to bear upon the recalcitrant and the 'traitors' to British rule.[5]

Hunter in this way arrives at the developmental argument for governing the minorities; an argument with which we are familiar today in more than one form. He said that reforms such as the Permanent Settlement had done enormous harm to the Muslim men of substance. Muslim peasants, and here he was specifically referring to the deltaic land of Bengal, had become dispossessed of land and wealth. British rule had damaged the Islamic system of education, thus ruining the leading stratum of Muslim society. The colonial system of administration had no scope for the educated men of Islamic society. Recruitments in the army of the Muslims were completely closed. Disaffection was thus bound to spread. He used interchangeably the two terms,' Islamic' and 'Muslim', in his analysis. Muslims as the ruling race had lost power with British conquest, and could not compete with the Hindus in absorbing modern education, and lagged far behind in competition to get into the modern educational system, bureaucracy, and other establishments. In the modern professional avenues also they lagged behind.

Today these arguments seem banal, but through these one hundred and forty years the basic reasoning has remained same. Identity and development: these two are the intersecting axes of the task of government of the minorities.[6] As we shall see in the following pages, this line of reasoning would lead soon to a combined strategy for governing the disaffected groups: one, the strategy of representation (ie, mechanisms of representation of a minority group to make the latter obedient subjects); and second, shaping the civilian way of doing things in the same orderly way in which military affairs are conducted. Indeed the civilian will begin at every stage of government from the military roots, and if possible with the military model in mind. On both these lines of thinking Hunter left enough hints in this classic tract.

We shall pass the next phase very quickly. Within forty years of Hunter writing the *Indian Musalmans* the first conscious move by the administration was made toward this direction, first in the form of the Partition of Bengal and then the Government of India Act 1909 or the Indian Councils Act of 1909, commonly known as the Morley-Minto Reforms. We need not re-travel the story of the first partition of Bengal. We must, however, recall the rationale cited by the government for the order to partition.

On 19 July 1905 a *Gazette Extraordinary* published the resolution of the Government of India on the partition of Bengal. By this resolution a new province was to be created

> with the status of Lieutenant-Governorship consisting of the Chittagong, Dacca, and Rajshahi Divisions of Bengal, the District of Malda, the state of Hill Tipperah, and the present Chief Commissionership of Assam. Darjeeling will remain with Bengal, in order to maintain associations and links, which are highly valued in both areas. (Entitled as Eastern Bengal and Assam) the capital of the new province will be Dacca with subsidiary headquarters at Chittagong. It will comprise an area of 106,540 square miles and a population of 31 million, of whom 18 millions are Muhamedans and 12 millions are Hindus. It will possess Legislative Council and a Board of Revenue of two members; and the jurisdiction of the High Court of Calcutta will be left undisturbed. The existing province of Bengal, diminished by the surrender of these large territories on the east and of the five of the Hindi states of Chota Nagpur, but increased by the acquisition of Sambalpur and five Uriya states, will consist of 140,580 square miles with a population of 51 million, of which 42 millions are Hindus and 6 millions are Muhamedans. In short, the territories, now composing Bengal and Assam, will be divided into two compact, self-contained provinces, by far the largest constituents of each of which will be homogeneous in character, and which will possess clearly defined boundaries and be equipped with complete resources of an advanced Administration.[7]

On the basis of this resolution Bengal was partitioned on 1 September 1905. The first large protest meeting was held on 7 August 1905 in the same place of first protest: the Calcutta Town Hall. The meeting called for a dialogue and reconsideration of the government stand. The All India Muslim League was born next year in Dhaka. Hindu nationalists and Muslims did not totally agree on the partition issue, but not all Muslims supported partition unconditionally. Tagore and many others protested against partition, while they also saw the entangled nature of the issue, complicated by high landlordism (mostly Hindu landowners), religion, access to education and public employment, and other such issues. Likewise, Muslim leaders like Akram Khan, Maulana Maniruzzaman Islamabadi, Ismail Shiraji associated with nationalist endeavours while continuing dialogues with the Congress, the predominant nationalist forum of the Hindus.[8] Similarly the militant nationalists, who were the early terrorists, also worked in the mainstream opposition to partition. Finally, the partition was annulled in 1911 in the face of continuing militant public protest, but Assam became separate from Bengal. Led by Tagore and joined by several others such as Krishna Kumar Mitra, Jagadish Chandra Bose, Maulavi Ekinuddin Ahmed, Arabindo Ghosh, Surendranath Banerjea, Pramatha Chaudhury, Sister Nivedita, Ramananda Chattopadhyay, Kumudini Mitra, Bipin Chandra Pal, Rokeya Sakhawat Hossain, Akram Khan, Maniruzzaman Islamabadi, Maulavi Abdul Karim, and Pulin Behari Das, the debate and the dialogue became what Tilly has chosen to call 'contested conversation'. Dimensions of organization, agitation, pamphleteering, petition, secret activity, fund raising, publicly arguing, mobilizing, boycott of foreign goods, bomb throwing, assassination, processions, night vigils, public fast, all kinds of political practices were discussed.

The strategy of right sizing the territory and right shaping the population by creating a Hindu and a Muslim Bengal within the Bengal Presidency by itself showed how far the colonial rule had advanced in terms of the techniques of government. Right sizing and right shaping were important policies towards securing consent of at least part of the population. We, of course, know today that the first Bengal partition had to be annulled in 1911, and violent protests and secret societies became a part of nationalist movement. Both John Morley, the Liberal Secretary of State for India, and the Earl of Minto, the hard right wing Viceroy of India, believed that suppression of terrorism in Bengal was necessary but not sufficient to establish stability of rule. They believed that a noteworthy step was required to retain loyalty of the subjects or at least the wealthy part of them, and retain the Muslim aristocracy on their side. They produced reforms known by the name of the Indian Councils Act of 1909, which did not cover any significant distance towards meeting nationalist demands for home rule, but introduced elections of Indians to various legislative bodies for the first time. Limited electoral power also had separate provisions for the Muslims. The Act of 1909 was therefore important for the following reasons: first, it effectively allowed the election of Indians to the various legislative councils in India for the first time, though the majorities of the councils remained British government appointments, and the electorate was limited to specific classes of Indian nationals. Second, the introduction of the electoral principle laid the groundwork for a parliamentary system with acknowledgement of the existence of minor groups. Third, the Act of 1909 stipulated that Indian Muslims be allotted reserved seats in the Municipal and District Boards, Provincial Councils and Imperial Legislature, and that the number of reserved seats would be in excess of their relative population (25 per cent of the Indian population). Finally, only Muslims were to vote for candidates for the Muslim seats, to be known soon as the infamous separate electorate system. As we know, while majority-centric nationalist opinion all along thought that this was a divisive ploy, as further constitutional reforms were introduced, in 1919 and 1935, Muslims became ever more determined to hold on to, and if possible expand, reserved seats and their weight. This was the classic instance of an *aporia* where a solution of a problem was found wanting in terms of the structure of the problem. In this case the problem was that governmental reason (here it was related to the logic of representation) wanted to find its own feet and a way to rationally administer the society including inter-group relations, while the solutions that it found took it back in one way or another to the problematic of sovereignty.

Governmental reasoning, of course, did not stop there. In exactly ten years another major attempt was initiated to strengthen civilian administration through another round of constitutional reforms, known as the Montagu-Chelmsford Reforms, once again to introduce gradually self-governing institutions. Edwin Samuel Montagu, the Secretary of State for India and Lord Chelmsford, then Viceroy of India joined hands to author a report that became the basis of the Government of India Act, 1919. They met Indian leaders like Gandhi and Jinnah to discuss possibilities of introducing limited self-government and protecting the rights of minority communities. The changes introduced at the provincial level were significant, as the provincial legislative councils contained a considerable majority of elected members. In 1921 another change recommended by the report was carried out when elected local councils were set up in rural areas, and during the 1920s the electoral basis of the urban municipal corporations was widened in order to Indianize them, which meant that the divisions introduced a decade back would now become deeper. The Report had stated that there should be a review after 10 years. John Simon headed the review committee, popularly known as the Simon Commission. It recommended further constitutional change. Three round table conferences were held in London in 1930, 1931 and 1932 with representation of the major interests. Gandhi attended the 1931 round table after negotiations with the British government. The major disagreement between the Congress and the British was on the issue of separate electorates for each community. The Congress opposed it, but it was retained in Ramsay MacDonald's Indian Communal Award. As the nationalist leadership had failed to come up with a constitutional solution of the communal issue, the British Prime Minister Ramsay MacDonald announced his own formula for solving the problem. Communal Award was announced on 16 August 1932. By this, the right of separate electorate now not only belonged to the Muslims of India but also to all the minority communities in the country. The Award also declared the Untouchables (as they were called then; their preferred term 'dalits' was coined post-Independence) as a minority and thus the Hindu depressed classes were given a number of special seats, to be filled from special depressed class electorates in the areas where their voters were concentrated. Under the Award, the principle of weight was maintained with some modifications in the Muslim minority provinces. The principle of weight was also applied to the European community in Bengal and Assam, Sikhs in the Punjab and North West Frontier Province, and Hindus in Sindh and North West Frontier Province. The Award could not satisfy any section of the Indian population. Muslims were not happy it as it had reduced their majority in Punjab and Bengal to a minority. However, they were prepared to accept it. On the other hand, the Hindus refused to accept the award; they could not accept the Untouchables as a minority. The Congress rejected the Award in toto. Gandhi protested against the declaration of the Untouchables as a minority. He undertook a fast unto death. However he signed the Poona Pact with B. R. Ambedker, their leader, to meet many of the Untouchables' demands.

In the end, the Constituent Assembly deliberations gave shape to this still unclear strategy of protection: protecting the unequal minorities. Protecting the weaker, the vulnerable, and the backward sections of the society was accepted as an essential task of government. It was to be the governmental strategy to cope with the inequalities of society. If the government could not make all equal, at least it could protect them: this became the norm of governance of the minorities, because the category of 'minority' congealed in it all the weaknesses, backwardness, discrimination, and inequalities of society. After all, the reality was that all *peoples* ('people' as legal category) could not be equal, some would be majority and some minority. In this specific form of power relation where constitutionalism could soon become inadequate in facilitating resolutions of conflicts arising out of the negotiation of claims by groups and populations for recognition from a state that builds up its political power on the basis of producing majorities and minorities, protection became the governmental strategy of universal rule. Minority rights therefore become in such milieu mainly the right to get protection of the state, and protection became the core of state's support to the right of the group to maintain its specific culture. Protection in this way came to redefine citizenship. Since minority rights, as most of the Constituent Assembly members thought (and therefore the proposed special section of minorities was dropped from the draft of the Constitution), appeared as a problem for democracy, one of the most effective governmental strategies was to protect the minorities as unequal groups with their specific cultures in an overall nationalist agenda.[9]

The Constituent Assembly discussions focussed on the nature of the claims for protection, and indicated the legal-institutional path of protection of minorities in a context of violence and everyday forms of domination of minorities. Grant of autonomy in special cases became a part of this strategy of protection by the same government that was producing majority-centric rule. It impacted on the type of federal governance obtaining in the country. In some cases, autonomy became the governmentalized form of protection; in others the government took the initiative to set up rights institutions such as the National Minorities Commission, National Human Rights Commission, and so on, and in still others cultural pluralism became the official doctrine. Article 371 A to Article 371-1 of the Indian Constitution contain special provisions, Article 370 is also a special provision relating to Jammu and Kashmir. Besides the operation of the Sixth Schedule in Assam, Meghalaya, Mizoram, and Tripura, Manipur and West Bengal have such councils outside the schedule. Yet, as indicated above, this proved inadequate. Therefore, apart from the well-known recommendations of the Sarkaria Commission, soon there were demands for statehood from many groups that are essentially minority groups so that political units would correspond to 'ethnic boundaries'. 'Ethnic boundaries' are now in this way being reproduced in various ways and various forms. The federal question is now a part of the nationality question, which contains the minority question. The claims and conflicts around the federal and nationality question remind us of Michael Walzer's argument (*Spheres of Justice*, Basic Books, 1983) on democracy that the democratic political arrangement is clearly one of the political ways of allocating power. In discussing the institutional nature of minority protection in the country, we have to therefore again and again revert back to the more fundamental question relating to the protection-based discourse that appears as rights-based discourse under conditions of post-colonial governance.

As we know, the proposal for political safeguards for religious minorities during the final stages of the making of the constitution was withdrawn at the last moment. The issue of safeguards of minority rights had been referred to the Constituent Assembly to an Advisory Committee on Fundamental Rights, Minorities, Tribal and Excluded Areas whose creation had been mandated by the Cabinet Mission Plan in 1946. Under the republican and liberal slogans of universal adult franchise, equality as individuals and equality as justice, non-discrimination, national integration, and cohesion, the Constituent Assembly decided to scrap the proposals of group representation because these were thought to be contradictory and harmful to territorial representation. Preferential provision was arranged for Scheduled Castes and Scheduled Tribes to help them overcome their historic social and economic disabilities, but the Scheduled Castes and Tribes were not to be regarded as minorities. This provoked differences within the minority groups, who now competed among themselves to prove why they were more eligible than others in getting protection either on grounds of numerical preponderance or cultural distinctness or political distinctness. The backward castes, for example, claimed that they were a part of Hindu society, but they were 'political minorities', and different from religious minorities. Some thought that political safeguards were not necessary, but affirmative actions were needed to remove the historic disabilities. Secularism and republicanism were the signs of high nationalism. While the term 'minority' was popular among and therefore invoked in the Constituent Assembly by all groups claiming special provisions, the term 'minorities' was removed altogether from the constitutional provisions dealing with group preference.[10] A benevolent majority community cast in the mould of easy-going, responsible, protective, self-sacrificing, and accommodative nature, was going to be the best guarantee of minority protection.[11] The same model of protection was adopted to protect rights of a weaker section or an individual within a group. The Shah Bano case of 1985 and the Muslim Women Protection of Rights on Divorce Act of 1986 both indicate this reproduction of the form.[12] Similarly in states reorganization the same form was repeated. The report of the States Reorganisation Commission, which was formed in 1954 and whose report came out in 1956, also based itself on the same strategy, namely, the quarantining of the minority problem within a broad framework of equality and rights, and thus in this case while it went someway in recognizing the political identity of linguistic groups, it territorially contained linguistic minorities.

Thus while it is true that in constitutional thinking there were two parallel ideas of nationalism and democracy,[13] the disjunction we are speaking of here cannot be solely or mainly traced to this. It has to be traced rather to the way in which nationalism and democracy in their respectively republican and nationalist versions combined to root out communitarian ideas, and along with this an effective programme of equality of groups. The new governmental strategy was forged in this milieu. Protection became another form of a quarantining strategy of the government, though we know that in the sixty years of post-Independence, this strategy did not stop riots or marginalization of minor groups and weaker sections of society. With the persistence of riots and attacks on minorities the government was back to the classic question that Hunter had faced nearly one hundred and fifty years ago, namely: Should the government try to preserve and protect the identity of the Muslims, a minor people in India, or should it harness its efforts to develop them? And in the event the second answer is valid, what would constitute development?

The committee headed by Justice Rajendra Sachar was the 'Prime Minister's High Level Committee on Social, Economic, and Educational Status of the Muslim Community of India'. Appointed on 9 March 2005 the committee submitted its report on 17 November 2006. Six other experts were members of the committee. In the report the committee did not raise any new issue except in a secondary way; the reason for its quick fame has to be sought elsewhere. As I have just mentioned, it was because of the way the committee tried to cover *all* aspects of the life of a minority group vis-à-vis governmental duties, obligations, and practices that the report became well known in a short time and began to be discussed in the public sphere. In election campaigns political parties used the report in their own respective ways. The entire life of a minority group, almost all its socio-economic aspects, was brought possibly for the first time within the framework of a governmental technology. At the same time the destiny of the Muslims as members of a minority community under a majority-centric rule, communalization of security and law and order forces, and the schizophrenic milieu involving the three nations belonging to an erstwhile united subcontinent, were kept out of discussion and hence the report. The underlying thought comes out as one of a developmental logic, namely, if the socio-economic indicators of the Muslims improve, then there can be an end to discrimination; therefore the need for socio-economic investigation, report, analysis, and appropriate specific recommendations. The committee of course did not ask why discrimination persists. Does powerlessness lead to discrimination or the other way round? However we need not go into that way of circular thinking, but see how the committee has viewed governmental need to develop a minority community in strictly developmental terms, which mean basically socio-economic terms.

The committee examined population size, distribution, and health conditions of the Muslims; their educational conditions; economy and employment; access to bank credit; access to social and physical infrastructure; poverty, consumption pattern and standards of living; their situation in government employment and programmes; Muslims OBCs (Other Backward Classes) and the need for affirmative action; leveraging community initiatives and discussed the special case of *wakfs*. The committee recommended on the basis of investigations of these dimensions. Significantly the report began with two entries (chapters one and two): one on the context of the report, approach, and methodology, and the second on public perceptions and perspectives.

I have already mentioned that the report avoids direct political discussions on the powerlessness of the minorities. On one exceptional occasion the report however does refer to the 'terrorist' tag on the Muslims.[14] However, the report does not enter into that discussion and the profound implications of the tag. We can give one instance, namely, what happens to a community when it is branded as a security threat, if not formally but in all kinds of practices, and the insecurity the members of the community face? The committee thus ignores the implications of the policy of the national security establishment to build what I have termed elsewhere as an architecture of macro-security, which precisely due to its nature provokes micro-insecurity at all levels. In fact, the report therefore while on the one hand demonstrates the pervasive socio-economic insecurity of the Muslims in all conceivable aspects, on the other hand it does not draw lessons from groups turning against groups, communities against community, and the brazen manner in which sections of indigenous population were marshalled against the Muslims in Gujarat, and the perpetrators of the carnage got away because after all they were dealing with people who were security threats. It is this aspect—the fact of ignoring threats and actual acts of murders and pogroms (consider the Srikrishna Commission Report on Mumbai massacres in 1992-93[15])—that results in ignoring the pervasive micro-insecurity of the lives of vulnerable population groups. The bio-power (a form of power that is directed to the human body across whole populations under the state's control) that the Committee wishes to invoke to save and develop the Muslims remains fundamentally at odds with the bio-politics (politics of the body) of security/insecurity.

We can push this point little more. Consider the issue of race: a sensitive theme in India since the colonial times. It is a sensitive theme to all who study minority situations and the minor peoples. But here I am not referring to racial stereotypes. Democratic politics did away with many stereotypes, but brought in new uncertainties in its wake. Thus the Sachar Report had to engage in an elaborate exercise and explain its methodology for that exercise, namely: Do Muslims form a backward community, in governmental language an OBC group? How do they compare with the dalits or indigenous population groups, or even with 'other' OBCs? What about differentiation within the Muslim community? More important, given all the similarities and dissimilarities, do Muslims form a community in a wide ranging sense, or is it that only as believers in the same faith and observing certain common practices that they can be considered as forming a community, while in many other socio-economic aspects they may be considered as parts of other communities or classes? The committee's report therefore is perched on an anxiety as it sets out on its mission to bring out a 'general' picture: one can say capturing the Muslim as occupying an almost homogeneous subject position. This is the tension between the identity argument and the developmental argument. The report tends to take the later line of analysis.

Thus the question remains, and to give an instance to clarify the point: What sense will the government make of a woman called Shah Bano, who fights a long legal battle to win maintenance after being dispossessed and evicted from her home, then spurns the low maintenance award given by the court, then goes up to the highest court of the land only to denounce later the Supreme Court's verdict as interference against Muslim personal law, and then again seeks restitution this time of her *mehr* (contractual gift) under the newly reconstituted Muslim Women Act? In short what will the government make of someone who refuses to occupy a single subject position (the situation being complicated by class, gender, religion, and sexuality)?[16] This is exactly the same sensitive nature that we can notice in any discussion in India on race, and the report goes to extreme lengths to avoid this in order to establish the developmental paradigm. The goal is to make sense of the impoverishment of the Muslim masses in socio-economic terms, yet establishing at the same time that the impoverishment is due to discrimination. What invisible histories will one need to excavate to combine both the arguments? What sense shall we make of the last sixty years of riots, dispossession, suppression, cordoning, and manipulation to arrive at today's socio-economic backwardness and the developmental recipe?

The first two chapters of the report are thus extremely significant from the view of studying emerging governmental technology, and future historians of minor peoples may well say that the Sachar Report is a landmark in the erasure of the political problematic of minorities in a democracy and puts an indelible stamp on the issue as a rational question of development and economics and sanitized demography. The first chapter thus invokes the principle of equality, and significantly sets out the three items of inquiry, namely, issues relating to *identity*, those relating to *security*, and finally issues relating to *equity*.[17] Yet the inquiry is almost along transcendental lines: all the issues finally are resolved in the developmental argument. As I have said, the strategy is that of a comparative perspective. In this perspective the report places the facts of 'ghettoization and shrinking of common spaces' and the relation between 'political participation, governance and equity'.[18] Yet this is not all, for while the report requires a perspective, the main goal is to capture the entire life of a minority group (Muslims in this case) in the frame of *underdevelopment* and *backwardness*, which would then call for developmental measures. This is a classic case of the emergence of bio-power as the core of governmental rationality. Hence the population size of a group is important; it is sensitive particularly when it is compared with that of another, but must be discussed in developmental terms. So as the report states, the birth rate among the Muslims is higher, but as development happens, it will come down and approximate the national average, with the national average also coming down in turn.

Educational conditions show that Muslims are at a double disadvantage, literacy rate is lower than other socio-cultural groups, the madrasas do not function and are starved off funds or are irrelevant for technically oriented jobs, and finally Urdu-medium schools languish. Of course, the committee does not inquire what happens when Urdu does not happen to be the mother tongue, or when except in two states Muslims take to the local language strongly (Tamil, Malayalam, or Bengali, for instance). The report notes the pattern of ownership of physical assets and human capital, and the known fact that most Muslim poor like most other Indian poor (population groups) are in small scale employment concerns, and in broadly what can be called the unorganized sector.

Who is then a Muslim today? With the extravagance of sample surveys shown over the television channels but with the explicit exclusion of the political-security dimensions of life in those presentations, we do not have much choice in this definition. Characterized by faith in Islam and near dispossession in many ways, the minor group must get money (and other resources from the government) to get life. In this way the lives of the minor groups are more than ever shaped by governmental reason. An agenda of inquiry inspired by radical history will be able to sift through the material of the last sixty years on intermittent wars between Hindus and Muslims, pogroms against the latter, increasing legitimacy of the dynamics of group representation, and the political economy of reservation for backward communities in order to make sense of the rationality the Sachar Report represents. Indeed in two significant chapters—ten and eleven—the report discusses at length the issues of 'Muslim OBCs and affirmative action' and the need of 'leveraging community initiatives—the case of Wakfs'. The significance lies in not only reinforcing the community identity of a group, but precisely, because it is now a community, in establishing that principles of social justice must apply here.[19] In this background it discusses three different experiences of affirmative action for Muslims OBCs: in Kerala, Karnataka and Bihar. What else will strengthen the community besides affirmative action? The report as an answer turns to the issue of wakfs, refers to the Joint Parliamentary Committee on *Wakfs* (1996-2006), and speaks of the strategic significance of community institutions and initiatives.[20]

In short, in a context dominated by immense difficulties for a state to combine individual rights and group rights[21] (and this difficulty is much greater in South Asia than it is in Western Europe), this rationality does not represent the classic liberal governmentality based on rights and rules (which take it as their primary aim to combine individual rights and group rights). It tells us instead more of the post-colonial reasons of governance, where development, democracy, and multiculturalism must go together, and democracy's legitimacy, by inference government's legitimacy, can be secured only with developmental language meant to develop a community. *Life's security must be achieved through life's development*; and forms of claim-making must conform to this principle. The right of the minorities to develop must be seen in this perspective. Yet the issue remains, if the sovereign power has to agree to different forms of life, and thereby settle for a much nuanced way to rule, how will it combine the strategic task of governing, which to a substantial extent calls for uniformity of the subjects of rule—the classic homogeneous juridical subject of rule of law, in other words, the *citizen*—while agreeing to the community mode of life of the minor groups? The tension will torment democracy throughout its life.

As the insistent existence of minorities *qua* minorities poses challenges to sovereign power, it appears that sovereignty cannot exist without being shared. This is where governmental operation becomes critical. It creates the impossible: sovereignty seems to dissipate in the deep waters of micro-management of society, without necessarily dissolving the power to coerce. That is the moment when development appears as the deux ex machina of modern governmentality.

NOTES

1. W.W. Hunter, *The Indian Musalmans*, rpt (New Delhi: Rupa, 2002); original title, *Our Indian Mussulmans: Are They Bound in Conscience to Rebel against the Queen?* all citations are from the 2002 edition, and noted as taken from *IM*.
2. I am summarizing his arguments in ibid: Chapter 2.
3. Ibid: 61.
4. Ibid: 100-37.
5. All citations in this paragraph are from ibid: Chapter 4: 138.
6. The famous Bengali Muslim essayist Qazi Abdul Wadud in his *Saswata Banga* (Dhaka: BRAC, 1983 [1959]) repeatedly refers to Hunter's report and describes how Hunter's book influenced the educated Muslim discourse in India in the early part of the twentieth century.
7. *Gazette Extraordinary*, 19 July 1905, reprinted in Rathin Chakraborty, ed. *Bangabhanga Pratirodh Andolan: Satabarsha Smarak Sangraha* (Kolkata: Natyachinta, 2006).
8. I have written on their response elsewhere, 'Leaders and Publics – Stories in the Time of Transition', *Indian Economic and Social History Review* 37, 4 (October-December 2000).
9. For details on the issue of autonomy; see, for instance, R. Samaddar, ed., 'Introduction', *The Politics of Autonomy* (New Delhi: Sage, 2006).

10. A member of the Constituent Assembly had remarked, 'I only wish, Sir, that the phrase "minorities" should be wiped out from the history. The ten years that have been given to them is a sufficiently long period and I hope that when we meet in the short period within ten years, these minorities will come and say "we are happy, we do not want anything".' Speech of R. K. Wadha, 27 August 1947, *Constituent Assembly Debates* (hereafter CAD), Official Report, 1946-1950; vol 5: 209.
11. Rochana Bajpai notes in details the process in which the minority issue was marginalized in the resolutions of the Constituent Assembly as a result of the contradictory co-existence of two constitutional spirits: republicanism and the spirit of group interest. See 'Minority Rights in the Indian Constituent Assembly Debates, 1946-1950', Queen Elizabeth House Working Paper 30, December 1999.
12. Kalpana Ram in an essay, 'The State and the Women's Movement – Instabilities in the Discourse of "Rights" in India', in *Human Rights and Gender Politics – Asia-Pacific Perspectives,* edited by Anne-Marie Hilsdon, Martha Macintyre, Vera Mackie and Maila Stivens (London: Routledge, 2000): 60-82, discusses the case, and points out how the state takes the role of the male custodian in defining the protection that the woman needs, and how this contributes to the identification of a religious community as a site of female identity.
13. Bishnu Mohapatra notes this in 'Understanding the Discourse on Minority Rights in Contemporary India', unpublished paper presented at a seminar on Minority Rights in India, organized by the International Center for Ethnic Studies, Colombo, in New Delhi, 25-26 August 2001.
14. *Prime Minister's High Level Committee on Social, Economic, and Educational Status of the Muslim Community of India,* 2006, Prime Minister's Secretariat, New Delhi; hereafter referred to as *SR* (Sachar Report): p.11.
15. The Commission was appointed in 1995 by the Maharashtra government to probe into the riots and violence against the Muslims that rocked Mumbai on 6-10 December 1992 and then again 6-20 January 1993. The Commission submitted its report on 16 January 1998. The recommendations of the Commission were never implemented, and the guilty, identified, were never prosecuted. The report has been since then a mobilizing point of human rights activists all over the country against a government they perceive to be quick on appointing commissions and committees but singularly failing in acting on their findings, and implementing their recommendations.
16. On this, Ashgar Ali Engineer, *The Shah Bano Controversy* (Hyderabad: Orient Longman, 1987); also, Zakia Pathak and Rajeswari Sunder Rajan, 'Shahbano', *Signs* 14, 3, (Spring 1989): 558-82.

17. *SR:* 3.
18. Ibid: 24.
19. Ibid: 190-95.
20. Ibid: 217-41.
21. See Dietmar Rothermund, 'Individual and Group Rights in Western Europe and India', in *Pluralism and Equality: Values in Indian Society and Politics,* edited by Imtiaz Ahmed, Partha S. Ghosh, and Helmut Reifeld (New Delhi: Sage, 2000): 320-43.

Part II

Minorities of Europe

5

MINORITIES IN EUROPE: An Overview on National Regulations

EMMA LANTSCHNER and ANDREAS EISENDLE

INTRODUCTION

A GENERAL IDEA of minority protection systems in Central and Eastern Europe is presented by focussing on the legal framework of six countries, namely, Austria, Hungary, Italy, Romania, Slovakia and Slovenia. They have been selected because all have national minorities and their territories, or at least parts of their territories, belonged to the former Austro-Hungarian empire. All the six countries under consideration are very different in terms of constitutional construction, which is reflected also by the various models of minority rights adopted by these countries. Italy, Slovenia and to some extent also Austria have an asymmetric protection where some minorities enjoy maximum standards while others have fewer benefits or are not even recognized (e.g., Roma in Italy, Serbs and Croats in Slovenia). Romania, Hungary and Slovakia have developed unitary models of protection in the sense that there is no difference among minorities when it comes to the legal framework applicable to them. However, in practice, the situation of national minorities is different in these countries because the small minorities cannot benefit from the existing laws to the same extent as the large minority groups.

The six countries under consideration represent a mix of old and new European Union member states and collaborate by several multilateral and bilateral treaties. It will be shown how the different interpretation of these treaties as well as the peculiarities of the countries' legal systems influence their standards in minority protection, considering the fields of education, right to use the mother tongue, political participation, media, economic participation and culture.

This chapter is based on a comparative legal study drafted in the framework of the project 'Practice of Minority Protection in Central Europe' (www.eurac.edu/mimi). Detailed legal studies on each country are also available on the project's website. The country studies on Hungary, Romania and Slovak Republic are drafted by Sergiu Constantin; the ones on Austria, Italy and Slovenia by Emma Lantschner.

WHO ARE THE MINORITIES?

Before giving an overview of the legal framework of minority protection, it is opportune to clarify the concept of a minority. Even though it is true that there is no clearly formulated definition contained in an international treaty which is generally accepted, we can say that traditionally in Europe a minority is a group in a non-dominant position whose ethno-cultural features are manifestly different from the rest of the numerically superior society of a country. In general there are two different concepts of minorities in Europe: On the one hand, there are 'national minorities' that share their cultural identity with a larger community that forms a national majority elsewhere (e.g., Germans in Italy, Hungarians in Romania). On the other hand, there are the so-called ethnic minorities that do not make up the majority of the population anywhere (e.g., Ladins in Italy). Traditionally in Europe the most important distinctive feature of a minority is the language and unlike Asia there is nearly no reference to religious and caste-related minorities.[1] Finally citizenship is often a further relevant element of the minority definition, in order to avoid a broader interpretation of this concept, which would include also newly settled groups and immigrants (Benedikter 2008: 8-10).

Austria defines minorities in its Minorities Act of 1976 as groups of Austrian citizens, traditionally living in parts of the Austrian territory whose mother tongue is other than German and who have their own tradition and culture (§ 1[2]). Based on this definition, the government has to adopt regulations—in agreement with the main committee of the parliament and after consultation with the government of the relevant *Land*—determining the national minorities for which Advisory Councils are established (§ 2[1][1]). In compliance with this provision, the government has established the Advisory Councils for the Croatian, Slovene, Hungarian and Czech minorities in 1977, for the Slovak minority in 1992 and finally, in 1993, also for the Roma. Apart for the Roma and the Hungarian minority, the status of 'recognized' minorities derives, however, from different earlier and higher ranking sources of the First and Second Austrian Republic. The Czechs and the Slovaks, for instance, were already granted special protection by the bilateral treaty of Brno (1920). The Slovenes and Croats are mentioned specifically in Art. 7 of the State Treaty of Vienna (1955).

Hungary recognizes national minorities as a constituent part of the state (HU Const Art. 68 [1]). Article 1[2] of the Minority Act (1993) defines national or ethnic minorities as those groups, which have lived on the territory of the Republic of Hungary for at least one century. Their members are Hungarian citizens who are distinguished from the majority of the country's population by their own languages, cultures and traditions. Generally they do not live in compact groups in certain areas but rather are scattered throughout the country in around 1,500 settlements and constitute a minority also in these settlements (Ministry of Foreign Affairs, Budapest 2000). It is worth noting that the Jewish community is not among the 13 officially recognized national minorities. In 2006 a proposal for the recognition of the Jewish population of Hungary as a national or ethnic minority failed because the initiators were not able to collect the 1,000 signatures required by Article 61 of the Minority Act, although official data showed that 12,871 persons were belonging to this religious denomination (Hungarian Central Statistic Office). Last but not least the special situation of the Germans must be mentioned. Once one of the largest minorities in the country, their numbers decreased dramatically due to mass expulsions after World War II (Kartesz 1953; Prauser and Rees 2004/1).

Italy accepts language as the only distinctive criterion of minorities, avoiding any reference to ethnic, political or national elements and can therefore be described as a country that recognizes linguistic pluralism (Palermo and Woelk 2008: 242-3). Article 6 of the Constitution of 1948 provides the protection of linguistic minorities by special laws, which were enacted only sporadically, leading to the paradoxical situation that for many years certain minorities were protected very well,[2] while other groups were not even recognized. This situation has changed only with the adoption of the Law on the Protection of Linguistic-Historical Minorities (IT Minority Act 1999), which follows the general principles laid down by European and international organizations and enlists further minority groups that mainly live concentrated territorially (Palermo and Woelk 2008: 242). However, the level of protection between the minorities already protected before the Minority Act of 1999 and those recognized through the law is quite different.

Romania has 20 officially recognized minorities but there is no clear legal definition of this concept. The Draft Law on the Status of National Minorities, discussed by the parliament since June 2005, handles this paradox situation by closing the legal vacuum of the countries' minority protection system. The Venice Commission expressed various concerns regarding the draft law and criticized particularly the introduction of citizenship as an objective element of the definition of minorities (Opinion 345/2005: 6). With regard to the demographic evolution of the minorities in Romania it is worth mentioning the dramatic influence of the communist regimes that ruled the country from 1948 until 1989. After the fall of the Iron Curtain, the new phenomenon of economic migration combined with low birth rates contributed to the decrease of the number of persons belonging to national minorities (Andreescu 2005: 43). An exception to this general negative trend is the non-homogeneous Roma minority, which according to the official data increased in the last decades from 0.6 per cent in 1956 to 2.5 per cent of the total population in 2002 (Tismaneanu et al. 2006: 575-76). Actually there are about forty different Roma groups in Romania (O'Grady and Tarnovschi 2001: 16 and 39).

The Slovak Constitution refers in its preamble to 'national minorities and ethnic groups' but there is still no legal definition of the term 'minority' in the Slovak legislation. The 12 officially recognized minorities are enlisted in the Statute of the Council of the Government of the Slovak Republic for National Minorities and Ethnic Groups, which is a governmental advisory and coordination body for the area of minority policy and for the implementation of the European Charter for Regional or Minority Languages in Slovakia (SK Third State Report under the FCNM: 6). The minorities' basic rights are protected by various constitutional provisions: The general non-discrimination provision of Article 12 ensures everyone's right to decide on his or her nationality and forbids any form of pressure and assimilation. Part IV of the Constitution guarantees that the membership to any minority group cannot have any negative consequences and foresees the right to practice and foster their own language, culture and tradition (Arts. 33 and 34). All the provisions on equal treatment have been collected in the Non-Discrimination Law 365/2004 but in reality there are still many problems. The Roma community in particular suffers under discrimination (e.g., in employment and in the education system). As a consequence their members often do not declare themselves to be members of the Roma community (Pan and Pfeil 2006: 491-93).

Slovenia's legal framework of minority protection can be described as similar to the Italian regime, as an asymmetric system. While the Constitution does not include specific provisions regarding the protection of the so-called 'new ethnic minorities' (most of them persons belonging to the nations of former Yugoslavia), the comparatively small communities of the autochthonous Italians and Hungarians enjoy a relatively complete legal protection. The rights of the Italian and Hungarian are guaranteed, apart from the constitutional provisions (Arts. 5, 11 and 24), by about eighty other laws and regulations. Also the protection of the Roma community is explicitly foreseen by the Slovene Constitution (Art. 65) and furthermore by the basic protective law on the Roma (SI Roma Community Act 2007). It is worth mentioning that certain traditional communities (e.g., Germans and Jews) due to different historic reasons almost disappeared and do not enjoy any specific additional minority protection (Zagar et al. 2006: 20-1).

EUROPEAN CONTEXT

In the last century there have been different historical events that have influenced the evolution of minority protection in Central and Eastern Europe. World War I ended in the dissolution of the Austro-Hungarian empire, which left disputed new borders and large national minorities living outside their kin-states so that the situation of national minorities became for the first time an important issue on the international community's agenda. The first attempts to deal with this issue have been the so called 'Minority Treaties' signed under the auspices of the League of Nations that were interrupted by World War II which made the situation of minorities even worse. After that it took decades to build a positive European context in which the states were able to cooperate at a multilateral and bilateral level within an international framework.

Finally, the fall of the Iron Curtain, followed by the dissolution of the Soviet Union, Czechoslovakia and Yugoslavia, marked the start of a new era and an important step of development of the European standards. After that the countries started to face the minority issue collectively, tending to a standardized international framework.

In respect of the multilateral cooperation, it is worth mentioning that in the mid-1990s all six countries have ratified the Council of Europe's Framework Convention for the Protection of National Minorities (FCNM). With regard to the European Charter for Regional or Minority Languages (ECRML) the situation looks a bit different. Italy has not yet ratified this important document in the field of minority rights and Romania did it only in 2008, although it had signed it already in 1995. Other countries did not or still do not include in their ratification laws different language groups among those to be protected.[3] Their membership in the Organization for Security and Co-operation in Europe (OSCE), which created the post of the OSCE High Commissioner for National Minorities in 1992, is also important. The Commissioner's main tasks are to provide early warning and mediation procedures whenever tensions involving minorities seem to threaten peace and stability in the continent (Benedikter 2008: 120-21). Although in the European Union (EU), the integration process has been first of all an economic project, its influence on political issues is more and more important. In 1993, the Council of Europe, which is the supreme decision-making body of the EU, adopted the Copenhagen Criteria as fundamental premises for accession (108-09). Slovenia joined the EU in 2004 together with Hungary and Slovakia, and Romania in 2007. These four countries had to comply first with the 1993 Copenhagen criteria, including the respect for, and the protection of minorities. Austria, which had joined the EU already in 1995 and Italy, one of the founding states of the European Communities, did not have to deal with this type of minority protection conditionality.

In the 1990s the former communist countries made particular efforts for the improvement of their international relations and concluded several bilateral treaties of friendship like the Hungarian-Slovak and the Hungarian-Romanian bilateral treaties on Good Neighbourliness signed in 1995-1996 (Lantschner 2009). They were clearly interested in developing comprehensive systems for the protection of the minorities by appealing for reciprocal protection for their kin minorities, living in the neighbouring states and looking for a win-win solution based on compromise and cooperation. Moreover they have established Joint Intergovernmental Commissions for the implementation of their bilateral agreements (Lantschner and Constantin 2003).

EDUCATION

The right of minorities to education in their mother tongue is foreseen in the constitutions of all six countries. This principle is further implemented by national (in Hungary, Romania, Slovakia, Slovenia), federal (in Austria) and regional (in Italy) laws according to the constitutional structure of each state.

In all six countries persons belonging to a minority group have the possibility to study in their mother language in kindergarten, primary/elementary and secondary schools. The application of this right is often subjected to conditions, which limit the possibility of education in minority languages: In Italy education in German and Ladin is provided only in South Tyrol and in Slovenia schools with tuition in Italian are established only in the ethnical mixed municipalities. In Austria Article 7 of the State Treaty of Vienna (1955) speaks about a 'proportional number of secondary schools' with tuition in Slovenian and Croatian. In Hungary, authorities have the obligation to establish classes and schools for minorities 'according to local possibilities and demands' (HU Minority Act 1993, Art. 43 [2], [3] and [4]), similar conditions are foreseen in Romania and in Italy. People who cannot access these facilities have the opportunity to study at least their mother tongue, culture and traditions as separate subjects. Normally the extra costs of the education in a minority language are covered by the state, regional or local authorities. In all the countries under scrutiny the minorities enjoy the right to establish and run their own private educational institutions.

Another important aspect is the examination of the countries' different solutions regarding their minority educational systems. It is usually not possible to choose between a monolingual or a bilingual school, which either can be the consequence of the existing legal framework or of a legislative vacuum. In some countries, persons belonging to a minority group have, at least in theory, the possibility to study either in a bilingual school or in a monolingual school. For the Slovenes, Croatians and Hungarians living in Austria, the respective Minority School Acts of Carinthia (Arts. 12 and 16 [3]) and Burgenland (Arts. 3 and 8) foresee the possibility to establish mono- and bilingual primary schools; in practice, teaching takes place mainly in the bilingual form, only Slovenes in Carinthia have a monolingual grammar school. Also in Hungary there is the possibility to choose bilingual education in kindergartens and schools according to the local need and demand (HU Minority Act, Art. 42[2] and [3]; HU Public Education Act, Art. 5). By contrast in Romania and Slovakia, the existing legal framework does not provide for bilingual education. People belonging to a minority group have only the option to choose between a school or class with tuition in their mother tongue or one where the teaching is exclusively in the official language. According to the Romanian law on the ratification of the ECRML, Hungarian and German are the minority languages that enjoy the maximum protection and promotion in the field of education (Constantin 2008: 575-84). The asymmetric legal frameworks of Italy and Slovenia form a third category of educational systems: While for certain minority groups living in given territories constitutional regulations provide clearly for separate education systems,[4] other minority groups have only the option of a bilingual education.[5]

There are also minority groups that enjoy an education system with very specific features and therefore do not fit in a scheme. For example, Ladins in South Tyrol (Italy) study in their mother tongue in kindergarten and primary schools but then switch to a bilingual (German and Italian) education, where they continue to study the Ladin language as a separate subject (Baur and Medda-Windischer 2008: 235-58). The Roma minority represents also a special case handled by different solutions which often are not satisfying. Italian framework law on linguistic minorities does not even recognize the Roma, although the Italian government agreed to apply the FCNM also to the Roma. The Slovenian Constitution speaks about the 'special rights' of Roma but regulations in the field of education can be described as discreet. In Romania there are places reserved for Roma candidates at universities, but there is still a lot to be done at the level of primary and secondary education. Slovakian authorities do not provide any teaching in Romańi and children who fail linguistic tests are often placed in schools for children with special needs. This practice has been criticized by the Committee of Independent Experts responsible for carrying out the ECRML's monitoring mechanism retaining the actual practice contrary to the Charter and basic human rights (Crniæ-Grotiæ 2008: 392).

With regards to university education in minority languages, the six countries can be split in two groups. In Austria, Italy (except for the trilingual University of Bolzano), Slovenia and Hungary there is no university education in the minority languages because of their rather small minorities. Their bilateral agreements allow and encourage people belonging to minorities to study in their kin-states' universities: For example, the Agreement between Austria and Slovenia on cooperation in the field of culture, education and science was signed in Ljubljana in 2001. By contrast, Romania and

Slovakia have large Hungarian minorities. In both countries there are monolingual minority private educational institutions and state universities which have faculties with tuition in Hungarian.[6]

USE OF LANGUAGE

The right to use the minority languages in relation with authorities is stipulated by constitutional legislation in all six countries. With regard to the implementation of this principle, it is possible to make a distinction between three situations. In Slovenia the law mentions explicitly the territorial administrative units where persons belonging to the Italian or Hungarian languages can address public administration and judicial institutions in their mother tongue (SI Administration Act 2002 Art. 4 [2]). In contrast there are countries that use a threshold for the identification of the municipalities where the minorities can use their mother tongue in relation with public authorities. In Romania and Slovakia rules regarding the use of minority languages shall be applied in municipalities where a minority is at least 20 per cent of the population. These regulations have been considered as a positive development by the Advisory Committee of the FCNM on the one hand (Opinion on Romania 2006: 24-25; Opinion on Slovakia 2006: 22) but criticized by the Committee of Experts on the other because of the high threshold of 20 per cent which does not allow an appropriate implementation of the minority protection (Report on Slovakia 2007: 9). Finally, there is a third solution where both the clear determination of the territorial units and the percentages are used. The Italian legal framework foresees determinate areas for the protection of the German and Ladin (IT Autonomous Statute of South Tyrol), French (IT Autonomy Statute of the Aosta Valley) and Slovene minorities (IT Slovene Language Law 2001) whereas the other linguistic minorities are protected in those provinces and regions where they make up at least 15 per cent of the population (IT Minority Act

1999). Article 7[3] of the Austrian State Treaty of Vienna foresees that the Croats, the Slovenes and the Hungarians may use their mother tongue in relation with public authorities in the mixed administrative and judicial districts of Carinthia, Burgenland and Styria. In 2001, the constitutional court introduced the threshold of 10 per cent in order to define the meaning of the term 'mixed population', which was welcomed by the Advisory Committee of the FCNM (Opinion on Austria 2002: 3) but in practice has never been implemented.

In most of the cases, the public bodies and institutions that shall make use of minority languages are those authorities that are carrying on their activities within the territorial administrative units determined according to the various systems analysed above. There are also countries that differ from this territorial principle where in some conditions authorities and administrative offices located outside these areas have to allow the use of the minorities' language if their respective body is responsible for issues related to a minority group's interest. In Austria, federal and *Länder* authorities are obliged to allow the use of minority language if their competences cover mixed population settlements (10% threshold) even if they are located outside of these areas. The same is true for the Ladins living in South Tyrol (Italy), who are allowed to use their mother tongue also outside their municipalities if the respective body is responsible for their issues and interests. In other countries the law is even more precise and extends the list of institutions that can be addressed by the members of a recognized minority community in their mother tongue: In Romania a person who belongs to a minority group is allowed to use the native language in relations with the institutions subordinated to the public administration, with the deconcentrated public services of the central bodies and with the various institutions subordinated to the local councils. In ethnically mixed municipalities of Slovenia bilingualism is stipulated not only in the local and national bodies but also in public enterprises and all public agencies.

Furthermore, it is important to compare the status of the minority languages in the six countries and to analyse what their linguistic rights guarantee. Slovenia, Austria and Italy recognize minority languages as official in certain territorial units.[7] By contrast, the only official languages of Slovakia and Romania are their state languages. Hungary is somehow in-between, allowing the representative body of the minority self-government or the body of the national minority self-government to determine the official language (beside the Hungarian) of the procedure falling into its competency.

The basic right of persons belonging to national minorities is to address the public authorities, orally and in writing, in their mother tongue and to receive the reply in the same language. The costs for an interpreter or a translator shall be covered by the public authority. In general this is a guaranteed right everywhere but there are some special cases. In Italy, Germans and Slovenes have the right to receive an administrative act in their mother tongue not only at the provincial level but also from the regional authorities.[8] The situation is different in Slovakia and Austria where the law does foresee a very limited right to be served in oral dealings by civil servants.

All six countries have regulated the right to use the minority language before the courts with the help of interpreters and translators and without extra charges for parties. In general, the procedural papers and judicial decisions are drawn only in the state language, but the situation is different when a minority language is declared official. This is the case for the Italian and Hungarian languages in the mixed municipalities of Slovenia and the German language in South Tyrol (Italy). As a consequence, the members of the minorities have the possibility to conduct monolingual or bilingual judicial proceedings, and the documents of the court are drafted accordingly.

Each of the countries allows the public authorities to issue documents of public interest, regulations and decisions taken in their procedures also in a minority language, imposing various conditions. In general, it is possible to distinguish between legal frameworks where acts are made public automatically and others that publish their regulations and announcements in the minority language only upon request. The Romanian system is somewhere in-between, by making a distinction between the decisions of individual character that shall be communicated in the minority language only at request and the decisions of normative character that shall be published in the minority language in the municipalities with at least 20 per cent minority inhabitants.

With regard to the use of the minority toponymy (street names, signs on public bodies), it is a fact that this is allowed in all six countries but in practice there are still problems of implementation to be resolved. The main problem is that in various territorial units the minority population does not reach the threshold laid down by law or provisions are not implemented. A positive example is the ethnically mixed municipalities in Slovenia, where the use of bilingual signs is extended to private enterprises, economic organizations and associations.

POLITICAL PARTICIPATION

There are different ways in which the participation of persons belonging to national minorities in public affairs can be ensured: one possibility is to provide for their representation in elected bodies, at national, regional or local level. Another one is to establish consultation mechanisms and a third one is to provide for cultural or territorial autonomy.

Among the six countries under consideration, Austria and Slovakia are the only countries which do not provide any legal provision regarding the representation of persons belonging to minorities in elected bodies. While the Hungarian minority in Slovakia, which represents 9.7 per cent of the overall population, is strong enough to enter the parliament and local bodies without such a mechanism, for the smaller minorities it is difficult to gain any representation. Similar is the situation in Austria, where the minorities represent only a small percentage of the population. As a consequence of this situation there is a strong wish within the minorities for special mechanisms that permit their political representation.

Unlike in these two countries, Article 68[3] of the Hungarian constitution ensures the representation of the national minorities living in the territory of the country. This is further specified by Article 20 of the Minority Act, which stipulates that Minorities have the right—as determined in a separate Act—to be represented in the National Assembly, but this provision has never been implemented.

In Romania, the Hungarian national minority represents 6.6 per cent of the overall population and does not need any provisions to be represented in policy: in the election held on 30 November 2008 they got 31 seats in parliament. For the smaller minorities, Article 62 of the Constitution guarantees the representation of one organization per national minority in the parliament,[9] as long as their share of the votes in the elections is at least 10 per cent of the average number of validly cast votes in the entire country necessary for the election of a deputy (RO Election Law 2008) or 5 per cent of the total number of valid votes expressed in the respective electoral district in local elections (RO Election law 2004). A similar provision is foreseen in the Italian region of Friuli Venezia Giulia where a party representing the Slovene minority can be represented in the regional assembly under the condition that it receives at least 1 per cent of the votes region-wide and makes a coalition with another party that enters the assembly.

Beside these systems, there are two countries which have implemented autonomy systems to protect their minorities. In the territorial autonomy of South Tyrol in Italy the representation in public administration of the three linguistic groups living in this area is guaranteed according to a proportional system reflecting the strength of the respective groups. The cultural autonomy adopted in Slovenia provides for the representation in parliament for Hungarian and Italian minorities. Members of these groups even have a double voting right: one vote cast for the election of representatives, equal to all other Slovene citizens, and one for the election of the representative of their community.

Whenever representation in elected bodies is not possible, the provision for other mechanisms of representation is very important. All the countries under consideration have advisory bodies on minority issues, which are involved in the proposal and commenting on legislative initiatives and the distribution of funds for activities of minority organizations.[10] They differ very much in terms of composition and mandate. While some are composed by minority representatives only, most of them also have a strong presence of governmental officials or are even established as a governmental body.

MEDIA

Three of the six countries under consideration incorporate minority protection in relation to media in their constitutional provisions. In Austria, Slovene and Croat minorities living in Carinthia, Burgenland and Styria have the right to develop and access media in their own languages (AT State treaty of Vienna Art.7). Article 34 of the Slovak Constitution foresees the right of citizens representing national minorities to disseminate and receive information in their mother tongues. In Slovenia, the autochthonous Italian and Hungarian minorities have the right to develop activities associated with public media and publishing (SI Const Art. 64).

Each country provides regulations for the public broadcaster with regard to minorities in general and broadcasts in minority languages in particular by ordinary legislation. In Hungary, the Television and Radio Broadcasting Act (1996) provides that public TV and Radio broadcasters have to respect the dignity and essential interests of the nation as well as of the minorities, and shall not offend the dignity of other nations. Moreover national as well as regional and local broadcasters shall foster culture and languages of the minorities by providing information in the minority languages and using subtitles in television programming or multi-lingual broadcasting. Similar is the situation in Slovenia where the public broadcaster Radio Television Slovenia (RTV) shall further 'support the creation and development of cross-border radio and television projects' and 'promote ties between the ethnic communities and their mother countries' (SI Radio and Television Corporation Act 1996).

Equally vague are the laws concerning the amount of time to be dedicated to minority language programmes. The Austrian public broadcaster ORF has to dedicate an *appropriate share* to programmes in minority language and can fulfil this task also by cooperating with private broadcasters. With regard to private broadcasting, Austrian legislation foresees that for the distribution of radio and TV frequencies the diversity of opinion in the broadcasting area and the cultural context are criteria to be kept in mind. Article 18 of the Hungarian Minority Act demands the production and broadcasting of programmes for national and ethnic minorities on a *regular* basis. The Romanian Audiovisual Law (2002) foresees that distributors have to ensure the *necessary services* for the broadcasting of shows in the minority language only for localities where a national minority amounts more than 20 per cent. Romania has been criticized repeatedly by the Advisory Committee of the FCNM for the fact that smaller minorities are underserved because of the percentage clause (Opinion on Romania 2006: paras. 115-9). It needs to be mentioned that Romanian TV programmes broadcast in the minority language have to be translated into Romanian by way of subtitles, dubbing or simultaneous translation, except for music videos and educational programmes for teaching foreign languages. Slovene legislation is quite ambiguous in this field: while for the Roma ethnic community the provisions are rather vague, the creation of one radio and television channel is granted for the autochthonous Italian and Hungarian ethnic communities and must be broadcasted by the RTV Slovenia in at least 90 per cent of the area inhabited by the respective community (SI Act on Radio and Television Corporation Arts. 3 and 8). The Italian Law Minority Act (1999) provides that in the convention between the Ministry of Communication and the public broadcaster RAI the protection of linguistic minorities has to be ensured. Furthermore, it foresees the possibility of additional conventions between the regions on which minority territories are located and the public broadcasting company. The Slovakian Act on Radio (2003) and on Television (2004) foresees that one of the main activities is the broadcasting of programmes in the language of minorities balanced in their content and regional coverage.

With regard to media bodies, four of the countries have specific provisions concerning the representation of minorities in such bodies and the tasks to be undertaken for the minorities. The Austrian Federal Law on Broadcasting Corporation (2001) guarantees that at least one of the 35 members of the ORF's Audience Council is a representative of a national minority. The Audience Council has to be consulted when it comes to the definition of the length of programmes broadcast in minority language. Similar are the provisions in Hungary, where the national minority self-governments shall be represented in boards of trustees of the public broadcasters (HU Act on Television and Radio Broadcasting). In the Romanian National Audiovisual Council (NAC) minority representation is not prescribed by law but it constitutes a positive practice that one of the eleven members belongs to the Hungarian minority. One of the NAC's tasks is to take measures for the correct use of the Romanian language and the languages of national minorities (RO Audiovisual Law 2002). The strongest and most consistent representation is foreseen in Slovenia, where two of the 29 members of the RTV

Slovenia's Program Board shall be appointed by the Hungarian and Italian ethnic community respectively (SI Radio and Television Corporation Act 1996). Article 10 of the Statute of RTV Slovenia provides the establishment of two Programme Committees, one for the Italian and one for the Hungarian national community program. Six of the nine members of each of the Programme Committees are appointed by the Italian and Hungarian self-governing national communities respectively.

The reception of broadcasts from neighbouring countries is either allowed through national legislation, or the acceptance of the respective undertaking from the ECRML. Article 9 of the agreement between Austria and Slovenia (2001) foresees the exchange of cultural programmes and authors in order to encourage the cooperation in the area of publishing, radio and TV broadcasting. The Hungarian treaties with Romania, Slovakia and Slovenia provide, for example, for the right of minorities to have access, in their mother tongue, to information in electronic and printed media, as well as to freely exchange and disseminate information. Article 11 of the ECRML foresees several provisions in the field of media but the states mostly accepted only the undertakings which were already in place in their respective countries.

The publication of printed media in minority languages is fostered in each of the six countries by financial support. In Austria, for example, print media published in minority languages do not need to sell a minimum number of papers in order to have access to federal funds in support of their media (AT Press Law 2003). In Slovenia the Italian minority cooperates with the Italian minority from Croatia where an Italian daily newspaper is published. Their publishing house as well as the Hungarian-language weekly and a newspaper for the Roma community are co-financed by the state (SI First State Report under the FCNM: paras. 81 and 83). A similar system of direct support is also foreseen in Italy, Romania and Slovakia where minority daily newspapers in Slovenian (Italy), German (Italy and Romania) and Hungarian (Romania and

Slovakia) language are published. In addition to that Italy and Romania also foresee an indirect press support by providing non-financial measures in order to deliver the selling and circulating of the daily papers. Both foresee a reduced added tax and furthermore, Italy guarantees reduced postal tariffs and support for journalistic trainings (Ebner and Rautz 2005: 51-83).

ECONOMIC PARTICIPATION

Legislation in the field of economic participation of persons belonging to national minorities is rather scarce. Regarding public employment there are different solutions of a 'preferential' treatment of persons belonging to national minorities. In Italy, the Autonomy Statute of South Tyrol, which has the rank of a constitutional law provides for the proportionate representation of all linguistic groups (German, Italian, Ladin) in public administration (Art. 89). In Romania the law requires the employment of civil servants and police persons who are able to speak the minority languages in the administrative-territorial units where the inhabitants belonging to a national minority represent 20 per cent of the population. Other countries foresee the disbursement of extra pay to civil servants who speak the respective minority language and are employed in areas with minority populations.

Concerning the private labour market, one of the best solutions has been adopted by Slovenia to limit the emigration of members of the autochthonous minority groups (SI First State Report under the FCNM: para. 51). There are funds reserved for favourable loans to persons belonging to the Hungarian and Italian national communities or legal entities in the majority ownership of members of an autochthonous national community for 'investments in the development of farms, secondary activities on farms, co-operatives, small business, and for the investments in other production and service facilities in economy' (SI Economy Regulations 1997

Art. 3). In Italy, Article 15[1] of the Autonomy Statute of South Tyrol provides that the Ministry of Industry, Commerce and Artisanry assigns to the Provinces of Bolzano and Trento 'quotas of the annual allocations contained in the state budget for the implementation of state laws to finance increases in industrial activity'. Important in this area are also provisions on non-discrimination (e.g., in job advertisements, access to work, contracting and conditions of employment). Especially delicate in this regard is the situation of the Roma community, which in all countries under consideration is severely affected by disadvantages in the field of economic participation. Romania has confronted this problem by adopting specific programmes for the professional training and reorientation of the Roma people and supporting young Roma graduates in getting jobs. Moreover, the strategy foresees landownership programmes for the agricultural activities of the Roma communities and a soft credit system for the small and medium-sized enterprises owned by members of the Roma minority.

With regard to international agreements, Article 13 of the ECRML, which, as mentioned earlier, has been ratified by all countries under consideration (except Italy), offers different solutions in the field of economic and social life. While Austria has chosen only the general subparagraph 1[d] in order 'to facilitate and/or encourage the use of regional or minority languages', Slovenia has accepted all provisions for the Hungarian and Italian ethnic communities.[11] The other countries range somewhere in between, accepting only some subparagraphs and some of the languages protected under the charter. In addition, there have been stipulated several bilateral agreements in order to foster economic cooperation across the border. One of the best examples in this field is the agreement between Hungary and Slovenia, which provides plans on regional and economic developments, supporting all forms of trans-boundary cooperation in order to prevent the emigration of the respective inhabitants (HU-SI agreement 1992: Art. 7).

CULTURE

Acceptance of a minority's cultural diversity is of utmost significance in the framework of minority protection and is enshrined in the constitutions of all six countries under consideration (AT Const Art. 8[2]; HU Const Art. 68[2]; IT Const Art. 6; RO Const Art. 6, SK Const Art. 34; SL Const Arts. 61 and 64). While in general, the countries avoid providing group rights in the framework of minority protection, all countries but Romania lean towards this form of collective approach in the field of culture. So the Slovak Constitution provides citizens belonging to national or ethnic groups the right to develop their own culture and the Austrian constitution acknowledges the cultural diversity which finds expression in the autochthonous ethnic groups. In Italy, the linguistic groups living in South Tyrol even enjoy cultural autonomy (IT Autonomy Statute of South Tyrol Arts. 2, 15[2] and 19) and in Hungary and Slovenia minority self-governments play a decisive role in the field of culture.

In financing the cultural development, all apply different mechanisms and institutions. In general, there are two different solutions as to how they decide on the distribution of the budget among the respective minorities. While, for example, in Slovenia the budget is disbursed depending on the cultural needs and demands submitted by organizations of the respective minority, in the Slovak system the total available amount is divided according to the real size of the minorities, while raising the amounts adequately for the smallest minorities (Petocz 2010: 731-54). The Autonomy Statute of South Tyrol in Italy provides the distribution of the funding for cultural activities in direct proportion to the size of the three linguistic groups (German, Italian and Ladin).

Usually the cultural funds are covered by the countries' state budgets but there are also examples where even the regions and provinces (as in Austria and Italy), can support with their budgets, the creation of cultural institutions. In general the disbursement of cultural funds is the responsibility of the respective governments. The institutions responsible for the disbursement of cultural funds are: in the case of Austria, the federal Chancellery (while the Minority Advisory Councils can issue recommendations on the use of promotional funds); in the case of the Autonomous Province of South Tyrol, the cultural departments of the three linguistic groups in the provincial administration; in the case of Romania, the National Department for Interethnic Relations (DIR). The DIR monitors the use of the funds and stipulates protocols with each of the organizations, which have full responsibility on how they spend the subsidies. In Slovakia, the Ministry of Culture, in particular, its section for minority cultures, is the main element of the government's policy of support for regional or minority languages (Committee of Experts Report on Slovakia 2007: para. 167). Within the ministry, a committee is established that assesses the applications for funding of various groups of speakers and adopts 'recommendations to the Minister on the amounts of subsidies to be granted' (para.169).

One of the most important treaties which influence the countries' protection system in the field of culture is the ECRML. While in Romania, Slovakia and Slovenia, most of the provisions are realized, in Austria only a few attained fruition. A further measure for the preservation of culture derives from the different bilateral agreements like Hungary's treaties on good neighbourliness and cooperation with Slovakia (1995) and Romania (1996), and the agreement between Austria and Slovenia on cooperation in the fields of culture, education and science (2001).

CONCLUSION

This study provides an insight into different minority protection systems in Central and Eastern Europe. As discussed, the last century has been a very turbulent time for the six countries under consideration which experienced two World Wars, in which borders changed several times and nationalistic ideologies split the continent. Finally, after the fall of the Iron Curtain the countries joined together and began to collaborate not only on economic projects but also in important fields as minority protection. The multilateral and bilateral treaties that have been drawn in this context were very important in order to provide standards in this field and scrutinize their implementation.

Besides these positive developments, there are still many aspects that need to be improved. While non-discrimination is an accepted principle, many countries are still reluctant to adopt positive measures of active minority protection with the consequence that there is no substantial equality between members of a minority and the majority population. Moreover, whenever countries provide positive measures, they are only supposed to guarantee individual rights; most ignore the important aspect of group rights (Benedikter 2008: 135-36). This is reflected also by the fact that international systems of minority protection are often too abstract to guarantee an efficient minority protection and do not have any legal binding mechanisms to enforce their implementation.

One reason for the problems that still persist in the field of minority protection is the protectionist behaviour of nation-states as well as the fear of possible secessions. All the more it seems obvious that an efficient minority protection system can work only collectively: under an international aspect, the countries have to be more courageous in finding innovative solutions and not just weak compromises. Under a national aspect, peaceful co-existence shall be understood as a challenge for the majority population as well as for the members of minorities. Both have to understand that diversity must be seen not as an obstacle but a cultural treasure, which has to be protected, maintained and fostered.

APPENDIX

Table 6.1 AUSTRIA

	2001	%	Self-estimation	%
Population (2001)			8,032,557	100
German-speaking Austrians			6,991,388	87.0
Ethnic groups:				
1. Slovenes	17,953	0.2	50,000	0.0
2. Croats (incl Burgenland-Croats)	45,194	0.6	42,000	0.5
3. Hungarians	25,884	0.3	20,000 – 30,000	0.4
4. Czechs	11,035	0.1	15,000 – 20,000	2.0
5. Romany-Sinti	4,348		10,000 – 20,000	2.0
6. Slovaks	3,343		5,000 – 10,000	0.1
	107,757	1.3	142,000–172,000	2.1
Others	116,450	1.4	158,612	2.0
Foreign nationals	710,926	8.9	710,926	8.9

Source: Pan and Pfeil 2006: 367; Statistic Austria, census 2001.

Table 6.2 HUNGARY

	2001	%	Self-estimation	%
Population (2001)			10,162,000	100
Hungarians			9,066,000	89.2
National minorities:				
1. Romany	190,046	1.9	400,000 – 600,000	5.9
2. Germans	62,233	0.1	200,000 – 220,000	2.2
3. Slovaks	17,692		100,000 – 110,000	1.1
4. Croats	15,620		80,000 – 90,000	0.9
5. Romanians	7,995		25,000	0.2
6. Poles	2,962		10,000	0.1
7. Serbs	3,916		5,000 – 10,000	0.1
8. Armenians	620		3,500 – 10,000	0.1
9. Ruthenians	1,098		6,000	
10. Slovenes	3,040		5,000	
11. Greeks	2,509		4,000 – 4,500	
12. Bulgarians	1,358		3,000 – 3,500	
13. Ukrainians	5,070		2,000	
	314,059	3.1	1,096,000	10.8

Source: Pan and Pfei: 607.

Table 6.3 ITALY

	Self-estimation	%
Population (2002)	56,305,000	100
Italians	52,876,900	93.9
National minorities		
1. Sardinians	1,660,000	2.9
2. Friulians (Rhaeto-Romanics)	720,000	1.3
3. Germans (census in South Tyrol)	304,500	0.5
4. French speakers (incl. Franco Provencals)	200,000	0.4
5. Occitans	178,000	0.3
6. Sinti-Romany	130,000	0.2
7. Albanians	90,000	0.2
8. Slovenes	53,000	0.1
9. Ladins (Rhaeto-Romanics)	43,000 – 57,000	0.0
10. Greeks	18,000	
11. Catalonians	15,000	
12. Croats	2,600	
	3,428,100	6.1

Source: Pan and Pfeil 2006: 240.

Table 6.4 ROMANIA

	1992	%	2002	%
Population	22,760,449	100.0	21,680,974	100.0
Romanians	20,095,449	88.3	19,399,547	89.3
National minorities:				
1. Hungarians	1,622,364	7.1	1,433,073	6.6
2. Romany	409,723	1.8	535,140	2.5
3. Vlachs (Aromanians)	250,000	1.1	50,000	0.2
4. Germans	119,436	0.5	59,764	0.3
5. Ukrainians/Ruthenians	66,833	0.3	61,098	0.3
6. Lipoveni/Russians	38,688	0.1	35,791	0.2
7. Turks	29,533	0.1	32,098	0.2
8. Serbs	29,080	0.1	22,561	0.1
9. Tatars	24,649	0.1	23,935	0.1
10. Slovaks	20,672	0.1	17,226	0.1
11. Bulgarians	9,935		8,025	

Table 6.4 ROMANIA (*cont.*)

	1992	%	2002	%
12. Jews	9,107		5,785	
13. Macedonians	6,999		731	
14. Croats	6,955		6,807	
15. Czechs	5,800		3,941	
16. Poles	4,247		3,559	
17. Greeks	3,897		6,472	
18. Armenians	2,023		1,780	
	2,659,941	11.7	2,307,786	10.6
Others/no details	4,527		23,591	0.1

Source: Pan and Pfeil 2006: 418.

Table 6.5 SLOVAKIA

	1991	%	2002	%
Population	5,274,335	100.0	5,379,455	100.0
Slovaks	4,519,328	85.7	4,614,854	85.8
National minorities:				
1. Hungarians	567,296	10.7	520,528	9.7
2. Romany	75,802	1.4	89,920	1.7
3. Czechs	59,326	1.1	46,968	0.9
4. Ruthenians	17,197	0.3	24,201	0.4
5. Ukrainians	13,281	0.3	10,814	0.2
6. Germans	5,414	0.1	5,405	0.1
7. Croats			890	
8. Jews	134		218	
9. Poles	2,659		2,602	
10. Bulgarians	1,400		1,179	
11. Russians			1,590	
	742,509	14.1	704,315	13.1
Others	12,498	0.2	60,286	1.1

Source: Pan and Pfeil 2006: 502.

Table 6.6 SLOVENIA

	1991	%	2002	%
Population	1,913,335	100.0	1,964,036	100.0
Slovenes	1,689,657	88.3	1,631,363	83.1
National minorities:				
1. Hungarians	8,000	0.4	6,243	0.3
2. Italians	2,959	0.2	2,258	0.1
3. Romany	2,259	0.1	3,246	0.2
4. Germans (incl. Austrian heritage)	424		680	
	13,642	0.7	12,427	0.6
Others	167,701	8.8	145,921	7.4
No details	42,355	2.2	174,325	8.9

Source: Pan and Pfeil 2006: 519.

LEGAL PROVISIONS:

Austria (AT)

- Federal Constitutional Act of 1920
  (AT Const)
- State Treaty of Vienna BGB1. No. 152/1955
  (At State Treaty of Vienna 1955).
- Federal Law on the Austrian Broadcasting Corporation,
  BGB1. I No. 83/2001.
  (AT Broadcasting Corporation Act 2001)
- Minorities Act, BGB1 No. 369/1976.
  (AT Minorities Act 1976)
- Minority School Act of Burgenland,
  BGB1 No. 641/1994.
  (AT Minority School Act of Burgenland 1994)
- Minority School Act of Carinthia No. BGB1 101/1959
  (with amendments)
  (AT Minority School Act of Carinthia 1959)
- Federal Law on the Promotion of Press,
  BGB1. I No. 136/2003.
  (AT Press Law 2003)

Hungary (HU)

- The Act No. XX from 1949 – The Constitution of the Republic of Hungary.
  (HU Const)
- The Act No. LXXVII of 1993 on the Rights of National and Ethnic Minorities.
  (HU Minority Act 1993)
- Act No. LXXIX of 1993 on public education.
  (HU Public Education Act 1993)
- Act No. I of 1996 Hungarian Act on Television and Radio Broadcasting.
  (HU Act on Television and Radio 1996)

Italy (IT)

- The Italian Constitution of 1948
  (IT Const)
- Autonomy Statute of the Aosta Valley of 1948
  (IT Autonomy Statute of the Aosta Valley)
- The Autonomous Statute of Trentino-South Tyrol of 1972
  (IT Autonomous Statute of South Tyrol)
- Law No. 482/1999 on the protection of historic linguistic minorities
  (IT Minority Act 1999)
- Law No. 38/2001 on the Protection of the Slovene Linguistic Minority in the Region Friuli-Venezia Giulia
  (IT Slovene Language Law 2001)

Romania (RO)

- The Constitution of Romania of 1991, amended and completed by the Law No. 429/2003.
  (RO Const)
- Audiovisual Law No. 504/2002
  (RO Audiovisual Law 2002)
- Law for election of the local public administrative authorities No. 67/2004.
  (RO Election law 2004)
- Law on the election of Chamber of Deputies and Senate No. 35/2008.
  (RO Election law 2008)

Slovakia (SK)

- The Constitution of the Slovak Republik of 1992.
  (SK Const)
- Minority Language Law No.184/1999.
  (SK Language Law 1999)
- Act on Slovak Radio—Law No. 619/2003
  (SK Radio Act 2003)
- Act on Slovak Television—Law No.16/2004
  (SK Television Act 2004)
- The Non-Discrimination Law No. 365/2004.
  (SK Non-Discrimination Law)

Slovenia (SI)

- Constitution of the Republic of Slovenia of 1991.
  (SI Const)
- The Act on Radio and Television Corporation No. 05/96
  (SI Radio and Television Corporation Act 1996)
- Regulation on Criteria, Conditions and Procedures of Allocating Funds for Creating the Economic Basis for the Autochthonous National Communities No. 33/97, 16/99 and No. 62/01
  (SI Economy Regulations 1997)
- The Act of Roma Community in the Republic of Slovenia No. 33/07
  (SI Roma Community Act 2007).
- The Act on Public Administration No. 52/02, . . ., 126/07
  (SI Administration Act 2002)

International treaties

- Bilateral treaty of Brno between representatives of Austria and Czechoslovakia of 1920.
  (Treaty of Brno 1920)
- Convention on Providing Special Rights for the Slovenian Minority Living in the Republic of Hungary and for the Hungarian Minority Living in the Republic of Slovenia of 1992.
  (HU-SI agreement 1992)
- Treaty on Good Neighbourliness and Friendly Cooperation between Slovakia and Hungary of 1995.
  (HU-SI treaty 1995)
- Treaty on Understanding, Cooperation and Good Neighbour-

liness between the Republic of Hungary and Romania of 1996. (HU-RO treaty 1996)

- The Framework Convention for the Protection of National Minorities of 1998
(FCNM)
- The European Charter for Regional or Minority Languages of 1998.
(ECRML)
- Agreement between the Government of the Slovak Republic and the Government of the Republic of Slovenia on Cooperation in the Fields of Science, Education, and Culture. Bratislava, 14 December 1999.
(SK-SI agreement 1999)
- Agreement between Austria and Slovenia on cooperation in the field of culture, education and science of 2001
(AT-SI agreement 2001)

NOTES

1. For a detailed overview see the Tables 61-6 in the Appendix.
2. Germans and Ladins in South Tyrol, Slovenes in Friuli Venezia Giulia, the francophone minority in the Aosta valley.
3. E.g., Hungary extended the application of the ECRML to the Romani and Beash languages only in 2008 and Slovenia still doesn't include the Croatian, Bosnian and Serbian in the list of protected minority languages considering them as immigrant languages and therefore not covered by the provisions of the charter.
4. E.g., For German-speaking South Tyroleans in Italy and Italians in Slovenia the only choice available is a monolingual school.
5. E.g., French-speaking population of Aosta in Italy and Hungarians in Slovenia.
6. E.g., University Babes-Bolyai in Romania and University of Nitra in Slovakia.
7. E.g., in Italy German language in South Tyrol, while it is not the case for the Slovene language in Friuli Venezia Giulia.
8. Germans in the province of South Tyrol and the Region Trentino-South Tyrol. Slovenes in the provinces of Trieste, Gorizia and Udine and the Region Friuli Venezia Giulia.
9. The one which has obtained the largest amount of valid votes among the organizations of the same minority.
10. Minority Advisory Councils in Austria; Department of National and Ethnic Minorities within the Prime Minister's Office as well as Minor-

ity Self-Governments in Hungary; Commission of Six in Italy (South Tyrol); Council for National Minorities in Romania; Council of National Minorities and Ethnic Groups in Slovakia; and Minority Self-Governments in Slovenia.

11. For the other languages protected under the charter (Croatian, German, Romany) only Part II applies.

REFERENCES

Andreescu, Gabriel. 2005. *Schimbari in harta etnica a Romaniei.* Cluj: Ethnocultural Diversity Resource Center.

Advisory Committee on the Framework Convention for the Protection of National Minorities. 2002. *First Opinion on Austria. ACFC/INF/OP/I(2002)009.* Strasbourg (2003): Council of Europe. http://www.coe.int/t/dghl/monitoring/minorities/3_FCNMdocs/PDF_1st_OP_Austria_en.pdf.

Advisory Committee on the Framework Convention for the Protection of National Minorities. 2006. *Second Opinion on Romania. ACFC/OP/II(2005)007.* Strasbourg (February): Council of Europe. http://www.coe.int/t/dghl/monitoring/minorities/3_FCNMdocs/PDF_2nd_OP_Romania_en.pdf.

Advisory Committee on the Framework Convention for the Protection of National Minorities. 2006. *Second Opinion on Slovakia. ACFC/OP/II(2005)004.* Strasbourg (June): Council of Europe; http://www.coe.int/t/dghl/monitoring/minorities/3_FCNMdocs/PDF_2nd_OP_SlovakRepublic_en.pdf.

Baur, Siegfried, and Roberta Medda-Windischer. 2008. The Educational System in South Tyrol. In *Tolerance through Law: Self-Governance and Group Rights in South Tyrol,* edited by Jens Woelk, Francesco Palermo and Joseph Marko: 235-258. Leiden: Martinus Nijhoff.

Benedikter, Thomas, ed. 2008. *Europe's Eethnic Mosaic. A Short Guide to Minority Rights in Europe.* Bolzano: European Academy.

Committee of Experts. 2007. *Report on the Application of the European Charter for Regional or Minority Languages in Slovakia. First Monitoring Cycle. ECRML (2007) 1.* Strasbourg (February): Council of Europe. http://www.coe.int/t/dg4/education/minlang/Report/EvaluationReports/SlovakiaECRML1_en.pdf

Constantin, Sergiu. 2008. The Romanian Law on Ratification of the European Charter for Regional or Minority Languages. In *European Yearbook of Minority Issues,* vol.6, 2006/7: 575-84. Leiden: Martinus Nijhoff.

Crniæ-Grotiæ, Vesna. 2008. The Work of the Committee of Experts of the European Charter for Regional or Minority Languages between June 2006 and June 2007. In *European Yearbook of Minority Issues,* vol.6, 2006/

7: 387-407. Leiden: Martinus Nijhoff.

Ebner, Toni Rautz, and Günther Rautz, eds. 2005. *Minoritiy Dailies Association MIDAS.* Bolzano: Athesia AG.

EURAC research. European Academy of Bolzano – Institute for Minority Rights. www.eurac.edu/mimi.

European Commission for Democracy through Law (Venice Commission). 2005. *Observations on the Draft Law on the Statute of National Minorities of the Republic of Romania. CDL (2005)070 Opinion no. 345/2005.* Strasbourg (August): Council of Europe. http://www.venice.coe.int/docs/2005/CDL(2005)070-e.pdf.

Hungrian Central Statistic Office. Population by Religion, Denomination and Main Age Groups, 1920–1941, 2001. http://www.nepszamlalas.hu/eng/volumes/26/tables/load1_2.html.

Kertesz, Stephen. 1953. The expulsion of the Germans from Hungary: A study in postwar diplomacy. *Review of Politics,* 15, 2: 179-208.

Lantschner, Emma. 2009. *Soft jurisprudence im Minderheitenrecht: Standardsetzung und Konfliktbearbeitung durch Kontrollmechanismen bi- und multilateraler Instrumente.* Baden-Baden: Nomos.

Lantschner, Emma and Sergiu Constantin. 2003. *Comparative Summary of Bilateral Agreements for the Protection of National Minorities. SP/ba(2003)002.* Strasbourg (December): Council of Europe. http://www.coe.int/t/dghl/monitoring/minorities/6_Resources/PDF_SP_BA(2003)002per cent20ComparativeSummary_BilatAgr_en.pdf.

Ministry of Foreign Affairs Budapest. 2000. The National and Ethnic Minorities in Hungary. In *Fact sheets on Hungary, no. 3/2000.* http://www.mfa.gov.hu/NR/rdonlyres/9F2D180E-538E-4363-AA5E-3D103B522E3B/0/etniang.pdf.

MIRIS. The Minority Rights Information System database. http://www.eurac.edu/miris.

O'Grady, Cathy, and Daniela Tarnovschi, updated by Tibor Szasz. 2001. *Roma of Romania. Minorities in Southeast Europe.* Center for Documentation and Information on Minorities in Europe – Southeast Europe (CEDIME-SE).

http://www.edrc.ro/resurse/rapoarte/Roma_of_Romania.pdf.

Palermo, Francesco, and Jens Woelk. 2008. *Diritto costituzionale comparato dei gruppi e delle minoranze.* Padova: Cedam.

Pan, Christoph, and Beate Sibylle Pfeil. 2006. *Minderheitenrechte in Europa. Handbuch der europäischen Volksgruppen Band* 2. Wien: Springer.

Petocz, Kálmán. 2010. Participation of National Minorities in Decision-Making in Slovakia. In *European Yearbook of Minority Issues,* vol.7, 2008/2009. Leiden: Martinus Nijhoff.

Prauser, Steffen, and Arfon Rees (eds). 2004/1. *The Expulsion of the German Communities from Eastern Europe at the end of Second World War.*

European University Institute Working Paper HEC. Florence.

Republic of Slovenia. 2000. *First State Report Submitted by the Republic of Slovenia Pursuant to Article 25, Paragraph 1 of the Framework Convention for the Protection of National Minorities. ACFC/SR(2000)004.* Strasbourg (November): Council of Europe. http://www.coe.int/t/dghl/monitoring/minorities/3_FCNMdocs/PDF_1st_SR_Slovenia_en.pdf.

Slovak Republic. 2009. *Third State Report Submitted by the Slovak Republic Pursuant to Article 25, Paragraph 1 of the Framework Convention for the Protection of National Minorities. ACFC/SR/III(2009)008.* Strasbourg (Juli): Council of Europe.

http://www.coe.int/t/dghl/monitoring/minorities/3_FCNMdocs/PDF_3rd_SR_SlovakRepublic_en.pdf.

Statistic Austria. Official Census 2001. http://www.statistik.at/web_de/statistiken/bevoelkerung/volkszaehlungen/bevoelkerung_nach_demographischen_merkmalen/022886.html

Tismaneanu, Vladimir et al. 2006. Raportul final al Comisiei prezidentiale pentru analiza dictaturii comuniste din Romania', Bucharest.

Zagar, Mitja, Miran Komac, Mojca Medvešek and Romana Bešter. 2006. *The Aspect of Culture in the Social Inclusion of Ethnic Minorities. Evaluation of the Impact of Inclusion Policies under the Open Method of Co-ordination in the European Union: Assessing the Cultural Policies of Six Member States. Final Report: Slovenia.* ECMI Working Paper No. 33. Flensburg: European Centre for Minority Issues. http://www.ecmi-eu.org/fileadmin/media/download/Working_Paper_33_Slovenia.pdf.

6

KOSOVO IN ABKHAZIA OR THE UNIVERSALITY OF DE FACTO STATES

BENEDIKT HARZL

INTRODUCTION

The expression *sui generis* was effectively created by scholasticism in order to raise an idea or a reality which cannot be included into a wider concept. Literally meaning that something is unique in its characteristics, the term was generously applied to describe the legal nature of the European Union, the relationship between France and Caledonia, the profession of soldiering, and last, but not least, the case of Kosovo. Whereas Kosovo's alleged uniqueness has been justified in the first place by the large extent of international engagement and the far-reaching legal powers given to the UN Administration in Kosovo (UNMIK), supporters of the *sui generis* school of thought have even expanded Kosovo's uniqueness over other conflict elements referring to the 'just cause' approach of separatism. According to this philosophy, Serbia has put into question—due to massive human rights violations—its legitimacy to govern Kosovo. However, in the same vein, it is argued that allegedly no repressions can be reported from Georgia that had equally provoked both Abkhazia and South Ossetia to secede from Tbilisi (Erb

2008). Even though such a mindset is the direct result of lacking knowledge and probably lacking interest for a region which appears to be 'out of reach' for European foreign policy, the question of whether or not severe human rights violations justify secession is controversially discussed. Hilpold (2009: 55) argues that 'the right to self-determination should be interpreted in the sense that it [only] produces influence on the national constitutional systems requiring them to provide for participatory rights'. But even if such an interpretation is anachronistic as well as unsatisfactory for an ethnic minority group which is being subjected to repression, what makes Kosovo so unique as to be awarded only to the Albanians as the golden price of external self-determination? The answer to this question gives an insight into the inadequacy and inconsistency of such an interpretation: That Kosovo represents a *sui generis* case and hence does not set a precedent is actually a denial of the argument that massive human rights violations and ethnic cleansing justify remedial secession. Otherwise, what would be the sense of denominating Kosovo as unique (Muharremi 2008: 435)?

This article attempts to prove that the application of a *sui generis* methodology to distinguish Kosovo from other ethnopolitical conflicts, especially those in the Caucasus, is analytically insufficient. Even though there is an indisputable necessity for differentiation, the *sui generis* approach falls short to analyse and comprehend the underlying dilemma of post-communist ethnic engineering against the background of ethno-political power-seeking. In the following, the approach of a Balkanese *sui generis* case will be challenged by juxtaposing the Georgian-Abkhazian conflict with the Serbian-Kosovar confrontation in a phase-by-phase manner.

THE STRUCTURAL DIMENSION OF COMMUNIST FEDERATIONS: THE INHERITANCE OF CONFLICT

It is a commonplace that frontiers, drawn on maps, are the creations of politicians and reflect particular eras of history and corresponding strategies chosen at that time. In the cases of both the Caucasus and Kosovo, arbitrary boundary drawing accompanied by outright suppression and discrimination of minority groups stimulated myths and contributed to the widespread belief that historical injustices have to be corrected by playing the territorial card. Attempts were made to move the origins of conflict deeper into past ages of history. The Abkhazian side often refers to the early medieval feudal state of the Abkhazian kingdom which lasted from AD 780 until 1008 (Gigineishvili 2003) in their quest to justify independence whereas Albanian academics reacted to Serbian nationalism by masterminding an alleged ethnic and cultural continuity between the early Illirians and the medieval Albanians (Selemi 1998). The creation and the subsequent demise of the respective Communist federations appear to be more plausible for use as an initial point of orientation.

Indeed, Soviet ethnic engineering and the transfer of its underlying basis to the Balkans after World War II had a major impact on the development of conflict and still serves as the main explanation of why both the Soviet Union as well as Yugoslavia were institutionally ill-equipped to prevent violence. The main architects of the ethno-federal dimension in the Soviet Union, Vladimir Lenin and Joseph Stalin,[1] were convinced that the only way to remove the support base for nationalism and the evil of capitalism that were intrinsically linked was to grant far-reaching autonomy and self-rule rights by territorialization of ethnicity. In order to operationalize this notion of 'Leninist' self-determination, a set of hierarchically structured subjects was created: First came the Union Republics (SSR) which even had the legal right to secede from the Soviet Union, followed by the Autonomous Soviet Republics (ASSR) of which there were more than 15 with their own constitution, legislation and the right to fly their own flag, and the list of this matrioshka-doll-like system was rounded off with autonomous regions *(oblasti)* and areas *(okrugi)*. The nation was, in Lenin's view, merely a community of belonging whereas a *class*, by contrast, represented a community of *interests*. Hence, a community of interests, preferably common interests, is said to be more stable than a community of belonging, where the bonding is looser. It was exactly for this reason that the indigenization campaign was deliberately chosen to override trivial differences of anachronistic national distinctiveness since it promoted class consciousness. Indeed, the supranational nature of the Communist Party was at the beginning of the 1920s very successful in neutralizing possible inter-ethnic tensions, political elites in the Caucasus felt closer to members of their own class in other regions than they did to their ethnic kin at home and likewise, Soviet functionaries understood one another much better than people of their own ethnic background (Ascher et al. 1999). Likewise, the Leninist indigenization policies concentrated in addition on the education of illiterate people of whom there were many after the demise of the tsarist empire.

Yet the well-intentioned but incorrect presumption, according to which at the end of this process of inter-ethnic equalization would come the erosion of the nation itself, resulting in the coming closer of nations *(sblizhenie)* and merging of nations *(slijanie)*, got lost in the reality of Soviet day-to-day political practice. Stalin recognized that the nationalities policies of the 1920s effectively created and amplified distinctions which could threaten the hegemony of the Communist Party. Therefore, Stalin shifted towards a primordialist interpretation of the nation and started to dismantle all the institutions of nationalities created in the 1920 and effectively reversed the wheel of Lenin's indigenization policies. Stalin's deportation policies and his strategy of rule and divide in regions of ethnic plurality reduced the number of official peoples from about 200 in the 1926 census to 59 by 1939 (Martin 2001: 114). Morality and justice aside, Stalin was right insofar as he was not convinced of the alleged 'transient' nature of nationalism as Lenin had predicted in the 1920s. And this can be exemplified by an illustrative fact. Given the situation in a transitional phase that some minorities hold territorial autonomy and certain other minorities are deprived of this privilege, one would—especially in a time of economic crisis and decline as in the late 1980s—suppose that the latter had more reasons to push for independence and would more likely put their claims into practice, also by using force. But surprisingly, none of that happened with the exception of the Gagauz people in Moldova, who, however, solved their initial confrontation peacefully with the central government of Kishinev already in 1994 by establishing the autonomous territorial entity of Gagauzia.[2] As a matter of fact, and this shall lead to the underlying problem of *universal structural factors* for ethnic conflicts in the post-Communist space, practically all secessionist or irredentist struggles on the territory of the former Soviet Union were carried out between (former) autonomous regions and their central governments (Cornell 2002).

STRUCTURAL DILEMMA AND ETHNO-POLITICS: ABKHAZIA

Abkhazia, which used to be a Soviet Socialist Republic on equal level with Georgia, was only under Stalin incorporated as ASSR into the Georgian SSR in 1931, allegedly as punishment for the Abkhaz Communist leadership and their failure to overcome the protest of the peasant population against Stalin's collectivization policies (Lang 1962: 256). What followed then was a massive 'Georgianization' of Abkhazia and its native people, and it seemed that history repeated itself: The tragedy suffered by the Abkhaz people during the Russian conquest in the nineteenth century and the forced emigration of the Muslim part of the Abkhaz people to Turkey was compounded by a repressive policy by Georgia.[3] Hence, Alexei Zverev reasons correctly that 'Stalinist repressions hit Abkhazia like the rest of the USSR, but here it had an additional ethnic colouring as it was carried out by Georgians' (Zverev 1996). The deportation and re-population policy resulted in the vanishing of the Abkhaz population in their own homeland, so that in 1955 Abkhazia comprised only 13.3 percent ethnic Abkhazians (Lakoba 1998). With his Georgian comrade Lavrenti Beria, Stalin also conducted systematic assaults on the Abkhaz culture: All schools that used the Abkhaz language were closed, the Abkhaz alphabet was eliminated and replaced by Georgian letters and Abkhaz newspapers were abolished (Mihalkanin 2004). Already in 1957, 1964, 1967 and 1978, mass meetings and demonstrations took place in Abkhazia, demanding the detachment of Abkhazia from the Georgian Union Republic (Mihalkanin 2004). And then finally in 1989, the national Abkhaz assembly 'Ajdgyrala' was founded and passed the 'Lykhny Declaration' asking the Central Committee of the Communist Party of the Soviet Union for upgrading of Abkhazia in order to restore the status of a Union republic. Even though the status of an ASSR and the extent of administrative and cultural rule had varied over time, the only element which differed from a Union republic was that an ASSR fell short of having the right to secession. But even if the law to secede was unreachable for Abkhazians, their claim for independence was purely from a legal viewpoint indisputable, at least in 1990. According to Art. 3 of the 'Law on Procedures for resolving questions related to the secession of Union Republics from the USSR (3 April 1990)', *'the peoples of autonomous republics and autonomous formations shall retain the right to decide independently the question of staying in the USSR or in the seceding Union republic'* (Hannum 1993: 751).

Nevertheless, the manifestation of unrest to stay within a new and alien state triggered an equally dangerous explosion of nationalism from the Georgian side: tens of thousands Georgians gathered and held nationalist protest rallies in the cities of Gali, Sukhumi and finally in Tbilisi. And the Georgian capital became the place of a tragic occurrence: On 25 March 1989, troops of the Soviet Ministry for Internal Affairs opened fire on the protesters, killing twenty and injuring hundreds.[4] The brutality of this action, from which Mikhail Gorbachev desperately tried to distance himself, marked a crucial turning point in the conflict history and further radicalized the irreconcilable positions of the conflict parties. And this event also cemented the view of the Georgians that their minority groups are only political tools of Moscow.[5] From that time on, official Georgia is reformatting the Georgia-Ossetian and Georgian-Abkhaz dimension into a Georgian-Russian conflict. Mikhail Saakashvili's outrageous interpretation of the Abkhazian conflict reads as follows: 'When one day Russian Generals woke up and discovered that their dachas were suddenly part of a foreign country and realized that they lost property they started to bomb Georgia'.[6] The fact that there is an indigenous ethnic minority who has been repressed and nearly liquidated by the Georgian army and paramilitary units in 1992 does not even appear in a footnote in the official Georgian conflict interpretation. The assumption that Russia was preparing for a conflict, using local unease to egg on Georgia's territorial integrity became a question of how Georgia understood this conflict. If anything, only comparisons with animals were raised by Saakashvili when speaking about minorities themselves: 'I know that Georgia's ill-wishers, the hyenas [sic] ensconced in the government buildings in Sukhumi, are looking up at us and thinking: let us see when they will falter and when they will fall down so that we can devour them.'[7]

What is furthermore remarkable is the fact that Georgia has one of the highest numbers of PhDs and professional academics throughout the former Soviet Union, but not even such a well educated society was immune to the deadly policies of ethno-nationalism. To the contrary, Georgian academia became an important megaphone of nationalism and joined the political class in portraying the Abkhaz people as guests on Georgian soil. Some shocking comments, like the one of the well-known and highly reputed historian Mariam Lordkipanidze, can illustrate this: 'The so-called independent Abkhazian SSR was an artificially created entity, whose existence in isolation from Georgia was absolutely unnatural and untenable historically and culturally. . . The existence of Abkhazian autonomy in any form within the boundaries in which it took shape under Soviet rule is absolutely unjustified . . . Abkhazians were never molested by Georgians, they only attacked and plundered one another' (Tishkov 1997). The ethnic entrepreneur Gamsakhurdia, who was interestingly a philologist, early found out the way to make use of such statements and to translate them into political actions. And Saakashvili, promoted and supported by Western Europe and America, obviously followed the footsteps of the first Georgian president in radicalizing the language. Already in 2007 he intimated that Georgia planned to solve its conflicts in violation of international law by the use of reckless force, something which happened then in 2008: 'We have been patient for 14 years. I want to say for the whole world to hear that our patience is reaching its limits and is running out. As of today we are beginning a countdown to our return to Abkhazia. We will all certainly return. I firmly promise you this once again. We began preparing for this several years ago.'[8]

STRUCTURAL DILEMMA AND ETHNO-POLITICS: KOSOVO

Likewise, Slobodan Milosevic illustrated the Kosovo conflict as being triggered in a conspiratorial relationship between Austria, Germany and the Holy See and even denied the existence of ethnic conflict which—if anything—according to this view, was created by Western media. Asked by the *Washington Post* in 1998 about the alleged foreign factor in the Kosovo crisis, Milosevic answered, 'You know the implosion [of Albania occurred] a year before Kosovo. Their army disappeared practically and they are living in chaos. Albania is a factor of instability in [the] whole region. There is not one single terrorist faction in the whole world [that does not have a] base in Albania. And [there is an] Albanian narco-mafia which is . . . giving money to foreign journalists and politicians—bloody money [because] they are earning it dealing with drugs' (*Washington Post* 1993). The picture of a similarly situated dilemma gets even clearer when taking into account the underlying pre-war institutional dilemma.

The Soviet Constitution of 1936 served as a main source of inspiration for the decision to create a federal Yugoslavia with six equal constituent republics, taken during the second Anti-Fascist Council for the People's Liberation of Yugoslavia (AVNOJ) Conference in the town of Jajce in 1943 (Mappes-Niediek 2005). This structural fact of an autonomous province within a superior republic applies to the Serbian-Kosovar confrontation as well, since the latter conflict party had enjoyed the privileges of far-reaching autonomy rights within a clearly defined territory in the frame of a Socialist Autonomous province. The confrontation between an *uti possidetis* approach according to Socialist—or in the Georgian case even Stalinist—boundary drawings, where the golden price of recognition was only awarded to former Republics, and the call for self-determination in other entities, became already noticeable at the beginning of the 1990s. There was unease since the 1960s. Demonstrations took place already in 1968 in Kosovo, whereas in Abkhazia, Albanians for the first time proclaimed a 'Kosovo Republic', in such a way so as to shift the objective towards upgrading the autonomous status of Kosovo under the Socialist Republic of Serbia into equal republic status within the Yugoslav Federation (Cohen 1993: 51).

The federal level of Yugoslavia reacted to the growing unease in Kosovo by eliminating the Serbian term *Metohija* from the provincial name in 1968, and finally the adopted federal constitution of 1974 provided Kosovo with far-reaching rights such as veto rights concerning the change of borders as well as constitutional changes for all provinces and republics of Yugoslavia (Vickers 1998: 178-79). This constitutional reform has enormously enhanced the position of Kosovo within Yugoslavia: Kosovo had its own legislative and executive branch, even a supreme court. However, the only difference—as already discussed in the case of the Abkhazian Autonomous Republic—was that the right to secession was only assigned to *nations* in the institutional dress of federal republics (such as Serbia, Croatia, and so on) and not to *nationalities,* of which Kosovo was one. In retrospect it turns out that the reconciliation of a state aiming to build a communist ideal where all ethnically-related and cultural differences would easily dissolve in a state based on the principle of ethno-federalism and the linkage between ethnicity and territory were already questionable from an ideological dimension. In this situation of central political planning with a simultaneous ethnic accommodation, the overall system did not take into account two crucial as well as relatively interrelated issues (of which one is the subsequent result) which came to a head in Kosovo and in Abkhazia as well: the lack of historical consciousness and insecurity.

On the one hand, the ahistorical and to a certain extent even anti-historical party line of the Communists left old wounds unhealed and on the other, opened by its deliberate indifference the stage for ruthless power-seeking of ethnopolitical entrepreneurs in the transitional period. By inventing the category 'Yugoslavs' at the censuses which were taken decennially, the ruling Communists in Yugoslavia attempted to foster a certain kind of nation-building which was, however, only successful with army members and children of mixed marriages (Baltic 2007: 27). Likewise, the postulated ideology of the Communist Party of the Soviet Union was the creation of a new *sovietskij narod* (Soviet people), a new human species, an archetype of a people with all the characteristics which were emerging in the Soviet Union despite its cultural, linguistic and ethnic diversity in the background. And the niches of this grey zone of ethnic accommodation in the environment of an authoritarian one-party system was soon filled with new political activism. 'In reality, the order in Yugoslavia was based entirely on political decisions, made in concrete centres of power within the party. The self-governing myth made every thought of limiting political power pointless, given that the system's sustainable functioning was, according to that myth, based exclusively on deliberation, agreement and a never-ending search for equilibrium and balance' (Kovacevic 2008). In other words, the fact that Yugoslavia and the Soviet Union never fulfilled the minimum requirements to be categorized as fully-fledged federations, which traditionally aim at establishing a political union of *really* self-governing states or regions united by a federal government, gives an answer to the question as to why both federations were unable to channelize and moderate ethno-political claims. Thus, the Yugoslav system of complete party control and infiltration of society—Yugoslavia had more political prisoners than any other country ruled by Communists (Bideleux 1985: 184)—was sustainable as long as the Communist Party was flexible enough to provide 'incorporating authoritative elements of society into one whole' (ibid: 10). Hence, the state's decentralization process which accompanied the simultaneous defragmentation of the party, created insuperable security dilemmas which were difficult to tackle. This was so also for the international community and, least of all, for the academic communities of Serbia and Georgia: Just to the contrary, Zviad Gamsakhurdia's nationalistic battle cry 'Georgia for the Georgians' which culminated in the renaming of South Ossetia into 'region Tskhinvali' (Tishkov 1997: 14) and the famous 1987 memorandum of the Serbian Academy of Sciences and Art which drew historical analogies to the myth of victimization at the battle of Kosovo polje (Cohen 2002: 99) was part of the same ethno-political deal. The deliberate analogies drawn between historical self-sacrifice and present victimization where 'the other' has savagely betrayed one's right to exist could not have found a more fertile institutional basis than that of communist ethno-federalism.

THE PHASE OF CONFLICT IN ABKHAZIA

One of the triggering events for war in Abkhazia was the re-adoption of the old 1925 Constitution by the Abkhaz Supreme Soviet, shortly before the collapse of the Soviet Union in 1991, which provided for a treaty relationship with Georgia. The declaration was issued in both Abkhazian and Georgian and did not mean, at least for the time being, fully-fledged independence. And under the pretext of this event, but also given the internal struggle between Shevardnadze and supporters of the then president Zviad Gamsakhurdia (the so-called 'Zviadists'), Georgia started its assault on Abkhazia in order to 'restore the constitutional order'. The Georgian invasion of Abkhazia in 1992 was in its initial stage quite successful as well as brutal: Together with ethnic Georgian residents of Abkhazia and former prison inmates who were released under the condition to fight in Abkhazia, Tengiz Kitovani's troops took the capital Sukhumi already on 18 August 1992 (HRW 1995).[9] The Georgian forces quickly took control of Abkhazia 'in a bout of killing and looting characteristic of the undisciplined militias' (Cornell 2002, 169). An official Abkhazian publication, the so-called 'White Book of Abkhazia' listed only for the period between August 1992 and March 1993 a total number of 2,000 non-Georgian civilians (also Armenians), killed by the Georgian military either in battle or during ethnic cleansing.[10] In a mood of victory and high spirits, the then Georgian President Shevardnadze announced via radio on 17 August 1992: 'Now we can say that Georgian authority has been restored throughout the entire territory of the republic' (Zverev 1996).

The whole subregion of the Caucasus, having roughly the size of Romania, is the homeland of approximately fifty different ethnic groups which speak languages that belong again to totally different language families. The collapse of the Soviet Union and the subsequent emergence of nation-states did not assign the minorities a crucial place in the respective national conception. This is compounded by the fact that many of these minorities often had relatives who lived previously across (Soviet) administrative borders but within one country (Soviet Union) and now were separated by internationally recognized borders. This was not only true for the divided group of the Ossetes, it also applied to the Armenian minority in Abkhazia and other connections based on a certain kinship. And what the Georgian war strategists underestimated in the first place, was the strength of ethnic sentiments. The first immediate response and assistance for the liberation of Abkhazia came from (para-)military units of the North Caucasus and anti-Georgian movements such as the Confederation of Mountain Peoples of the Caucasus. This military organization, which allegedly committed grave human rights violations during the war, called young men of all North Caucasian ethnicities to join the battle against the Georgians, and pro-Abkhazian demonstrations under the slogan 'Hands off Abkhazia' were organized in many cities in the North; solidarity was even manifested in Chechnya. Volunteers began to arrive in Abkhazia by narrow mountain paths and were trained and equipped, also by the Chechen military leader Shamil Basayev: Paradoxically, some years later in the war against the Russians, the very same Shamil Basayev commanded his 'Abkhaz Battalion' successfully; it had gained direct combat experience in the battle against the Georgians. And this is one of the crucial peculiarities of the Caucasus subregion: Ethnic groups in this region cannot be downsized to either pro- or anti-Russian chess figures: some equations such as 'the enemy of my enemy is my friend' represent in view of the Caucasian complexity totally oversimplified speculations. If 'the enemy of my enemy is my friend', the 'friend of my enemy shall be my enemy as well'. But as just discussed such simple models do not work in this particular region and their application by Western media leads to totally wrong political decisions. Apart from irregular troops from all corners of the Northern Caucasus, Cossacks joined the war on the side of Abkhazians together with soldiers of the Fourteenth Soviet Army who arrived directly from another troubled spot, namely, Transnistria.

Georgia received considerable assistance from the extreme anti-Russian and anti-semitic 'Ukrainian National Assembly—Ukrainian National Self-Defence',[11] which motivated its supporters to join the war against, what they saw as, Russia. Some sources even state that sportswomen snipers from the Baltic states joined the Georgians for mercenary reasons (ibid). To sum up, Abkhazia became the battlefield of different actors, mercenary units and entrepreneurs of which Russia was only one, albeit a very dominant one.

Russia's role in the conflict shifted from an initial reluctance to intervene to open support for Abkhazia. At the outset of the conflict, Russia urged both sides to come to terms peacefully in a diplomatic way, but after Abkhazia has been overrun by the Georgians and a new security dilemma began to unfold at the very fragile southern belt of the country,[12] the Russian military started jointly with northern volunteers to push the Georgian military forces back. It further strengthened the view of Georgia, which was undoubtedly convenient, that ethnic conflicts do not exist; only some extremists are motivated by an ancien regime to hijack Georgian territories. But for the sake of clarity and fairness, some grossly neglected facts have to be emphasized as well: The Abkhaz soldateska became more and more uncontrollable for Moscow, which did not wait to create trouble till a ceasefire was brokered by Russia, which was then, very much to the anger of the Kremlin, breached by the Abkhaz. In addition, Russia was responsible for the humanitarian costs and consequences. Russia became part of this conflict automatically since it evacuated tens of thousands Georgian as well as Abkhaz civilians from the conflict regions (HRW 1995), and provided food and accommodation for endless streams of refugees. Despite contrary claims from the European Union, it has been less directly affected by Caucasian security dilemmas as compared to Russia, and it is ill-conceived to accuse Russia of having inspired the Georgian-Abkhaz conflict. This totally oversimplified suggestion implies that Russia not only provoked the military invasion of Georgia, but also means that Russia—a collapsing empire in a turbulent transitional period, an ancien regime at the verge of a civil war—would have been absolutely sure of the course of subsequent events in the highly unpredictable region of the Caucasus.

Finally, Georgia lost control over Abkhazia, and Abkhazia began to institutionalize its de facto republic, viewing independence as non-negotiable. Moreover, the 200,000 ethnic Georgians who were expelled from Abkhazia and are living today in inhuman conditions in provisory housing were the ones that paid the price for a totally unnecessary escalation of what could have been resolved peacefully; for instance, by inviting Abkhaz officials to discuss the implementation of autonomy. Atrocities beyond description were carried out on both sides and give proof that complexities of ethnic diversity must not be solved by force. In this light, the most recent Georgian military assault against South Ossetia represented probably the last nail to be hammered into the coffin for the prospects for refugee return, let alone Georgian re-unification ambitions.

THE PHASE OF CONFLICT IN KOSOVO

Like the Soviet Union, Yugoslavia too fell short of instruments to cope with the hard security-related implications resulting from ethno-political agitation in the late 1980s. In Kosovo, probably the most critical factor which was often referred to as cultural genocide by Serbian ethnic entrepreneurs has been its specific demographic situation. From 1961-1981, the proportion of Albanians in Kosovo rose from 67 to 78 per cent (Independent International Commission on Kosovo 2000: 38). The reason for this obvious demographic explosion was on the one hand a comparatively high birth rate of Albanians, and on the other hand, the out-migration of Serbs and Montenegrins, which too caused this substantial change in Kosovo's ethnic composition. Yet both factors were not discussed objectively by Serbian ethno-agitators; they were furnished with ethno-nationalistic tones in order to demonstrate what they allegedly 'had always known about the goals of Albanians in Kosovo'. Serbian nationalists successfully exploited the fear of their people of an increasingly alienating homeland by interpreting demographics in ethno-national categories: Considering the high birth rate of Albanians, Serbian nationalists suspected a deliberately planned strategy to outnumber Serbs in Kosovo by switching on 'silent birth machines'. Even though women occupy a subordinate position in Albanian society (Vladisavljevic 2006: 58), this argument was by and large in line with the widely spread image of Albanians in Serbia, who were described as a culturally underdeveloped and hardly literate people. In the nineteenth century, the former Serbian prime minister Vladan Djordjevic said Albanians were thin, short, and that their Roma and Phoenician traits made him think of primates who slept hanging in trees. He continued his hate speech by stating, 'whereas other human beings had lost their simian tails in the course of evolution, it seemed that the Albanians had their tails well into the nineteenth century' (Banac 1984: 293). The same style of interpreting demographics by referring to defamation held true to a certain degree for the issue of Serbian out-migration from Kosovo: Indeed, surveys conducted in 1985-1986 among Serbs who left Kosovo indicated that a high percentage of the emigration resulted from verbal pressure, damage to property, attacks on children, that is, non-economic factors (Vladisavljevic 2006: 58). Even the Albanian member of the presidency of the Central Committee of the League of Communists, Ali Shukrija, criticized Albanian nationalism in 1981 by saying 'what nation and what honorable person can be proud of the fact that the girls of Serbian nationality dare not go to school, that graves are desecrated or that church windows are broken? How would Albanian families feel if their graves were desecrated and their religious objects damaged?' (ATA Tirana 1991)

Nevertheless, the Serb nationalists as well as the media exaggerated the suffering of Serbs and praised it as 'ethnic martyrdom' (Malcolm 1998: 338) but economic factors of Albanian nationalism, even though the Yugoslav Communist party was well aware of poverty and economic decline in the region, were silently and deliberately neglected. Kosovo was

Yugoslavia's poorest region where most of the managerial positions and state jobs were held by Serbs. This inequality was not mentioned as mobilizing factor on the part of Albanians. Though the translation from economic crisis and inequality in public life to war is not automatic, it has to be pointed out that economic circumstances can influence ethno-nationalism: Although the economic gap between Kosovo and other parts of Yugoslavia has always been enormous, at least during Communism special funds were given for improving infrastructure, electricity and industry.[13] However, this gap continued to grow during the Yugoslav economic crisis in the 1980s and co-generated ethnic unease that later on escalated dramatically. Unemployment reached 27 percent in 1980 and increased rapidly to 40 percent in 1990 (Independent International Commission on Kosovo 2000: 38). This economic drama around Kosovo was seen by Albanian activists as a result of their insufficient constitutional positioning, and they were sure that a Republic status would give them more economic control, which would introduce automatically more favourable policies. On the other hand, long before the rise of Milosevic, Serbian political debates were marked by the demands for re-capturing control of the autonomous budgets of Kosovo and Vojvodina in order to correspond to pressures for government reform by the IMF (ibid: 37–38).

The local Serbs' response to these dilemmas of Albanian pressure were efforts to ensure their security, however, by nationalistic means. The result was a greater nationalist agitation in both camps since the Albanians started to abandon their former pro-republican approach in favour of secession.[14] Instead of coming to terms peacefully, the explosive situation was fuelled and, as explained by both sides, by digging out alleged historical truths of the dusty historical relic of ethnomobilization, and it turned out also that the pseudo Federation of Yugoslavia fell institutionally short to moderate this conflict. Indeed, it was exactly this federation which co-generated the Kosovo drama. The suspension of the Kosovar autonomy by Milosevic was just another step within this struggle that brought the region to explosion.

Throughout the 1990s, the situation for Kosovar Albanians remained unsustainable in the province. At the beginning of 1998, the Democratic League of Kosovo (LDK) as the main political organization of Albanians with its charismatic chairman Ibrahim Rugova began to lose its influence on the de facto political landscape of Kosovo. The continuation of the peaceful approach to reach independence, one of the credos of Rugova, was in the eyes of many Kosovar Albanians discredited and demonstrated nothing else but flagrant irrationality given the Serbian suppression policy in the region. Ignoring international calls for restraint and dialogue, Serbian forces accelerated counter insurgency and ethnic cleansing activities throughout Kosovo and thereby indirectly contributed to the formation of the Kosovo Liberation Army (KLA), which came more and more involved in skirmishes against police and army units of Belgrade. The death toll of this conflict was tremendously high: from March to June 1999, there were an estimated number of 10,000 civilians killed, most of them Albanians, and approximately 860,000 Albanian civilians were forced to seek refuge outside of Kosovo.[15] Since diplomatic efforts, which were culminating at the Rambouillet negotiations, failed, NATO decided to start an air campaign against strategic targets in Serbia and Kosovo in order to bring an end to ethnic cleansing and displacement in Kosovo. This campaign, even though controversial, as discussed in the media and within the academic community, stopped the systematic oppression of Kosovar Albanians. Yet, NATO was not able to prevent ethnic counter-cleansing, when Serb military and police units withdrew from the province in June 1999. Approximately 200,000 Serbian and Roma residents of Kosovo became the victim of Albanian revenge and had no choice but to flee from this province which also used to be their homeland (HRW 2004). It is also for this reason that, as in the Abkhazian case also, Kosovo carries the hardly flattering image of having benefited from massive post-war displacements against the Serbs, resulting in an 'acceptable' ethnic composition of the country.

DIFFERENT INTERNATIONAL RESPONSES

In order to bring an end to the Serbian-Kosovar conflict, the international community has put all of its capacity into the scale of possible solutions and adopted, also with green light from Beijing and Moscow, SC Resolution 1244, which provided for a fully-authorized civil and military presence in Kosovo. Yet, even though this resolution established full legal authority of UNMIK over Kosovo, the thorny status issue was left open in the legal wording. The text of the resolution referred to the commitment of all member states to respect the territorial integrity of the Federal Republic of Yugoslavia, and called furthermore only for 'substantial autonomy and meaningful self-administration for Kosovo'.[16] However, this stipulation was particularly anachronistic and also unrealistic as it did by no means reflect the atmosphere in Kosovo, especially after what had happened during the conflict. Likewise, considerable segments of the academic community started to shift from the positivistic interpretation of the principle of self-determination to a more flexible model. Given the fact that Albanians had been systematically discriminated, tortured and murdered on the grounds of ethnic origin, Joseph Marko correctly argued already in 1999 that 'Kosovars are entitled to the right of external self-determination' (Marko 1999: 277). Indeed, the Kosovo incident gave shape to a new interpretation of the triangle between self-determination, territorial integrity and state sovereignty. This approach, of course, did not put into question the last two principles in essence, but it helped to view them in a more reasonable manner, so that states can rely on the principle of territorial integrity as long as they possess governmental structures which are representing the whole population of a state without discriminating on the grounds of race, religion, and so on. Nevertheless, from a purely positivistic view, the legal wording of Resolution 1244 remained clear insofar as it did not allow a secession of Kosovo without Serbian consent.

The unclear status question, however, had a huge contribution in a further destabilization of the region so that a resolution of the thorny statehood issue became top priority for the international community. In an attempt to balance the dogmas of international law and the climate of heightened security on the ground, UNMIK focused on the policies of 'standards before status' as well as 'earned recognition'. Soon, it turned out that the diplomatic efforts of the Special Envoy Martti Ahtisaari to bring both conflict parties, Serbian and Kosovar officials, together was doomed to failure. From the start of the status negotiation process, it had been evident even to outside observers of Kosovo affairs that an agreement between Belgrade and Prishtina would not be attainable since the two conflicting opinions of self-determination *vs.* territorial integrity are as a matter of fact hardly reconcilable. In February 2008, the Kosovar National Assembly finally declared its independence which was subsequently recognized by a number of states, above all the USA and most of the EU states.

The European attention towards the South Caucasian conflict zones was considerably lower so that Russia was thereby automatically assigned a significant role in the peacemaking process. Moscow managed to organize the Sochi truce agreement of 1993, but the fact that this agreement was breached by the Abkhaz forces demonstrates clearly that Russia's influence on the conflict was limited. Abkhazian forces, using a window of opportunity in the form of a ceasefire, overran Sukhumi and began to displace Georgian residents. It is noteworthy in this regard that the big wave of displacements of ethnic Georgians only started in the follow-up of the violation of the Sochi truce and subsequently the Georgian army was forced to withdraw to Tbilisi. Also in Kosovo, the big wave of displacements against the Serbian civilian population started only after the cessation of the NATO bombings, and have likewise been a clear violation of international law.

The violation of the Sochi agreement also changed the Russian stance to the Abkhazian question considerably. The agreement had called for the establishment of a Russian-Georgian-Abkhaz control group to monitor the ceasefire and a general memorandum was reached that allowed the Abkhazian Supreme Soviet to return to Sukhumi. However, it can be taken for granted that the Abkhaz side deliberately delayed the refugee question in order to create an accomplished fact for the sake of independence. Moreover, the ethnic cleansing, apart from personal tragedies, created a heavy blow for Georgian society: Although some estimated 60,000 refugees returned to Abkhazia since 1998,[17] Georgian refugees from Abkhazia are living in inhuman conditions, occupying until today hotels, dormitories and old Soviet military barracks throughout Georgia. According to some sources, the Georgian government does not encourage these refugees to integrate since it would lose its argument for re-establishing hegemony over Abkhazia (Dudwick 2002: 245). Sadly, both sides play a cynical game on the backs of thousands of refugees and, paradoxically, this particular issue strongly resembles the present situation in and around Israel, and Abkhazian politicians are pointing in their statements to the Israeli blockade towards the return of refugees in the quest for legitimacy for their actions (Klussmann 2008).

Although the Sochi agreement, which also called for the deployment of international observers under the auspices of the UN, looked as a very promising first step towards peace, it became irrelevant when Abkhaz forces retook the whole territory. Efforts to settle the conflict were renewed in late 1993 and early 1994 and were compounded by the UN Security Council Resolution 858 (1993) in August in an unanimous decision which established the United Nations Observer Mission in Georgia (UNOMIG),[18] dispatching several hundreds of UN personnel to the region in order to verify the compliance of the Sochi agreement in both South Ossetia and Abkhazia. Despite all the huge diplomatic efforts in which Russia actively participated, the only progress seemed to be the absence of new hostilities, but even this was not always achieved. In sum, 32 Security Council resolutions were issued on the Abkhazian conflict since 1993, but none of them brought a fundamentally new approach to peace. A new attempt of Georgia and Abkhazia to come to terms was reached in April 1994, when both sides signed the 'Declaration on Measures for a Political Settlement of the Georgian-Abkhaz Conflict'.[19] It included approaches to power-sharing models and constitutional arrangements, but unfortunately, this document was not a breakthrough but a new obstacle. The document stipulated that Abkhazia would have its own constitution and legislation as well as coat of arms and flag, leaving only the realms of foreign policy, foreign trade and customs to the pillar of 'common activity' of both entities. And such a formulation of course opened the floor for heavy discussions and far-reaching interpretations, since it strengthened the view of the Abkhazians that both sides were recognized as equal and sovereign subjects which were delegating powers to each other, a view which was correspondingly refused in Tbilisi.

De facto until today, the peace process has been nothing else but a period of deadlock, this was especially true for the return of IDPs. The diplomatic efforts, including the Geneva process under the aegis of the UN of 1997, the UN-brokered document of Basic Principles for the Distribution of Responsibilities between Tbilisi and Sukhumi in 2001[20] and other initiatives fell short to give answers to the three most pressing questions: *(i)* security and non-resumption of violence; *(ii)* IDPs and refugee return; and finally *(iii)* social and economic issues. Moreover, the Rose Revolution which was carried on a wave of Georgian nationalism and which installed Mikhail Saakashvili as president made things even worse: Violating the 1992 agreement according to which the Kodori Gorge[21] shall be a demilitarized region, only observed by CIS peacekeepers and the UNOMIG, Georgian police and military forces entered the valley and used this region as an ideal area for attack and retreat when it came to a resumption of violence. Until 2008, the situation on the ground has been in a fragile stalemate, and until then the demands of Abkhazians and Georgians had little in common. While Tbilisi desired to solve the issue of refugees first before a serious discussion on the future status should be started, the Abkhazian view was diametrically opposed. Fearing that a mass return of mostly Georgian IDPs would change the ethnic balance in disfavor of the Abkhazians, Sukhumi insisted that the legal status has to be defined first.

Since August 2008, the situation changed dramatically. With the Georgian assault on South Ossetia, the shelling of Tskhinvali and the killing of Russian peacekeepers, Abkhazia used the window of opportunity to finalize its total secession from Georgia. The war in South Ossetia spread to Abkhazia, but this time, Russia openly fought on the side of the Abkhazians. Faced with an ultimatum to leave the upper Kodori Gorge, all Georgian forces were driven out of Abkhazia. The unnecessary and reckless escalation, which had only and exclusively been in the interest of Georgia, set the final end to any considerations for re-unification in Abkhazia as well, at least for the time being. Today, with the recognition of independence of Abkhazia by Russia, Nicaragua, Venezuela, and in addition probably Belarus and some Central Asian countries which are to be expected to follow in a not to too distant future, all plans for a settlement have to be re-evaluated and re-assessed and especially the stance of the EU will have to be re-positioned.

CONCLUSION: *SUI GENERIS* AS A CONTRADICTORY MODEL

Having analysed above the conflict biography in both cases, Abkhazia and Kosovo, one has to ask seriously which criteria the EU council uses when it denominates Kosovo as alleged *sui generis* case which does not call into question the principles of sovereignty and territorial integrity (Council of the EU

2008). According to the overwhelming majority of scholars and politicians who are advocating the just cause approach of secession, Serbia has lost, due to its far-reaching and systematic human rights violations, the legitimacy to govern Kosovo. Yet, to place such a re-modelled principle of public international law only and exclusively within the narrow boundaries of Kosovo, so that secessionist conflicts in other post-communist parts of the world should be regarded as the product of entirely different factors, is not only far from convincing, it also casts a dark shadow on political ethics (Coppieters 2007) and the logic of such an argumentation: Academics and politicians have weakened their own argument on the legitimacy to secession in Kosovo in such a way that the principle of *remedial secession* could never be developed, only a politically-motivated exception would have to be found.

Dogmatists of the *sui generis* school of thought refer very often to the overwhelming UN mandate in Kosovo as the crutches to their argument. They argue that Abkhazia, in contrast to Kosovo, has hardly seen any international engagement. Indeed, Abkhazia did neither enjoy the establishment of a robust UN administration nor global attention on equal level with Kosovo. But isn't this the result of a deliberate choice on the part of EU and NATO states? Until today 'international' engagement has only been undertaken if explicitly requested or approved by the metropolitan state Georgia (Caspersen 2008: 69). And this differs greatly from the Serbian-Kosovar confrontation, where the EU states intimated from the very beginning that Kosovo has to decide about its future status regardless of being supported or not in this by Belgrade. The lack of international engagement had tragic consequences for the civilian population on the ground: the Abkhazian de facto authorities, unlike Kosovar Albanians, have often unsuccessfully requested the UN to be provided with internationally recognized travel documents, but since EU states and the US supported the Georgian conflict interpretation, it was very difficult for the Kosovar Albanian population to live within this environment of political as well as economic blockade. Georgia's refusal to allow the issuance of UN travel documents might in this context be regarded as a partial justification for the Russian passport distribution policy, even though the distribution of citizenships as well as the payment of pensions are not neutral issues in an ethnic conflict. It is for this reason that Russia is being harshly attacked for its 'passportization' campaign by West European scholars (Nygren 2008). However, very few pay attention to the fact that a mass acquisition of Russian passports is regarded as problematic by the political elites in Abkhazia in their bid for real independence.

The comments of scholars like Islam Lauka (2007) (see 'Kosovo a universal case or sui generis?', the Albanian Institute for Political Studies, Tirana 2007) show a lack of knowledge and an anti-Russian bias when indirectly claiming that in contrast to Georgia, Serbia does not act in bona fides when offering autonomy.[22] Does this actually mean in return that Georgia acts with these much-trumpeted bona fides? Can it be seen as an expression of bona fides that only some months before Mikhail Saakashvili attacked South Ossetia, the Georgian president promised to both breakaway states South Ossetia and Abkhazia 'the farest-reaching autonomy' (Socor 2008)? Which interpretation of bona fides can be sustained when a man, who said in 1993 that 'only 10,000 young Abkhazians have to be killed in order to destroy the genetic fundament of the Abkhazian people' (Fedyashin 2009) becomes under the Saakashvili administration minister for 'conflict resolution'? What do bona fides mean for territorial integrity when the EU investigation group finds out that by 7 August 2008, Georgia mobilized 12,000 troops and 75 tanks to storm South Ossetia and started this catastrophe (Klussmann 2009)? This list of academic shortcomings can be further continued, probably one of the most appropriate descriptions for this insufficient approach was found by the

Republican congressman Dana Rohrabacher: 'We have a totally inconsistent position when it comes to some countries that might have areas that want to have their self-determination but are occupied by people who are somewhat pro-Russian' (Robinson 2008).

In order to round off the circle of thoughts on the universality of de facto states, the following conflict parallels will again sum up the narrative of this article by juxtaposing Kosovo and Abkhazia in a cross-conflict element approach:

- In both cases, Kosovo and Abkhazia could point to a pre-war constitutional status with clearly defined territories. The development of conflict was in both cases generated by the collapse of a multi-national Communist federation and the implementation of discriminating policies by the parent states.
- Displacement and systematic murder have shaped the ethnic composition in both de facto states, even though Abkhazia has used the immediate aftermath of the war to reverse this composition totally and to set Georgia before new realities.
- Both de facto states became the place of ethno-political agitation and ruthless power-seeking with involvement of military as well as paramilitary groups.
- Both de facto states claim that the respective metropolitan state is not able to provide for security and reasonable self-rule so that only secession can satisfy their legitimate demand.
- In turn, both metropolitan states have for a long time interpreted the conflict by not assigning the respective minorities a certain position within the conflict.
- International actors (especially states and international organizations) have decided in both cases to suspend a final resolution for the status issue for a very long time. They have moderated peace talks under the auspices of the UN, OSCE and EU, but in neither case were the conflict parties able to come to terms. The lack of an equally

far-reaching mandate of the UN in Abkhazia as in Kosovo can be explained with deliberate priority setting of EU states and the USA within the Security Council: the Georgian conflict interpretation has been their guideline in most diplomatic efforts.

- Even if the right to remedial secession is not justified, both Abkhazia and Kosovo can claim that their de facto statelets are existing realities. In the case of Abkhazia this is even more clear, Georgia lost its influence more than 15 years ago.
- Both statelets are partially recognized states. And in both cases, the recognition was exercised against the expressed wish of the parent state. However, the fact that Kosovo has been recognized by more states than Abkhazia is irrelevant in view of public international law. States do not come into being by recognition as a constitutive act; they are defined along the criteria of the Montevideo convention of 1933. Therefore, the extent of justification for secession cannot be quantified by the number of recognitions.

This chapter argued that the uniqueness of a conflict situation lies usually in the eye of the beholder. Whether certain situations, facts or acts are effectively *sui generis* depends to a great extent on whether one is interested in seeing them as cases of *sui generis* or not (Müllerson 2009). By supporting one-sidedly the Georgian position of territorial integrity obviously at all costs, the EU and the USA have succeeded in achieving the very opposite of what they have wanted in the first place, namely, consolidation of Russia's influence in Abkhazia, and effectively an enlargement of the Russian state territory, something which (contrary to popular myth) is by no means universally popular in Abkhazia itself. In an obvious attempt to counteract the awaited results of the EU investigation commission (which will probably bring very depressing news for Georgia's role during the August war 2008), several European intellectuals and politicians urged the EU to define a proactive strategy to help Georgia regain its territorial integrity.[23] Indeed, a proactive policy makes sense, but it should not nourish illusions and indulge in fantasizing about a return to the status quo ante bellum. Instead, the EU should help and assist Georgia to cope with the loss of both, South Ossetia and Abkhazia and should, equally important, not treat Abkhazia as a criminalized, illegitimate, aggressive and chaotic puppet state of Russia. The refusal to deal with de facto authorities and to take their demand seriously has minimized the international community's chances for conflict resolution. The most recent example has been the withdrawal of the UN Observer Mission to Georgia (UNOMIG). Its mandate expired in July 2009, and since Abkhazia as well as South Ossetia (with Russian backing) wanted the name 'Georgia' to be deleted from the title, the UN Security Council could not come to a unanimous decision. The result is that the observers have had to leave, giving the Abkhazians a convenient argument: The UNOMIG has left, ergo, the conflict is solved. It is evident, however, that this conflict is actually far from being solved.

NOTES

1. Stalin gained much reputation within the Communist Party with his book *Marxism and the National Question,* written in Vienna in 1913. He was henceforward seen as expert on the dimension of accommodating ethnic plurality in the Soviet Union.
2. For a more comprehensive analysis of the autonomy of Gaugazia see: http://www.oeko-net.de/kommune/kommune09-01/agagaus.htm (German)
3. Until today, the biggest section of the Abkhaz people are still living in Turkey and not in Abkhazia.
4. A good overview on this historical event can be found in the dictionary of Georgian national biography, available under http://www.georgianbiography.com/history9.html
5. Which is to a certain extent absurd, especially given the military assistance of volunteer Cossack and Chechen formations which were

fighting side by side with their Abkhaz comrades.

6. Speech of Georgian President Mikhail Saakashvili, delivered at the Atlantic Council Romania Bucharest, 3rd April 2008, available at http://www.theseminal.com/2008/04/03/saakashvili-speech/
7. Website of the Georgian President, press release under the title 'Saakashvili opens new rail link in upper Abkhazia', 29 September 2007, available at http://www.president.gov.ge/?l=E&m=0&sm=3&st=60&id=2349
8. Website of the Georgian President, press release under the title 'Saakashvili attends presentation of voice of Abkhazia radio in Zugdidi', 6 October 2007, available under http://www.president.gov.ge/?l=E&m=0&sm=3&st=60&id=2360
9. Kitovani was at that time a Georgian military commander with high profile involvement in the wars over Abkhazia and South Ossetia.
10. Belaya kniga Abkhazii (*White book of Abkhazia)*, 1992-1993, Moscow, 1993, pp. 143-147.
11. In Ukrainian: YHA YHCO, *Óêðà¿íñüêà Íàö³îíàëüíà Àñàìáëåÿ – Óêðà¿íñüêà Íàö³îíàëüíà Ñàìîîáîðîíà*, this party still exists in Ukraine and maintains excellent relationship with the neo-Nazi party NPD (National-Demokratische Partei Deutschlands).
12. Russia had to cope with the humanitarian consequences of the war and was concerned with how this war creates unease in the multi-ethnic Russian North Caucasus.
13. This was also due to the *bratstvo i jedinstvo* doctrine which forced richer regions to accept reallocation of money.
14. Very soon the discontent of Albanians about the deepening economic crisis erupted to which the Serbians responded with a wave of military force in which numberless Albanians were killed. The claim for secession was therefore from the beginning furnished with the argument of lacking Serbian legitimacy.
15. Independent International Commission on Kosovo, *The Kosovo Report: Conflict, International Response, Lessons Learned* (New York: Oxford University Press, 2000): 2.
16. Text of the UN SC Resolution 1244/99 available under http://www.unmikonline.org/press/reports/N9917289.pdf
17. UN High Commissioner for refugees, Background note on the Protection of Asylum Seekers and Refugees in Georgia, 2004, p.2.
18. UN Security Council resolution 858 (1993), available under: http://www.undemocracy.com/S-RES-858(1993).pdf.
19. The text of this agreement is available under: http://www.pcr.uu.se/gpdatabase/peace/Geopercent2019940404.pdf.
20 The UN Secretary General issued this document as a possible start-

ing point for new attempts to solve the crisis, however it is still refused by the Abkhazian conflict party since it emphasizes Georgia's territorial integrity.

21. A strategically important river valley in Abkhazia.
22. Some experts refer to the bona fide theory, a glimpse into this discussion can be seen under http://volksgruppen.orf.at/diversity/Stories/80300/
23. Available under http://aktualne.centrum.cz/czechnews/clanek.phtml?id=648263

REFERENCES

Ascher, Ivan, Alexandra Patten, and Denise Monczewski. 1999. State Building and the Reconstruction of Societies. Caucasus Conference Report 1999, Berkeley Program in Eurasian and East European Studies, University of California, Berkeley.

ATA Tirana. 6 January 1991. Transmitted in FBIS Daily Report (Eastern Europe) on 9 January 1981.

Baltic, Nina. 2007. Theory and Practice of Human and Minority Rights under the Yugoslav Communist System. Report in the frame of the FP6 project MIRICO. http://www.eurac.edu/NR/rdonlyres/5BC4CBE8-A754-4040-B69E-8A21E19E768B/0/ReportontheTheoryandPracticeofHumanRightsandMinorityRightsundertheYugoslavCommunistS.pdf

Banac, Ivo. 1984. *The National Question in Yugoslavia. Origins, History, Politics.* Ithaca, NY: Cornell University Press.

Bideleux, Robert. 1985. *Communism and Development.* New York: Routledge.

Caspersen, Nina. 2008. From Kosovo to Karabakh: International Responses to De Facto States. *Südosteuropa* 56: 58-83.

Cohen, Lenard J. 2002. *Serpent in the Bosom. The Rise and Fall of Slobodan Milosevic.* Oxford: Oxford University Press.

—— 1993. *Broken Bonds: The Disintegration of Yugoslavia.* Boulder: Westview Press.

Coppetiers, Bruno. 2007. Kosovo and the Principles of Just Secession, *CEPS Policy Brief* no. 147, Centre for European Policy Studies. http://www.ceps.be/files/book/1564.pdf

Cornell, Svante. 2002. Autonomy and Conflict—Ethnoterritoriality and Separatims in the South Caucasus—Cases in Georgia. Department of Peace and Conflict Research, Uppsala, Sweden.

Council of the European Union. 2008. Council Conclusions on Kosovo, Brussels, February 18. http://www.eu2008.si/en/News_and_Documents/Council_Conclusions/February/0218_GAERC5.pdf

Dudwick, Nora. 2002. No Guests at Our Table: Social Fragmentation in Georgia. In *When Things Fall Apart—Qualitative Studies of Poverty in the Former Soviet Union*, edited by Nora Dudwick, Elizabeth Gomart, Alexandre Marc and Kathleen Kuehnast: 213-58. Wasington: The World Bank edition.

Erb, Nadja. 2008. Kein Vergleich mit dem Kosovo. *Frankfurter Rundschau*, August 28.
http://www.fr-online.de/in_und_ausland/politik/aktuell/1585068_Kein-Vergleich-mit-dem-Kosovo.html

Fedyashin, Andrej. 2009. Saakaschwili will zurück in den Krieg. *RIA-Novosti*, August 6. http://de.rian.ru/analysis/20090806/122600112.html

Gigineishvili, Levan. 2003. Conflicting Narratives in Abkhazia and Georgia—Different Visions of the Same History and the Quest for Objectivity. Tacit Knowledge and Intuition Website, Harvard Graduate School.
http://web.archive.org/web/20070812141131/http:/gseweb.harvard.edu/~t656_web/peace/Articles_Spring_2003/Gigineishvili_Levan_ConflictingNarrativesAbkhaziaGeorgia.htm

Hannum, Hurst. 1993. *Documents on Autonomy and Minority Rights*. Dordrecht: Kluwer Academic Publishers.

Hilpold, Peter. 2009. The Kosovo Case and International Law: Looking for Applicable Theories. *Chinese Journal for International Law* 8, 1: 47-61.

Human Rights Watch Report (HRW). 1995. Georgia/Abkhazia: Violations of War and Russia's Role in the Conflict.
http://www.hrw.org/reports/pdfs/g/georgia/georgia953.pdf

—, (HRW). 2004. Kosovo Serbia – Protect Minorities from Ethnic Violence, March 18.
http://www.hrw.org/en/news/2004/03/18/kosovoserbia-protect-minorities-ethnic-violence

Independent International Commission on Kosovo. 2000. *The Kosovo Report: Conflict, International Response, Lessons Learned*. Oxford: Oxford University Press.

Klussmann, Uwe. 2008. Kosovo auf dem Kaukasus. *Der Spiegel*, May 11.
http://www.spiegel.de/politik/ausland/0,1518,552109,00.html

—, 2009. Georgia's Murky Motives: Saakashvili under Pressure from EU probe. *Der Spiegel International*, March 23.
http://www.spiegel.de/international/world/0,1518,615160,00.html

Kovacevic, Bojan. 2008. *The Experience of Yugoslavia's Federalism as Warning for Europe's Unfinished Federation*, published article for the IFF Summer University.

Lakoba, Stanislav. 1998. History: 1917–1989.In *The Abkhazians*, edited by George Hewitt: 89-101. New York: St. Martin's Press.

Lang, David Marshall. 1962. *A Modern History of Georgia.* London: Weidenfeld & Nicolson.
Lauka, Islam. 2007. *Kosovo: A Universal Case or Sui Generis? Tirana*: The Albanian Institute for Political Studies.
Malcolm, Noel. 1998. *Kosovo: A Short History.*, New York: New York University Press.
Mappes-Niediek, Norbert. 2005. *Die Ethno-Falle: Der Balkan-Konflikt und was Europa daraus lernen kann.* Berlin: Ch. Links.
Marko, Joseph. 1999. Kosovo – A Gordian Knot? In *Gordischer Knoten Kosovo/a: Durchschlagen oder Entwirren,* edited by Joseph Marko: 261-280. Baden-Baden: Nomos.
Martin, Terry. 2001. *The Affirmative Action Eempire: Nations and Nationalism in the Soviet Union, 1923-1939.* Ithaca, NY: Cornell University Press.
Mihalkanin, Edward. 2004. The Abkhazians: A National Minority in Their Own Homeland. In *De facto States – The Quest for Sovereignty,* edited by Zozun Bahcheli, Barry Bartmann, and Henry Srebrnik: 143-63. London: Routledge.
Muharremi, Robert. 2008. Kosovo's Declaration of Independence: Self-Determination and Sovereignty Revisited. *Review of Central and East European Law* 33, 4: 401-35.
Müllerson, Rein. 2009. Precedents in the Mountains: On the Parallels and Uniqueness of Kosovo, South Ossetia and Abkhazia. *Chinese Journal for International Law* 8, 1: 2-25.
Nygren, Beril. 2008. The Rebuilding of Greater Russia: Putin's Foreign Policy towards the CIS countries, New York: Routledge.
Robinson, Dan. 2008. US Lawmakers Debate Resolution Criticizing Russia. *Voice of America,* April 30.
http://www.voanews.com/english/archive/2008-04/2008-04-30-voa71.cfm?CFID=300976050&CFTOKEN=96051095&jsessionid=de305d75a9188dd1edf177a253678305a1e7
Semil, Pulaha. 1997. On the autochtony of Albanians in Kosovo and the Postulated Massive Serb migration at the end of the 17th century. *International Journal of Albanian Studies* 2, 1.
http://www.albanian.com/v4/archive/index.php/t-10405.html
Socor, Vladimir. 2008. Georgia Offers far-reaching autonomy to Abkhazia. *Eurasia Daily Monitor,* April 1
http://www.jamestown.org/single/?no_cache=1&tx_ttnewspercent5Btt_newspercent5D=33509
Tishkov, Valery. 1997. *Ethnicity, Nationalism and Conflict in and after the Soviet Union. The Mind Aflame.* London: Sage.
UN High Commissioner for Refugees. 2004. Background note on the Protection of Asylum Seekers and Refugees in Georgia.
Vickers, Miranda. 1998. *Between Serb and Albanian: A History of Kosovo.*

London: Hurst.

Washington Post. 1998. I Can Only Be Proud of My Role. Interview with Slobodan Milosevic. December 13.

Vladisavljevic, Nebojsa. 2006. Grassroots Groups, Milosevic or Dissident Intellectuals? A Controversy over the Origins and Dynamics of the Mobilization of Kosovo Serbs in the 1980s, in *Conflict in South-Eastern Europe at the End of the Twentieth Century,* edited by Thomas Emmert and Charles Ingra. New York: Routledge: 55-70.

Zverev, Alexei. 1996. Ethnic Conflicts in the Caucasus 1988-1994. In *Contested Borders in the Caucasus,* edited by Bruno Coppieter. Brussels: Vub Brussels University Press.

The historical narrative of the conflict development in Abkhazia is largely based on the findings of the FP6 project 'MIRICO', reports and articles available under:

http://www.eurac.edu/Org/Minorities/MIRICO/index.htm

7

EUROPE'S WORKING REGIONAL AUTONOMIES

A Comparative Analysis

THOMAS BENEDIKTER

MAPPING EUROPE'S TERRITORIAL AUTONOMIES

Europe's working territorial autonomies share numerous common features, and also reflect differences corresponding to their different genesis, development, geographical location, ethnic composition and political context. Usually autonomies are institutional and procedural systems based on complex legal provisions, starting from the basic autonomy statute or constitutional law, and coming to enactment laws and decrees embracing the legal provisions approved and adapted by the autonomous institutions.

In this overview the autonomous entities of the Russian Federation (federal subjects) are not listed as this state should be considered a special case, in fact, the most complex one of an 'asymmetrical federal system' with autonomous republics, regions, *oblasts* and districts. The label 'autonomous' of some of its 88 federal subjects reflects rather a historically distinct claim for a special relationship between the centre (federal government) and some of its entities, due to the presence of particular minorities or peoples, rather than a special territorial autonomy. Although regional autonomy in Russia substantially can be compared to the other remaining forms of autonomy in Europe, the prevailing organizational principles in that state are federal by nature. In contrast, Spain officially is not a federal state, but a 'state of autonomous communities' showing blurred boundaries to a federal structure. As all of its regions have their own specific status, the Spanish autonomy system is again different, for example, from the Italian regionalist state consisting of 5 special autonomies and 15 'regions with an ordinary statute'. However, generally regional autonomy in almost all states in Europe as in the rest of the world is a special political arrangement established for just some special cases of a given state (see Table 7.1).

Table 7.1 EUROPE'S REGIONS WITH TERRITORIAL AUTONOMY

State	Autonomous regions/entities	Capital	Population
1. Italy	Sicily	Palermo	5,031,081
	Sardinia	Cagliari	1,650,052
	Friuli-Venezia Giulia	Udine	1,204,718
	Trentino-Alto Adige	Trento	974,613
	Val d'Aosta	Aosta	122,868
2. Spain	Andalusia	Sevilla	7,849,799
	Catalonia	Barcelona	6,995,206
	Madrid	Madrid	5,964,143
	Valencia	Valencia	4,692,449
	Galicia	Santiago de Compostela	2,762,198
	Castile-Leon	Valladolid	2,510,849
	Basque Country	Vitoria/Gasteiz	2,125,000
	Canary Islands	Las Palmas de Gran C.	1,968,280
	Castile-La Mancha	Toledo	1,894,667
	Murcia	Murcia	1,335,792
	Aragon	Zaragoza	1,269,027
	Extremadura	Mérida	1,083,897
	Asturias	Oviedo	1,076,635
	Balearic Islands	Palma de Mallorca	983,131
	Navarre	Pamplona	593,472
	Cantabria	Santander	562,309
	La Rioja	Logrono	301,084

Table 7.1 EUROPE'S REGIONS WITH TERRITORIAL AUTONOMY (Cont.)

State	Autonomous regions/entities	Capital	Population
3. United Kingdom	Scotland	Edinburgh	5,094,800
	Wales	Cardiff	2,958,600
	Northern Ireland	Belfast	1,710,300
	Isle of Man	Douglas	80,058
	Guernsey	Saint Peter Port	65,573
	Jersey	Saint Helier	91,626
4. Finland	Åland Islands	Mariehamn	26,711
5. Denmark	Greenland	Nuuk	56,375
	Faroe	Torshavn	44,228
6. Belgium	German Community	Eupen	72,000
7. France	New Caledonia	Nouméa	230,789
	French Polynesia	Papeete	259,596
8. Moldova	Gagauzia	Comrat	171,500
9. Ukraine	Crimea	Sinferopol	2,000,192
10. Serbia	Vojvodina	Novi Sad	2,031,000
11. The Netherlands	Netherlands Antilles	Willemstad	220,000
	Aruba	Oranjestad	102,000
12. Portugal	Azores	Ponta Delgada	253,000
	Madeira	Funchal	265,000

SOURCE: all figures from the last available census dates or the most recent official estimated figures. Selection according to the criteria explained in Thomas Benedikter, *The World's Modern Autonomy Systems—Concepts and Experiences of Regional Territorial Autonomy*, EURAC Bozen 2009, Chapter 2:10; at: http://www.eurac.edu/Org/Minorities/IMR/Projects/asia.htm

NOTE: In Spain there are also two autonomous cities, Ceuta and Melilla. The Netherlands Antilles in Oct. 2010 will split in two groups of islands and shift to different kinds of status (*status a parte* within the Dutch Commonwealth, and overseas municipality).

Although the fundamental aim of an autonomy arrangement might be identical—territorial self-governance—the concrete 'design' is a result of the dialectical relationship between the autonomous community and the central state. Nonetheless, the performance of each autonomy arrangement, in terms of peaceful and harmonious relations among ethnic groups sharing the same territory, respect for minority rights, stability and positive social and economic development, can be evaluated only on the basis of generally shared criteria, an ambitious endeavour still to be done.

EXPERIMENTS IN INCORPORATING 'FUNCTIONS' OF AN AUTONOMY SYSTEM

Which are the 'functions' of an autonomy system to be compared? Generally, autonomy arrangements are established to meet specific needs and satisfy definable functions. The quality and the very success of an autonomy system depend essentially on how those functions are shaped and realized. We can consider these functions as the constitutive elements of every autonomy system. If one or some of these elements are seriously flawed or even missing, the stability, durability, indeed the system itself is at risk. In the past, some autonomy systems have failed because one or some of these functions were faulty. Although the list may not be exhaustive, among the most important functional elements are:

- *(i)* The political representation
- *(ii)* The scope of the autonomy
- *(iii)* The entrenchment and revision mechanisms
- *(iv)* The financial regulations
- *(v)* Provisions for regional citizenship
- *(vi)* International relations
- *(vii)* Language rights and protection of ethnic identity and minority rights
- *(viii)* The consociational structures and internal power sharing
- *(ix)* The control of economic resources
- *(x)* The settlement of disputes and legal protection mechanisms

These fundamental 'functional elements' have found different forms of application and solutions within Europe's working autonomy arrangements, which evidently in this short chapter cannot be compared in depth. This is a project for the future, based on more empirical research that should make it possible to draw an exhaustive evaluation of the performance of the distinct forms of territorial autonomy and even to determine the decisive elements of an 'optimum standard of autonomy' to be tailored to each single case. The following comparative analysis will concentrate on showing nothing else than the existence of different forms and qualitative levels of regional autonomies in relation to several of the 'functional elements' identified as fundamental to autonomy arrangements.

Political representation

All autonomous regions are governed by a democratically elected legislative body (parliament or council), which represents the whole population of the autonomous territory. The executive body of those regions in turn is elected by the legislative council or directly elected by the population, hence independent from the central government. The population of the autonomous regions—citizens of their respective states—is represented also on a national level, forming one or more constituencies for the election of members of the national parliament. In addition to that some states with a regionalist structure, such as Spain, and in the new future also Italy, have second chambers representing the separate regions as such, elected or appointed in accordance with a different representational system. In some cases as the Nordic islands, the Azores and Madeira, the constituencies of the autonomous territories are much smaller than those in the rest of the country, enabling the local communities to have their representatives in the national parliaments, although their numbers are insufficient.

Another special form of representation also at the executive level is the ex-officio membership of the Gagausian chief minister in Moldova's national government. In Italy, the president of an autonomous region is only entitled to take part in the session of the national government in Rome when some issues related to the autonomy are on the agenda. Some autonomous regions such as Åland Islands, Faroe and Greenland have even the right to be represented with a distinct delegate in international organizations such as the Nordic Council.

The scope of autonomy: legislative and executive powers

There are huge differences regarding the content of the autonomy in terms of the powers transferred to the autonomous entities. At the bottom ranks Corsica with autonomous powers merely limited to administrative competencies, which cannot be considered an 'authentic autonomy system', whereas at the top can be placed the Nordic islands—the Faroe, Greenland and Åland Islands—which rely on their respective states, Denmark and Finland, only as regards foreign affairs, defence, the monetary system and some aspects of the judiciary. Catalonia and the Basque Country are also vested with powers in the administration of the judiciary.

There is one basic feature characteristic of the whole range of European autonomies: this combines core issues related to the preservation of the cultural identity (the education system, language policy, cultural affairs) and territorial functions (labour market, regional sector economic policies, urban planning, health and social services, environmental protection, public transport, energy, local administrations and whatever refers to the management of local resources). Generally, the powers attributed to the autonomous regions are precisely enumerated in a closed list, whilst all the remaining policy sectors come under stately competencies for both legislation and administration.

Only the autonomous regions of the Azores and Madeira possess a general legislative power, leaving the remaining powers to the central state, Portugal. In the framework of power sharing with autonomies, there is an instrument of mutual control: the right to veto and the right to challenge decisions before the Supreme or Constitutional Court. The central government, in some cases, can exercise its veto regarding acts and decisions of the autonomous region, particularly of the legislative body if it exceeds its powers. In Greenland and on the Faroe a mixed expert commission is entitled to mediate. In all other working autonomies the conflicts over the exercise and division of powers are to be settled before the Constitutional Court. In the Republic of Crimea, the president of Ukraine can temporarily suspend an act set forth by Crimea, if he maintains it is not in line with the national constitution.

Entrenchment and revision procedures

Europe's autonomy regulations, in most cases, have found entrenchment at a constitutional level. The special status of the Azores and Madeira, the Republic of Crimea, Russia's federated subjects are entrenched in the respective state's constitutions. Also the autonomy statutes of South Tyrol and the Aosta Valley enjoy constitutional status. Although the autonomies of the Åland Islands and of Gagauzia are not a part of the Constitution, they can be modified only with a two-thirds (Finland) or a three-fifths (Moldova) majority of the national parliament. Spain in its constitution has recognized the general right to autonomy, but the single autonomy statutes, elaborated by the respective autonomous communities, are approved by the national parliament like nothing more than a normal act. However, such an autonomy statute can be amended only by the procedure set forth in the same statute or through a regional referendum. Only the status of the autonomous regions of Greenland and the Faroes do not have any constitutional entrenchment. Theoretically, these autonomies can be abolished with a simple national act without a qualified majority and thus are vulnerable to changing moods in the national parliaments. As these autonomies are even not based on international treaties, the readiness of the majority to cooperate with the national minority or autonomous community is essential for defending the autonomy.

But some scholars argue that even in the absence of a constitutional entrenchment granting autonomy, autonomy systems are implicitly imbued with the recognition of the principle of the right to internal self-determination of a national minority under international law. In that sense, autonomy regulations can be considered as protected by the general principle of self-determination of peoples. Hence, a given state, having once established autonomy, is not allowed to roll back these rights of a minority to any substantial extent, without the consensus of the concerned community and even less, abolish an autonomy statute. Still, there is no general mechanism of monitoring, controlling and guaranteeing autonomy regulations in positive international law. Such a provision would be an essential part of the proposed 'Framework Convention on the Right to Autonomy' as submitted in a draft version by the FUEN (Federal Union of European Nationalities) in 1994.

Autonomous regions do not have a constitutional legislative and executive power as federated states in a federal system. Normally, those representatives of federal units also have the right to propose new initiatives and provisions in order to reform the working autonomy or at least to be involved in joint commissions to shape reforms of the autonomy arrangements.

Who, then, is competent for the enactment and revision of the autonomy statutes? Do the regional communities and national minorities have any sovereignty to shape their own rules of the internal governing system? Generally, the autonomy statute (or regional constitution) is elaborated and approved by the state parliament, but the concerned minorities are involved in the elaboration of the status. In some cases (Basque Country, Catalonia, Crimea, Azores, Madeira), the autonomous regions are entitled to define for themselves the extent and the internal architecture of their autonomy within the given constitutional framework. Spain's autonomous regions, for instance, may elaborate and approve their own statutes that subsequently have to be approved by the central parliament. Thus, the population of the concerned region enjoys some constitutional powers, but they are limited by the state's constitution.

Financial regulations

A fundamental condition for a well-functioning autonomy is the structure of financial regulation. There are mainly two forms of financial regimes. The first consists of a financial transfer from the central government to the autonomous regions; the second one is based on the sharing of the tax revenues collected in the autonomous territory even to the extent of devolving the wholly locally earned taxes and tariffs to the autonomous entity. Fiscal federal system with effective powers for taxation is enacted presently only in the Basque Country and Catalonia; it exists in the Åland Islands, Gagauzia, the Azores and Madeira in a more limited form as these can raise their own taxes. Regarding expenditures, all autonomous regions with the exception of Corsica enjoy full freedom to spend their resources and budgets in an autonomous way.

Forms of 'regional citizenship'

Generally, Europe's autonomous regions and republics have neither a distinct citizenship nor any power to interfere politically on this matter. Indeed, going by recent trends, citizenship, the control of immigration, asylum rights and passports are even to be delegated to a supranational level, namely, that of the EU. Hence, these autonomous entities have no direct control on who is moving in and out of their territories and who is entitled to migrate and settle in their territories. Nevertheless, in some autonomous systems (Crimea, Åland Islands, Faroe, Greenland, South Tyrol and Gagauzia), there are some forms of 'regional citizenship', consisting basically of the entitlement to specific rights and privileges to be determined on the basis of the period of residence in the region

(Crimea, Åland Islands, Faroe, Greenland, South Tyrol and Gagauzia). A minimum period of legal residence is required to exercise political rights (franchise to social, regional councils), social rights (housing, social grants and scholarships), eligibility to the local civil service and preferential treatment in the regional labour market.

The Åland Islands went some steps further: persons, who do not master the Swedish language and have not resided in the area for a minimum of 5 years, may not purchase any real estate or open a commercial activity on the islands. Significantly, however, the person is not exempted from military service in Finland. Regarding 'regional citizenship', there is a huge difference between the smaller islands in Finland, Denmark and Portugal and the big regions, which are fully integrated in the common market as Catalonia, the Basque Country and Friuli-Venezia Giulia and so on.

Language policy and protection of national minorities

One feature common to all European autonomies is the fact that the minority languages along with the state language is accorded the rank of official language as the recognition, preservation and promotion of minority languages is the very rationale of establishing territorial autonomies (classical examples being: Gagauzia, South Tyrol, Basque Country, Catalonia and Galicia, Sardinia, Åland Islands, Faroe and Greenland). Again, in the Åland Islands, Swedish, remains the only official language. In most regions bilingualism is a formal requisite for being admitted to civil service jobs and each applicant has to be formally proficient in both languages. Also the topographic names regularly are bilingual or monolingual in the local language as in the Nordic Islands, Aosta Valley and some parts of the Basque Country. This is in contrast to the Swiss system based on the 'language territory principle' which has resulted in four language formula at the canton level, that is, it is recognized as the official language in the respective cantons, while at the federal level all three major languages enjoy equal rights. Most of Europe's autonomous regions are not monolingual or not even predominantly monolingual, for example, South Tyrol, Aosta Valley, Crimea, Corsica, the Spanish Communities, Wales, Gagausia. In all these regions, except Corsica, the minority language has the status of an official language within the region, and on equal footing with the national or state-language. In some cases, a complex legal system of bilingualism had to be worked out in order to ensure the right of each citizen of the region to use his or her mother tongue at each level and sector of the public administration. In some regions—South Tyrol, Catalonia, Crimea, Åland Islands—the use of minority language is also admitted in various levels of the judicial system.

The issue of the minority languages, strongly affects the promotion of minority rights, which frequently are in a weaker or even in an endangered situation. Hence, the autonomous governments are called upon to launch long-term policies to ensure the preservation and modernization for such 'lesser used languages' (e.g., Basque, Irish, Welsh, Faroese, Inuktitut, Corsican, Gallego, Ladin-Rheatoromanian, Gagauzian, Tatar in Crimea). Inevitably the language policy deeply affects the education system too. Several systems are operating in the European autonomy systems, beginning with the weakest form of promotion of a minority language as in Corsica, where Corsican is nothing more than an optional subject in comprehensive schools; then there are various forms of bilingual school systems as in Great Britain, Aosta Valley and the Basque Country) as well as strictly monolingual school systems in the respective minority languages.

Consociational structures and internal power sharing

Autonomy essentially is an internal arrangement for settling state-region conflicts or conflicts between the national 'majority' and minorities. They seek accommodation of conflicting group rights and claims without the redrawing of state boundaries. In complex conflicts in Europe, autonomy arrangements have had to negotiate not only the devolution of considerable power to the territorial unit but, in situations where there are different ethnic groups, they have had to build up overarching territorial loyalties and internal power-sharing structures. While territorial autonomy is meant principally to empower a specific group to exercise a greater degree of self-governance of its internal affairs, consociational structures in divided societies seek to ensure internal peace and stability, inter-ethnic cooperation and the participation of all relevant groups in an autonomous region in legislative and administrative power processes.

The institutional design of such 'regional consociations' and the legal and political provisions enacted to preserve that kind of power sharing depends on diverse local conditions. There are few such rules in the island autonomies with an ethnically quite homogeneous population, such as in the Nordic islands, the Azores and Madeira. The need to establish regional consociations arises in situations of internal heterogeneity as in the Basque Country (not even 30% of the population are active Basque speakers), South Tyrol (26% are Italians and 4% Ladins), Crimea (58% Russians and 12% Tatars apart from 24% Ukrainians), Northern Ireland (45% Catholics, 55% Protestants). Notably, there is one instrument for ensuring a first level of 'consociational power-sharing': democratic elections with the minimum representation guaranteed for all major groups. In South Tyrol the smallest group, the Ladins, has to be represented in the local parliament by law, whatever the turnout at the polls. In Crimea 14 members out of 100 seats in the Republic's parliament are reserved for the Tatars and one each for other indigenous peoples. A consociational way of governing has been established which encompasses the various ethnic groups and ensures policy coordination mostly through a political coalition. In order to set up stable coalitions for the governance of the region, minority forces have necessarily to enter into coalitions with parties representing other or smaller ethnic groups. This is also known as 'concordance democracy', following the Swiss model.

Four more provisions for safeguarding the rights of the national minorities can be observed in European autonomy structures:

(*i*) mandatory power sharing
(*ii*) segmental autonomy for each group
(*iii*) proportionality in all governmental functions
(*iv*) minority veto rights

Aspects of the functioning of these provisions can be found in several autonomy systems.

In Northern Ireland, to ensure participation of all communities in the Northern Ireland Assembly and to protect their rights, specific procedures for the allocation of committee chairs and ministries are applied. Key decisions have to be taken on a cross-community basis (parallel consent and weighted majority procedures). An 'Equality Commission' has been set up. The working of the Assembly is contingent on its members registering their identity by category—Nationalist, Unionist or Other—in order to ensure parallel consent and weighted majority procedures. The executive functions are allocated proportionally, according to the party strength in the Assembly as also at the municipal level. The Northern Ireland government has to include members of each community. The First and the Deputy First Minister cannot be members of the same community.

In South Tyrol, similar provisions are enshrined in the autonomy statute. The autonomous provincial government has to be composed of members from all three official communities and the ministries have to be allocated according to the numerical strength scored in the elections by each community within the provincial assembly. In addition to that, if any ethnic group considers itself discriminated against in ethnic terms, it can claim a separate vote in each group. Thus, each minority is entitled to cast a veto in a very important decision, like the annual budget. In South Tyrol, all governing institutions, including all administrative commissions, are composed in a proportional manner, according to the numerical relationship of the three official groups. Finally, there is a segmental autonomy for each group regarding cultural affairs: Germans, Italians and Ladins are entitled to manage their education systems and autonomously develop their cultural policies.

The Autonomous Republic of Crimea has established similar arrangements of 'segmental autonomy' regarding cultural affairs for the major ethnic groups living in the peninsula. All three major groups—the Russians, Ukrainians and Tatars—have to be represented in parliamentary commissions and in government. Apart from the proportionality, determined by a political party's numerical strength and power relations, provisions are made to ensure cross-community decision making processes. It should be added that there is no standard of an autonomy design structured along the lines of regional consociationalism that could be applied alike to all ethnic conflicts and autonomies in Europe.

Control of economic resources

If autonomy means territorial self-government, by definition, it has to ensure the possibility for the autonomous community to manage its social and economic development. This basic need includes the means to control and manage under its own responsibility the use of natural resources, an issue particularly important to many indigenous peoples depending for their very livelihood on natural resources such as land, forests and seas. In Europe, this concern has not found any expression in the form of exclusive collective property rights over certain land areas and natural resources by an ethnic community (as in the case of numerous peoples in India, Russia, America and Africa), but in most of the autonomous regions of Europe, ethnic minorities have been fully integrated not only into their national market economies, but also to the common market of the EU. In some case, this has led to the immediate danger of overexploitation of local resources, as for example, the fish grounds around the islands of Greenland and the Faroe, which previously were part of the European Community. Both islands decided to opt out of the membership in the EU to preserve their special rights in fishery. This legal possibility is not given to other regions in the EU, except the Åland Islands.

In the European case, then, the need for the community to exercise some control over the economic development of an autonomous region has to be met by means of a general economic and fiscal policy, that is, in accordance with national macroeconomic and monetary policy and with the policy set forth by the EU in Brussels. The division of powers offers a wide scope and political regulation in the field of economics: subsidies and regulations for the single sectors, regulation of the agriculture, development of infrastructures, direct intervention through public companies, environmental protection and energy control, urban planning and economic planning. Generally, a solid financial system for autonomy provides the most effective means to steer a local autonomy.

A COMPARISON OF THE EUROPEAN AUTONOMY SYSTEMS

Considering the whole range of these ten autonomy systems in Europe under the criteria just listed it is possible to form a first ranking, focusing on the real depth and extent of self-governance. Of course, this evaluation scheme is very rough and provisional, but it should help us understand that due to political, historical and social background autonomy systems have developed differently and are a flexible means to solve different problems.

The Ålands Islands obtain the most complete and far-reaching autonomy. Under the Act of Self-Government of 1991 the Ålanders enjoy legislative and executive powers in nearly all political sectors which matter to the peoples on the islands. The Åland Islands have even an administrative judiciary, whilst only the ordinary judiciary remains under the central state's powers. The Åland Islands also are vested with some financial autonomy with some limited powers of taxation. Eventually the permanent inhabitants of the Islands enjoy a form of 'insular citizenship', which is a prerequisite for the right to vote for the autonomous parliament. On the Åland Islands the local language is Swedish, which is the only official language. They are virtually a separate community, just linked to Finland by some parts of the juridical system (constitutional law, civil law and criminal law). However, the Åland Islands with its particular conditions are probably an exception even when compared with many regions with national minorities aspiring to territorial autonomy. Finally, Åland even has some powers entitling the autonomous region to be involved in international decision-making and to have representation in international bodies. Some Ålanders consider their region as 'a state in the state'.

In Greenland and the Faroe Islands, a wider degree of autonomy with quasi-statehood in most political sectors has been established as well. The legislative and administrative competencies are comprehensive, including a full budgetary freedom and a certain right of taxation. Only the judiciary is still controlled by the Danish state. Whilst sovereignty on the island formally lies with Denmark, the Faroe Islands have their own 'insular citizenship'. The high degree of self-government is underpinned by the right of the island's populations to participate even in foreign policy decisions if these have concerns pertaining to their interests. Greenland and the Faroes—along with the Ålands—are represented in the Nordic Council, in their own distinct capacity, along with their own state representatives. There is one major difference between Greenland and the Faroes and Åland Islands: on the Åland Islands, non-Ålanders have no right to purchase land or real estate (property of land is denied to non-Ålanders); however, in Greenland and the Faroes which are accessible to Danish citizens, the latter have the right to own property.

Unlike most other European regional autonomies, Greenland and the Faroe Islands obtained autonomy, regarding their participation in international or supranational organizations, as demonstrated by Greenland's opting out of the EU in 1985 in order to control its basic economic resources. If we take into account the fact that in the EU nearly one third of all regulations are enacted by Brussels, for a meaningful functioning of the autonomy system there has to be recognition that the degree of autonomy should not be measured only in terms of powers gained vis-à-vis the central government, but also in regard to the supranational structure of the EU. In an increasingly globalizing international market, autonomy systems of the future will have to be armed against the interference of decision makers at that level too if the autonomy is to be preserved in the core areas. The Nordic islands in Denmark and Finland are pioneers in this regard, whilst Åland's right for its possibility to regulate immigration by a sort of regional citizenship is a forerunner in that field.

The Spanish autonomous communities, and in particular the autonomy systems of the historical 'nationalities' of the Basques, the Catalonians and the Galicians, can be qualified as comprehensive autonomies with legislative and executive powers in nearly all internally relevant political affairs and a government which is responsible only to the regional autonomous parliament. They have not only budgetary autonomy, but also clear-cut powers of taxation, shared with the central state. Spain's autonomous communities have their own civil and administrative judiciary, but the Basque Country and Catalonia have even their own police force. The Spanish autonomous communities are also vested with a competence normally reserved only to federated member states of a federalist union, the power to elaborate their own autonomy statutes. The amount of autonomous powers of a region in Spain is in a high degree up to the region itself, which, within the constitutional framework, can freely regulate its own autonomy. Hence, Spain's regional autonomies are continuously extended and improved. However, the autonomy statutes have to be approved with simple majority by the central parliament of Madrid.

Spain is a highly complex and dynamic 'state of autonomies' with a continuous evolution in the relationships between the centre and the autonomous regions. Within this process, the historical smaller nations, Catalonia, Basque Country and Galicia, along with the Canaries, Valencia and Navarra, are continuously endeavoring to extend their 'autonomous statehood', forcing the central state to find new forms of equilibrium and coordination. The Spanish autonomy system, sometimes labelled as quasi-federal or as 'asymmetrical federalism without explicitly naming as such', is projected as a model for other European states hosting a number of powerful minority peoples or ethnic groups. However, despite the very advanced Spanish autonomy systems, it is evident, that major continental regions like Catalonia are not in the same empowered position as a remote island group with regard to controlling citizenship and immigration or integration in a supranational organization.

The Portuguese islands, the Azores and Madeira, in their progress towards an ever more advanced autonomy, are following Spain's autonomy models, although the two archipelagos are not distinct from the mainland regarding language and ethnicity. Hence, Madeira and the Azores represent the 'non-ethnic insular autonomy' claimed by so many island regions and states around the world, based rather on geographical reasons and needs than on cultural features. The new Portuguese constitution allows the two autonomous regions a broad range of legislative and executive powers, not specifically attributed to the central state. The general legislative competence, therefore, lies with the regional parliaments of the Azores and Madeira and the Islands are governed by an elected government, independent from Lisbon.

Of particular interest are the two autonomy systems established in the 1990s in the former communist states of Moldova and Ukraine. The autonomy of the regions of

Gagauzia in the Republic of Moldova is based on the state law, which has transferred autonomous legislative and executive competencies in areas of cultural, social, educational, economic and international affairs policy. The government of Gagauzia can also influence the composition of the personal staff of the judiciary on its territory. The supreme executive organ is headed by a governor, and along with a Gagauzian executive committee, vested with all governmental functions. The autonomy of Crimea, established in 1994, is reconstituting the former status of an 'Autonomous Republic' under the Soviet regime. In both cases—Crimea and Gagauzia—the central state has transferred extensive legislative and executive powers to the autonomous territories, also ensuring a certain degree of financial-budgetary autonomy. Moreover, these regions or republics, although very different in size, enjoy a distinct language policy regime aimed at safeguarding equality for the minority languages. They even have some freedom to regulate their international affairs, particularly in developing relation with their respective kin-states. The civil and criminal judiciary is still a central affair, but Crimea has its own constitutional courts. Crimea's inhabitants hold a specific Crimean citizenship, without losing their Ukrainian one, which provides for a certain control over the demographic evolution of the peninsula.

Italy is a hybrid combination of a regionalist and a federalist state (asymmetrically structured), particularly after the last devolution reforms approved in November 2005. Now all 20 regions have an extended range of legislative and executive powers, but no full financial autonomy. They have independent regional governments and can approve their own statutes. The exercise of all judicial matters is strictly reserved to the central state. Some 15 out of 20 regions are constituted as 'regions with ordinary statute', while five regions are 'regions with special statute' (Trentino-South Tyrol, Aosta Valley, Friuli-Venezia Giulia, Sardinia and Sicily). There are concrete plans to transform also the second chamber of the

Italian parliament into a diluted form of 'Chamber of the Regions', underscoring the new importance of the regions in the Italian devolution process. Italy, as well as Spain, is an 'asymmetrical regionalist state', moving towards federalism. But the backlashes of the old centralist tendencies, a fragile public finance for the regions and the North-South-dualism are holding back Italy from giving way to more self-governance at every level.

The German Community in Belgium in the framework of the transformation of the Belgian state into a federal state has achieved a considerable level of cultural and territorial autonomy, although it is still not considered on an equal footing with the two main constituent communities, the Flamands and the Walloons, as they do not have their own distinct regions. Nevertheless, as a part of the Region of Wallonia, the German Community is step by step establishing a special territorial autonomy, underpinning the asymmetrical character of the Belgian federalism.

The Netherlands Antilles are a hybrid construction combining features of an associated state with that of regional autonomy. Although the inhabitants of that island group are not directly represented in the Dutch parliament, they have a democratically elected representation with the Netherlands' government. Being geographically distant from each other in 2008, they have restructured their respective relations with the 'motherland', partially transforming into associated states. Curacao and Saint Maarten have switched to the identical legal status as Aruba already did in 1986, which is basically a 'free association', whereas the islands of Saba, St. Eustatius and Bonaire have been incorporated into the mainland of the Netherlands as 'municipalities' with a special autonomous status.

The case of the United Kingdom highlights an additional typical feature of territorial autonomy in Europe. The historical process of the formation of nation-states in Europe, has involved the integration or sometimes just the swallowing up of smaller historical nations. This happened in Spain, as in Great Britain, in Russia and in the Balkans. The devolution process in the United Kingdom is legitimized by the particular linguistic features of the regions, which are endowed with a high degree of self-governance, that is, Scotland, Wales and Northern Ireland. Indeed, in Scotland and in Northern Ireland, the minority languages are spoken by a very tiny part of the population. More significant in driving the devolution process has been specific historical reasons, which in turn have caused internal conflicts (Ireland) or centuries-old strife for regaining a certain degree of 'statehood'.

The Nordic islands, South Tyrol, Spain's historical autonomous communities, Catalonia, the Basque Country and Galicia, and Russia's Tatarstan, according to the functions delineated above, can be graded as having the most advanced forms of autonomy, whereas Corsica (a '*collectivité territoriale*' in France) is still at the beginning of the path towards a full-fledged autonomy. In between are a number of autonomy systems, which still could be improved and enlarged. Nevertheless, France has established an authentic regional autonomy, although not labelled as such, but as *pays d'outre mér* (overseas country). New Caledonia, a major island in Oceania, with a majority of indigenous population, shows all central issues of a territorial autonomy, and by an agreement signed in 1998; after 2011 it will be even more free to determine its further relation with France.

Claims for self-governance and autonomy at the regional level in Europe are deeply rooted in history and in the story of the building up of the European nation-state system. In Europe a strong consciousness of a regional identity largely based on cultural, linguistic and ethnic features can be felt nearly everywhere. Some European states tried to tackle this internal cultural complexity through federal structures (Switzerland, Belgium, Germany, Russia and recently Bosnia-Herzegovina); some states with 'asymmetrical regionalist autonomy systems (Spain, Italy, Serbia before 1989, and the United Kingdom).However, a conspicuous number of regional communities still are lagging behind and do not enjoy the same degree of self-governance, giving rise to harsh conflicts with central governments. Once the working autonomies prove to be a historical success or at least stand the test, the better will the conditions be to convince state majorities to aim for autonomy solutions.

CONFLICT RESOLUTION THROUGH TERRITORIAL AUTONOMY?

Looking at the world's map of autonomies, it is evident that throughout the world Europe is home to the majority of autonomy solutions. It is argued that in Europe territorial autonomy has in nearly every case proved successful for all conflicting parties involved: the national minorities, the regional communities, the central states, and some kin-states. In none of the eleven European states with working regional autonomies is there a serious debate about cutting them back. On the contrary, in most cases, the existing autonomy system is continuously being improved and deepened in order to grant an ever more appropriate system of self-government.

Spain leads the group of states with a dynamic development towards a more articulated 'state of autonomies'. Recently, in September 2005, Europe's largest autonomous region in terms of population, Catalonia, passed its newly reformed autonomy statute with a large majority of its regional parliament, subsequently also approved by the Spanish parliament. In Corsica, local political forces are working to reform the still weak model of self-government in order to enrich the system with more legislative powers. In Italy, the general devolution process of the central state's powers to the ordinary regions is pushing the state towards a federal structure, indirectly reinforcing the position of the five regions with special autonomy. Northern Ireland is facing the most critical situation, since real self-governance linked to a complex consociational arrangement between the parties involved is yet to take off. The conflict has shifted to a political level, but decades of violence and political cleavages have left deep scars. An ever-deepening process of European integration in the framework of the European Union has definitely been helpful to these autonomy solutions, as they are backed by a legitimate role of the respective kin-states.

The new autonomies in Eastern Europe have been operating only for about a decade and are still in a provisional phase, with at times contradictory developments in the inter-ethnic relations of the autonomous regions. In the Autonomous Republic of Crimea, for instance, the Russians retain their predominant rule, while the Tatar community, returning after deportation by Stalin in the 1940s, has yet to be accommodated. Tatarstan, on the other hand, presents a positive model of how national conflicts inside Russia could be resolved through an equitable balance of power between the centre (Moscow) and an ethnically mixed region (Tatarstan). Thinking about the ongoing conflict in Chechnya, a lesson to be drawn is that autonomy solutions should be envisaged before low-level violence escalates into a full-blown ethnic war. What makes these autonomies particularly important is their role as pioneers of autonomy regulations in a part of the continent, which since 1990 has been the site of rising new nationalism, state centralism and widespread hostility towards autonomy solutions. In this context, Gagauzia, Tatarstan and Crimea—if successful—are paving the way for a range of other regions aspiring to full autonomy (Abkhasians in Georgia, Albanians in Macedonia, Hungarians in Transylvania (Szeklerland), Serbia and Slovakia, Turks in Bulgaria, Ruthens/Rusyns in Ukraine, and other regions in the Northern Caucasus).

In this political context, three patterns of establishing regional autonomies can be distinguished. First, there is the 'traditional way' to grant autonomy as a special solution to a specific region in unitary states (Moldova, Ukraine, Portugal, France, Denmark, Finland, and the United Kingdom), due to its specific cultural, historical or ethnic features. Autonomy, here, appears as the exception aimed at accommodating a minority, whereas the state as a whole is not inclined to transformation in a federal or regionalist way. A second pattern is the establishment of autonomy in different (asymmetrical) forms to all subjects of a state, as has been happening in Spain and Italy since the 1970s. A third solution is the creation of different layers of self-government within a large and ethnically heterogeneous country, as in Russia, in quite an asymmetrical form in order to find appropriate solution for each specific regional reality.

Indeed, autonomy is increasingly being proposed as a remedy for other self-determination conflicts, while previously it had been seen as a step towards secession. Apart from granting autonomies to national minorities, multinational states were also faced with self-determination claims, like Bosnia-Herzegovina, Belgium and Macedonia, and have had to adopt extensive provisions for self-governance for ethnically differentiated territories. As they found a new equilibrium (though in two cases still uncertain) other states, faced with secessionist movements and acts like Cyprus (Northern Cyprus), Moldova (Transnistria), Georgia (Abkhasia and South Ossetia) and Azerbaijan (Gorni Karabagh) still have to find a way to re-integrate the break-away regions. The formerly autonomous Kosovo is actually gaining full independence, since a return to forms of autonomy under Serbian sovereignty is unacceptable to the huge majority of its population and the international community increasingly accepts its independence.

Even violent fringes of self-determination movements, like the ETA in the Basque Country and radical groups in Corsica, influenced by the example of the IRA in Northern Ireland, seem to be close to relinquishing the strategy of violent confrontation, if advanced forms of autonomy can be established. Protracted violent insurgency in those cases has eventually evolved towards a compromise on a form of autonomy. Apparently, a growing number of states have acknowledged that autonomy can serve to integrate national minorities into the state and to stabilize the conflict in situations otherwise prone to go out of control.

PERSISTING CONCERNS ABOUT EUROPE'S TERRITORIAL AUTONOMIES

The basic question to pose is whether territorial autonomy in Europe can achieve its objectives, namely, granting self-governance in a limited area and the protection of the national minorities living in that area. Generally, European states are still very sceptical about the right to autonomy. Often the argument used is that its content is too vague and that it cannot clearly be defined. But distinction has to be made between the right and the concrete form of application. Moreover, there is the concern that the interest of states to preserve full integrity of their territory should not clash with a possible right to autonomy. Autonomy, however, besides the conflict between the state and the concerned region, often has to tackle a double problem: to grant the protection of the national minority on its traditional homeland, but at the same time to include in the self-governance system all the groups living in that area. Territorial autonomy should benefit a whole regional community, not one group of the population only.

Every autonomy model in Europe has its unique features tailored to the specific problems to be solved. According to the specific premises and conditions of a region and national minorities, each autonomy system in Europe shows a particular 'architecture' and particular mechanism to ensure participation, conflict solving, power sharing, minority protection, stability. These autonomies are 'works in progress' involved in dynamic processes of reform, correction and transformation. By definition, they have to be dynamic, giving space to new answers for a developing society. On the other hand, there are some elements and conditions, which have turned out to be the key factors of success, as a detailed comparative analysis, will eventually demonstrate. New autonomy projects and negotiations have to take it into account, avoiding repetition of the harmful mistakes made in some other cases and adopting devices more likely to bring about a successful solution.

Keeping this basic information about working autonomy systems in mind, some lessons can be drawn from the European experiences:

(i) Autonomies are not a mere act of unilateral devolution of public powers. Establishing, entrenching and amending the autonomy must be based on a genuine negotiation process and constitutional consensus. This implies negotiations between political representatives of the concerned regional population and the central government.

(ii) Autonomy is an open, dynamic, but irreversible process, which has to involve at least three players: the representatives of the national minorities, the central government, and the representatives of other groups living in the same territory. All their interests have to be brought into a balance, with a strong role of the civil society and the media in building up a culture of common shared responsibility for peaceful coexistence.

(iii) Autonomy can offer the necessary institutional framework for minority cultures and peoples and languages, in so far as the regional institutions are endowed with all culturally relevant powers and means, especially in the field of education, culture and media.

(iv) An implementation plan is to be incorporated in the conflict settlement process. This sometimes is a very technical, long-lasting undertaking.

(v) There should be a possibly complete set of functions and powers to endow local institutions with true potential of self-governance. Sufficient powers make autonomy meaningful and should encompass legislative, executive and judicial powers, which have to be transferred in an unambiguous way

(vi) Autonomy has to be effectively entrenched, if not at an international level or bilateral level (kin-state), at least on a constitutional level, preventing it from being exposed to the vulnerabilities of changing political majorities in a central parliament.

(vii) There has to be a solid system of finance and sufficient provisions to allow the autonomous entity to control local economic resources, in order to ensure a positive social and economic development of the region.

(viii) Internally, when there are two or more ethnic groups sharing the same region, consociational arrangements for granting access and participation in power must be established for all relevant groups living in the same territory.

(ix) Regional integration, trans-border cooperation with kin-states or integration in regional supranational organizations are definitely helpful in ensuring autonomy solutions.

(x) There are even forms of participation of autonomous entities in international organizations, exerting influence when the concerned territory is affected.

(xi) In order to ensure the effective operation of autonomy, and in the case of overlapping powers between the state and the autonomous entity, there is a need of 'neutral instances' of mediation and arbitration or an effective mechanism of conflict solving. Such a role can be attributed to the Constitutional Court or Supreme Court of a state or various forms of joint commissions with an equal number of members of the state and the autonomous region.

BIBLIOGRAPHY

Ackrén, Maria, *Conditions for Different Autonomy Regimes in the World.* Åbo: Åbo Akademi University Press, 2009.

Basu Ray Chaudhury, Sabyasachi, Samir Kumar Das and Ranabir Samaddar, eds. *Indian Autonomies: Keywords and Key Texts.* Kolkata: Sampark, 2005.

Benedikter, Thomas, *The World's Modern Autonomy Systems – Concepts and Experiences of Regional Territorial Autonomy,* EURAC Bozen 2009, at: http://www.eurac.edu/Org/Minorities/IMR/Projects/asia.htm

Thomas Benedikter, ed., *Solving Ethnic Conflict through Self-Government – A Short Guide to Autonomy in South Asia and Europe,* EURAC Bozen 2009, at: http://www.eurac.edu/eurasia-net/PROJECT+DE;IVERABLES.htm

Ghai, Yash, ed. *Autonomy and Ethnicity: Negotiating Competing Claims in Multiethnic States.* Cambridge, Cambridge University Press, 2000.

Hannum, Hurst, *Autonomy, Sovereignty and Self-Determination: The Accommodation of Conflicting Rights.* Philadelphia: University of Pennsylvania Press, 1996.

Lapidoth, Ruth, *Autonomy Flexible Solutions for Ethnic Conflicts.* Washington, DC: US Institute of Peace Press, 1997.

Legaré, André, and Markku Suksi, Rethinking the Forms of Autonomy at the Dawn of the Twenty-First Century. *International J Minority and Group Rights* 15, 2-3 (2008): 143-55.

Marko, Joseph, Francesco Palermo, and Jens Woelk, *Tolerance Established by Law: The Autonomy of South Tyrol: Self-Governance and Minority Rights.* Leiden: European Academy Bozen and Brill, 2007.

Pan, Christoph, S. Beate, and S. Pfeil, *Minority Rights in Europe: A Handbook of European National Minorities,* vol. 2. Vienna: Braumüller 2002.

Samaddar, Ranabir, ed. *The Politics of Autonomy: Indian Experiences.* Delhi: Sage, 2004.

Schneckener, Ulrich, and Stefan Wolff, eds. 2004, *Managing and Settling Ethnic Conflicts.* London: Hurst, 2004.

Skurbaty, Zelim, ed. *Beyond a One-Dimensional State.* Leiden: Nijhoff, 2005.

Suksi, Markku, *Autonomy: Applications and Implications.* The Hague: Kluwer Law International, 1998.

Welhengama, Gnanapala, *Minority Claims: From Autonomy to Secession.* Aldershot: Ashgate, 2000.

Weller, Marc, and Stefan Wolff, eds. *Autonomy, Self-Governance and Conflict Resolution.* London: Routledge, 2005.

Weller, Marc, and Barbara Metzger, eds. *Settling Self-Determination Disputes: Complex Power-Sharing in Theory and Practice.* Amsterdam, Nijhoff, 2008.

Wolff, Stefan, *Ethnic Conflict: A Global Perspective.* Oxford: Oxford University Press, 2006.

—— ,Complex Autonomy Arrangements in Western Europe, in *Autonomy, Self-Governance and Conflict Resolution,* edited by M. Weller and S. Wolff. London: Routledge 2005.

8

EXPANDING CATALONIA'S AUTONOMY: An Interview with Aureli Argemì, the Founder and President of CIEMEN, Barcelona

THOMAS BENEDIKTER

INTRODUCTION

Spain by its constitution has accorded territorial autonomy to its 'nationalities' (smaller autochthonous peoples), the 17 so-called *Autonomous Communities* (regions) and two *Autonomous Cities* (Ceuta and Melilla). Three of those Communities are considered 'historical nationalities' with a longstanding tradition of regional self-government: Catalonia, Galicia and the Basque Country. Catalonia, the most populous of these historical autonomies, has enjoyed a far reaching autonomy during the second Spanish Republic, from 1932 to 1939, before being deprived of its power of self-rule by the fascist and centralist Franco-regime. The Autonomous Community of Catalonia is just one of the four autonomous regions of Spain populated by Catalans. It can be considered the 'Catalan mainland', as the Catalan language and culture is also widely present and deeply rooted in Valencia, the Balearic Islands and Aragon.

With a population of 7,248,300 (January 2009, see www.wikipedia.org) Catalonia is a major European nation without a state. The Catalan language is spoken in four European states (Spain, France, Italy and Andorra) and survived more than three centuries within a nation-state (Spain) with a different official language. Although a majority of Catalans consider Catalonia a 'nation', its autonomy is not linked to ethno-linguistic affiliation. First of all, Catalonia is a territorial body and whether a citizen belongs to one or another nationality or speaks Catalan as the mother tongue is simply not a matter of legal interest. In Spain autonomy first of all is a territorial concept and what is legally registered and relevant is not a citizen's affiliation to one of the recognized nationalities (peoples, minorities or ethnic groups), but his or her residency in one of its municipalities. The national character of an Autonomous Community like Catalonia—and alike for the Basque Country, the Asturias, the Balearic Islands and the Canary Islands—results from the ethnic, historical or cultural self-identification of the majority of its population and the concrete application of the autonomy in education, language, culture, media and other domains.

Catalonia's autonomy was first established in 1932 during the Second Republic. In 1939, after the Spanish Civil War, this first Autonomy Statute was abolished by General Franco, as Catalonia's population was mostly opposed to the fascist forces. During Franco's rule, the language rights of Catalans and Catalonia's entire system of self-government were suppressed. After the restoration of democracy in 1975, Catalonia's second autonomy statute was approved in a referendum in 1979. In 2003 Catalonia's Parliament embarked on a process of amending this autonomy in order to further expand the scope of the Catalan autonomy. A new statute was elaborated, which expanded the authority of the *Generalitat de Catalunya,* Catalonia's government, strengthened the competences and finance system of the Autonomous Community and redefined the rights and obligations of the citizens of Catalonia. The new (third) Statute of Autonomy was approved in a popular referendum on 18 June 2006 and became effective in August 2006. With a relatively low voter turnout of 48.85 per cent, 73.24 per cent were in favour of the new statute, 20.57 per cent against it. In 1979, 59.7 per cent of Catalonia's electorate had cast their vote, of which 88.1 per cent voted favourably. Subsequently, the new Catalan statute was approved by a majority of the Spanish Parliament, with the *Partido Popular* (PP, Spanish Conservative Party) opposing it.

It is highly significant that in the preamble to the statute, Catalonia is defined as a nation. Among the delegates of all parties, 120 out of 135 members of Parliament with the exception of the 15 delegates of the PP approved the definition. From the perspective of the Spanish government, this definition has a mere 'declaratory', but no legal value, since the Spanish constitution recognizes the indissoluble 'unity of the Spanish Nation'. Subsequently, the PP, along with the neighbouring Autonomous Communities of Aragon, the Balearic Islands and the Valencian Community, contested the statute before the Spanish Constitutional Court. The objections were based on various topics such as the disputed cultural heritage, but mainly on the statute's alleged breach of the principle of 'solidarity between the regions', which is enshrined in Spain's constitution for educational and fiscal matters. The Constitutional Court in 2009 has not yet issued its verdict on the new Catalan statute. Hence, possible stumbling blocks to the expansion of Catalonia's autonomy still exist. On the opposite side, Catalan left-wing parties, such as ERC or CUP, argue that the new autonomy statute does not give Catalonia enough scope for self-government. They cite the high abstention proof that Catalans wanted further self-government, but felt disappointed with the statute.

REFERENCES:

http://www.gencat.cat/index_cas.htm: official web of the Generalitat de Catalunya

http://www.nationalia.cat: CIEMEN's newsletter on minority issues

http://www.ciemen.cat: Catalan association for the rights of peoples

http://www.gencat.cat/generalitat/cas/estatut/index.htm: Catalonia's new autonomy statute

http://www.ciemen.org/mercator: European Network for Regional and Minority Languages and Legislation

CATALONIA'S NEW AUTONOMY

The following interview with Aureli Argemi, president of CIEMEN, Barcelona—originally taken in Spanish—was translated by Thomas Benedikter.

Aureli Argemí i Roca (born at Sabadell 1936) is a monk and activist of Catalan language. He entered the Abbey of Montserrat in 1951 and, after graduating in theology, was ordained as a priest in 1959. Later he collaborated with various initiatives of resistance against the Franco regime. In 1974 he founded the CIEMEN (Centre Internacional Escarré per a les Minorities Etnique i Nacionals) and is its director. In 1981 he was among the founders of 'Crida a la Solidaritat en Defensa de la Llengua, la cultura i la nació Catalanes' (Solidarity League for the Catalan Language, Culture and Nation), and later of CONSEU (Conference of Nations without a State in Western Europe). He is the director of 'Altres Nacions' and of the programme MERCATOR. Aureli Argemí is also the president of the Spanish Committee for the Lesser Used Languages, and one of the promoters of the 'Universal Declaration of Language Rights' (see the full text at: http://www.ciemen.org/pdf/ang.PDF).

B. Article 1 of Catalonia's new autonomy statute defined Catalonia a 'nation', but this sentence has been dropped by Spain's constitutional court. Subsequently, Catalonia's president Jordi Pujol stated: 'En realitat, que s'accepti que el Parlament de Catalunya defineix Catalunya com a nació és un reconeizxement important. Perquè, qui sinó el nostre Parlament ha de definir formalment què és Catalunya?'

(In reality, because the Catalonian Parliament has defined Catalonia as a nation, it is an important recognition. Who else than our Parliament is entitled to formally define what Catalonia is?) *Madrid, however, is afraid that such an article would be the equivalent of recognizing Catalonia's right to self-determination and that this right would be effectively claimed and exercised.*

ARGEMI: From a juridical point of view the issue, whether Catalonia should be considered a nation or not, has been disputed among the Catalan parties since the approval of Spain's constitution in 1978. Eventually, the term 'nationality' was adopted, which is not satisfying anybody. In Spain, however, the concept of 'regional communities', which in most of the cases have no distinctive linguistic features, has been established strongly. Catalonia's first autonomy statute thus defines Catalonia as a 'nationality'. During the recent debate about the new autonomy statute, 90 percent of the region's members of parliament were endorsing the definition of the Catalans as a nation, but this was rejected by the state's parliament in Madrid. Spanish jurists and politicians were, indeed, afraid of the implicit recognition of the right to self-determination in accepting Catalonia's 'nationhood'. Nevertheless, in the preamble to the statute the national character of Catalonia could not be denied. Moreover, the statute accepts the notion of the 'Catalan people'. All in all a rather incoherent solution applied by the Spanish parliament which was called to ratify the statute. Clearly, in Spain there are different connotations attached to Spanish people on the one hand, and to the Catalan people on the other.

B: *Catalonia's new autonomy statute has been contested before the Constitutional Court by the PP and the regions governed by the PP. Is there any chance for this claim to be accepted by the Court? Which are the current conflicts between Madrid and Barcelona?*

A: Today still we do not know how the Constitutional Court will judge on the appeal of unconstitutionality of the new Catalan statute. Probably it will determine more exactly how the statute shall be interpreted, if it is to be kept within the Constitutional limits. The court traditionally is biased to a more 'centralist view' and will set the limits of how far the statute and the autonomous policy can be further developed. The Spanish government is already applying the new statute, but in a rather restrictive way, especially when it comes to transfer of the new political and economic powers established by the statute.

B: *Is Spain in reality a federal system? Some authors consider this so-called state of autonomies substantially as a federal system, while jurist Arzoz distinguishes between a regionalist asymmetrical state (this would be Spain of today) and an asymmetrical federal state. According to Balaguer, Spain has achieved a federal result by following a regionalist path. Hence, the wrapping is still regional, but the content is federal. Do you agree?*

A: This debate still is not finished, but the Spanish governments hitherto have mostly opposed a federal concept of the state. The central state does not accept a plurality of sovereign actors, which might be entitled to build up a state responding to the claims and needs of the peoples who coexist within this state, open to federal solutions. According to Madrid, there is just a 'state of autonomous communities', which is a form of far-reaching decentralization, but not a federal state. Catalonia within this framework has a very unique position which transcends the dimension of decentralization, but the Spanish state is not willing to concede anything more than regional autonomy which should even be less asymmetric. In one word: all the autonomies should drink one coffee, served to everybody by the central waiter.

B. *If Spain would be effectively and legally transformed into a federal system, would there be any advantage for Catalonia and the other historical 'nationalities' of the Iberian peninsula? Or can the current autonomy be sufficient in order to preserve the identity and the culture of the Catalan people?*

A: A federal state would open up a major scope, for different ways of development, different forms of solidarity and cooperation among the regions. If we don't start to reform this state in a federal manner, conflicts and a major crisis may well occur. This could lead to the conviction that the only solution would be the creation of independent nations, however, as parts of the EU.

B. *The basic concept of Spain's regional autonomies is the territorial element. Thus, there is no registration of their inhabitants along their ethnic or linguistic affiliation, as it happens in other autonomous regions. A system made of quotas and proportionality regulations is deemed superfluous. Why?*

A: The foundation of the nations of the Iberic peninsula is not an ethnic one. It's a mix of citizens. The Catalan language has very different origins, while there is a nucleus of the population which has for centuries shaped the collective historic character. Catalans are people born in Catalonia or who have migrated from other countries, who identify themselves with the Catalan national community. They are willing to integrate into the Catalan people, with its language and culture. The concept of national identity therefore allows both for pluralism and inclusion. Due to the impact of the massive migration of recent decades, Catalan society is already a multilingual and multicultural one. However, the Catalan language and culture should be the common shared features of the whole community, where the diversities meet and coincide.

B. *Which kind of guarantees are given against a unilateral amendment of autonomy statutes in Spain? These statutes are nothing more than state acts; but in the case of an amendment also the consensus of the concerned Autonomous Community is required. Is this a sufficient guarantee?*

A: Theoretically the autonomy is safeguarded by the special way it is put into force. Nobody is allowed to amend the statutes unless both parliaments, the Catalan and the Spanish one, agree. The Constitutional Court gives a verdict on how the autonomy statutes are to be interpreted. There are only hypothetical assumptions about a possible power of intervention of International Courts whenever the rights of Autonomous Communities would be violated. The last word has to be spoken by the people with a popular referendum. But, again, the Spanish Parliament is in the position to determine the modalities of such a referendum and the Constitutional Court is called to interpret it. In that way the people's sovereignty is restricted by the highest court, as this court is allowed to amend the statute even after its approval by a popular referendum.

B. *Along with six other Autonomous Communities, Catalonia appears to have some legislative powers in the sectors of civil law, as the family law, the hereditary law, agricultural contract. Is this a feature which distinguishes Catalonia from other autonomous regions in Spain?*

A: Indeed, Catalonia has got some powers also in respect

of the civil law, which is different from that in force in other regions. But whenever a provision of the Catalan civil right diverges from the Spanish one, it is up to the courts to set the limits.

B. *Within Catalonia's new autonomy statute the powers of the Community have been defined much more precisely than in the previous statute. Are conflicts over competences with the central state, as happened so frequently between 1979 and 2006, to be tackled by this statute?*

A: This is true. The text of the new statute is much longer and more precise than the old one, but in some cases also ambiguous leaving room for interpretation. But the limits of the powers of the Central state have been defined more precisely. The central government often has considered the powers of the autonomous regions not as a right, but rather as a concession, keeping also with it the last decision in most important issues.

B. *Sufficient financial resources are essential for the proper functioning of autonomy. The new financial regulations for Catalonia have accommodated the Catalan claims or do you still need a better system of finance for the autonomy?*

A: The new fiscal system is not the same as in the Basque country called 'concerto economico'. This means that the autonomous government is entitled to levy the taxes and manage its own resources while both parties, the central government and the autonomous region have to come to terms regarding the amount of taxes to be paid to the state for covering the cost of the state's public services displayed in the concerned region. However, there is a major financial autonomy now for the Catalan government with a major scope for regional taxes and negotiation on the share of resources to be annually devolved to the

Centre. Again, these new rights of Catalonia have been contested by the Spanish Conservative Party, PP, before the Constitutional Court.

B. *In the Catalan Parliament a large majority has hailed the new autonomy. Which are the political forces opposing the new statute?*

A: The huge majority of about 90 percent is in favour of the new autonomy statute, although many Catalans are very critical with regard to the amendments applied by the Spanish parliament. Such amendments have curtailed some important features of Catalonia's autonomy. Only the PP and the Mixed Group, about 10 percent of the members of parliament in Barcelona, are opposing the statute.

B. *The Catalan language policy even at international level is considered one of the boldest with regard to the recognition and the legal position of the autochthonous language. The Catalan language now has been declared the 'lengua propia' of Catalonia, its main or 'original' language, and since 2006 every citizen of Catalonia has the duty to learn this language. Is this just a symbolic act or does it include also legal effects such as the right to give examinations in the school system?*

A: The new statute affirms that to know Catalan is not just a right, but also a duty. Recently the Parliamentary Assembly of the Council of Europe has hailed the Catalan system of linguistic immersion and the forms of positive discrimination applied in order to save the Catalan language. This 'immersion' is requested for operating against dividing the society, as Catalan is Catalonia's own language and also the language of social inclusion. Catalan and Spanish in Catalonia are co-official languages. The public administration is obliged to serve all citizens in their languages. But on a practical level, the Spanish language in daily life is still dominant. Thus major efforts are required to strengthen the role of Catalan and to operate a (system of) positive discrimination in order to make Catalan the normal language of all aspects of social life. The students can freely choose in which language they want to give their school-leaving examinations.

B. *Article 6.2 of the new statute reads: 'Totes persones tenen el dret d'utilizar les dues llengues oficials i els ciutadans de Catalunya tenen el dret e el deure de conèixer-les.'* (All have the right to use the two official languages and the citizens of Catalunya [Catalonia] have the right and the duty to know them). *Hence Catalan has also become the preferential language of public administration. Is this mirrored also in daily practice of the Catalan administrative system? If there is a duty of every public employee to know Catalan are there also official language examinations in the recruitment process?*

A: The autonomous administration on regional and municipal level uses Catalan preferentially Catalan for all official acts, but all acts and laws are promulgated in both languages. Public officials have to be fluent in both languages, which is ascertained in special exams. In the judiciary and in some state services, however, Spanish is still the dominant language.

B. *With the new autonomy statute the central state commits itself to engage for the recognition of the Catalan language at international level (e.g. within the European Union). Can Catalan ever become an official language of the EU?*

A: The Catalan language is not allowed to become an official language of the EU as it is spoken only in a part of Spain. But if the Spanish state is willing to get Catalan accepted with such a position, it could be legally feasible.

B. *The new autonomy statute is considered a milestone for further development of Spain's entire system of regional autonomies. On the other hand, the new statute of the Basque Country has been rejected by Madrid. Hence, the Basques will have to be content with what has been achieved by the Catalans?*

A: The Basque parliament has adopted a new autonomy statute where the Spanish state and the Basque country are put almost on an equal footing as if both were sovereign states. This approach hasn't been accepted by Madrid from the very beginning, leading to its rejecting the whole text. Then the Basque Country reacted with the intention to consult the people whether it should be entitled to the right of self-determination. Again the central state has strictly opposed any such referendum on that issue. With the new situation emerging after the Basque elections of 1 March 2009 we cannot expect any big step forward in the coming years. The old statute of Gurernika [Guernica] of 1979 keeps in force, but is clearly anachronistic. The Basque will not be accommodated with the new achievement for the Catalans.

B. *Which are the core points of the criticism of the Catalan left nationalists with regard to the new autonomy statute?*

A: The Catalan Left claims that Catalonia's new autonomy statute does not accommodate the claims of the majority of the Catalan people. Although enlarging the powers of the autonomous institutions, basically things remain the same. Sure, there is more scope for self-governance of the Catalans now, but this is not enough as expressed by hundreds of thousands in popular rallies in Catalonia.

9

TRANSNATIONAL MINORITY NETWORK AND MOBILIZATION IN EUROPE

BOJAN BREZIGAR

THE AFTERMATH OF World War II in Europe revealed substantial political changes. The continent was divided into two areas, dominated by the two states which had led the victory: the Soviet Union and the United States of America. The USA formally shared the responsibility for the area of its influence with France and the United Kingdom, while it was known that at least in the initial years almost all the main decisions were taken in Washington DC. On the other hand, the Soviet Union dominating over the Socialist Block concentrated all its power in Moscow.

The balance of power between the two blocks was the most important and, to a certain extent, the only political issue at that time, so much so that discussion of any particular or small problems seemed impossible. Among these problems, those related to ethnic and linguistic minorities have to be mentioned. Numerous changes in borders in Europe in the first half of the twentieth century produced instability along the borders. Most of the states were of the opinion that any discussion on minorities would have produced instability in the western block (the regimes in the East did not allow any discussion at all) and only some cases containing reference to minorities have been treated internationally. Important among them were the agreement of De Gasperi-Gruber on South Tyrol (1948); the London Memorandum on the Free Territory of Trieste (1954); the State agreement of Austria (1955); and the Bonn-København agreement on the German-Danish border (1956).

Most minorities in Europe felt isolated and oppressed. As soon as the political situation allowed, they started to contact each other with the purpose of acting internationally to obtain certain recognition at the international level; or to force their own states through international pressure to adopt measures to protect minorities and promote minority languages.

The vacuum left by politics has since that time been fulfilled by civil society. Within a few years after the end of World War II, hundreds of organizations have been established all over Europe. Most of them have worked on a voluntary basis: no public funding, no jobs, no staff, in most cases no reimbursement at all. These organizations have been working in the fields of culture, in education and later on in media as well. During my frequent interviews with the minorities I realized what real voluntary work means: people, families, who spend weekends selling everything and collecting money for opening schools, spending time and money for their language and culture. These voluntary initiatives and idealistic handling have saved many European minority languages from inevitable death.

As soon as conditions allowed, these organizations started networking amongst themselves, at times across borders. Based on the principle of 'we are stronger if we act together', they started activities within the minorities as well as between different minority communities, even those which had been 'enemies' not long before. The best practice in this domain has been developed in the German-Danish border area, with strong cooperation between the Danish minority in Germany and the German minority in Denmark. But there are other examples as well. By the 1960s minorities in Europe had established hundreds of NGOs that represented an army of civil society, democratically fighting for minority rights, using such democratic approaches as lobbying, signing petitions, forwarding proposals, wherever possible even going to court. If, on one side, just a few states were willing to recognize the principle of linguistic and cultural diversity, almost all of them accepted the freedom of association as the basic human right. Through the freedom of association minorities started their fight for linguistic rights. As soon as they became strong enough they joined their forces in transnational NGOs which have been the real engine for the long battle that led to the adoption and implementation of important international documents during the 1990s. Politicians often claim credit for those documents; they are right in a sense; these documents were adopted by international political forums. They would never have succeeded without the hundreds of organizations pushing for minority rights since the very beginning.

In this chapter the two most important transnational minority networks in Europe will be discussed and the results of their activity will be evaluated. These are the Federal Union of European Nationalities (FUEN) and the European Bureau for Lesser Used Languages (EBLUL).

FEDERAL UNION OF EUROPEAN NATIONALITIES (FUEN)

September 30, 2009 was a great day for the Federal Union of European Nationalities (FUEN), an organization that on this particular day celebrated 60 years of its existence. In the building of the Committee of the Regions in Central Brussels some 150 representatives of minorities gathered together to celebrate the event. Among others, the President of the Committee of the Regions and the representative of the European Commission congratulated FUEN for its activities. On the previous day and in the European Parliament (EP) several members of EP, belonging to the Intergroup for

Constitutional Regions and Minority Languages attended the joint meeting to celebrate FUEN's birthday. It was a great European event.

It had not been so before. As Jørgen Kühl writes, 'In 1949 the initiative was launched to create a European federalist association with the ambition to include regions, minorities, and ethnic groups which eventually would lead to the creation of European cooperation bodies closely affiliated with the pro-European and federalist movement' (Kühl 2000: 10). In April 1949 the First Congress of European Regions met in Paris. Some 160 delegates (among them there was a young French politician François Mitterrand, then secretary for the information policy of the French government) discussed federal issues and decided to create a permanent congress of European communities and regions representing groups and regions in Scotland, Wales, Cornwall, Friesland, Flanders, Wallonie, Britanny, Alsace, Provence, Aoste, South Tyrol, Friuli, Sicily, Sardinia, Swiss Cantons, Bavaria, Basque Country and Catalonia (ibid: 13-14). The second congress was scheduled to take place in Merano, South Tyrol, in September, but Italian authorities did not authorize it. So delegates met in November 1949 in Versailles for the Second International Congress of European Communities and Regions and in two days formally established the organization named Federal Council of European Minorities and Regions. The Congress requested the Council of Europe to appoint a subcommission for minorities, to include the right of use of vernacular languages in the Declaration on Human Rights and to appoint a commission with the task of drafting a charter on the rights and freedoms of the European ethnic groups (ibid: 15-17).

As could be seen the regions practically disappeared; the federalists went their own way and the Federal Council in 1955 changed its name to the Federal Union of European Nationalities (FUEN).

The first years of activity were very difficult. Minorities were not a popular issue in Europe; in a way they disturbed the new political order, the fixed borders and the principle of national states. It is thanks to a few idealists that FUEN resisted the prevalent trend at that time. There was the problem of post-war reconstruction everywhere and particularities, as minorities were, appeared in most cases as elements of disturbance. Cultural and linguistic diversity was not appreciated at all. Just a few exceptions had not influenced this general feeling. This lasted for more than twenty years. Still in 1966, when the yearly congress of FUEN was planned in Italy, in Gorizia, close to the border with the then Yugoslavia, on the day before the meeting, the Italian authorities prohibited the Congress and the delegates, who had already arrived in Gorizia, to meet, and they left after the President announced that the meeting was not been allowed (ibid: 95).

Later on, in the 1970s and 1980s the situation slowly changed and FUEN grew up, remaining in any case a Western European NGO. The iron curtain did not allow any cooperation with minorities in the East. At that time FUEN got some subventions from certain regional authorities, mostly in the German-Danish border, in South Tyrol and in Austria. These subventions allowed the organization to develop certain programmes, to establish the main office in Flensburg and to appoint the Secretary-General. Representatives of member organizations met every year, and in 1984 the youth organization, nowadays an autonomous body named YEN, was established. Nevertheless the political impact of FUEN has been very limited and until the mid-1980s the organization, due to the veto of the Italian government, had not been given the NGO observer status with the Council of Europe.

In 1989 the situation suddenly changed. After the fall of the Berlin wall, European institutions urgently needed organizations with a good knowledge of minority issues. FUEN was at that time the most important organization in this field. The fact that this organization had drafted a charter on the main principles for European minority rights already in 1956 (ibid: 85-86)—which were revised and supplemented in 1985—convinced the main international organizations, that FUEN could be a reliable, experienced and serious partner in dealing with minority issues in Eastern Europe as well. Since 1991 FUEN developed these principles further into a draft for a convention on the basic rights of European ethnic groups, and submitted its proposals to the international endeavours of the Conference on Security and Cooperation in Europe (CSCE), the UN, the Council of Europe and the European Parliament. FUEN has also strongly supported all endeavours of the Council of Europe in this respect. It placed great hope in the new mechanisms including those related to the European Charter on Regional and Minority Languages and the Framework Convention for the Protection of National Minorities. In recognition of its efforts towards attaining protection for European minorities, FUEN obtained participatory status to the Council of Europe in 1989 and a consultative status to the United Nations (UN) in 1995. It is also represented at OSCE (the former CSCE) conferences concerning national minorities and ethnic groups.[1]

With such policy FUEN strongly expanded in Eastern Europe, including Russia, Ukraine and Southern Caucasus; it often became a discussion partner for governments and parliaments in many states of Europe and in European and international institutions, representing the needs of minorities and the interest of states to maintain their cultural and linguistic diversity. It drafted several documents on these issues and influenced the policy of both states and international institutions. During the course of its existence, FUEN has become a respected organization through its consistent adherence to democracy and rights, its work for better protection of ethnic groups and its stance for peaceful dialogue.[2]

As regards structure, it appears from the web page of the organization that FUEN is the umbrella association of European national minorities. Full members are representative organizations of national minorities. Organizations initially wishing to become familiar with FUEN work or ones interested only in particular fields of minority policy become associate members. According to the web page in 2007 FUEN's membership consists of 45 full and 40 associated members from 32 European states. Four state institutions support FUEN with annual grants, while a large number of scientific institutes promote FUEN materially and ideologically.

The member organizations undertake to pursue the policy principles of FUEN. They base their activities on a democratic and constitutional state, they reject violence and separatism. FUEN's official languages are English, French, Russian and German. The political aim of the organization is clearly explained on the web page as well:

> According to its statutes, the Federal Union of European Nationalities serves the ethnic groups in Europe and pursues the goal of preserving their national identity, their language, culture and the history of national minorities. This objective is pursued only by peaceful means. It decisively takes a stand against separatism and the violent moving of national borders, and works towards a neighbourly, peaceful coexistence of majority and minority in one state or region. FUEN has now been convinced since 1949 that a minority can only find a harmonious relationship with the majority population on the basis of free democratic and constitutional principles in peaceful and constructive dialogue through the negotiation of political solutions.[3]

Finally, regarding the structure, the Congress elects the President and several Board members (all of them called Vice-Presidents). The main office and the Secretary General are located in Flensburg in Germany, close to the Danish border, at the centre of the Danish minority in Germany.

EUROPEAN BUREAU FOR LESSER USED LANGUAGES (EBLUL)

This organization originates from the commitment of the first elected European Parliament in favour of maintaining cultural and linguistic diversity in Europe. In 1981, two years after the first democratic elections, the Parliament adopted a resolution on a Community Charter of Regional Languages and Cultures and on a Charter of Rights of Ethnic Minorities.[1] Some Members of the Parliament, being aware that Europe could maintain its culture only if it kept the whole mosaic of its diversity, began to discuss how on a European level all languages could be promoted and safeguarded. The resolution considers this particular aspect and tends to promote and to safeguard languages as part of the European common heritage, with no specific relationship with the political aspect arising from the presence of a linguistic minority in a specific area.

Insofar as the European Parliament and the European Commission give importance to the linguistic aspects, the European Parliament has included in the yearly EU budget the budget line B3-1006 since the year 1983, when the amount was of 100,000 ECU only; since then the amount has been growing yearly, and it reached 1 million of ECUs in 1988, 2 million in 1991, and 4 million in 1998. The political body that has an overview of these activities is the Intergroup for Regional and Minority Languages of the European Parliament, consisting of some 50 MEPs of all the EU member states. The Intergroup (now called Intergroup for Traditional National Minorities, Constitutional Regions and Regional Languages, which after the 2004 elections enlarged its activities) still exists and meets on a monthly basis to discuss European matters as well as aspects of single communities related to the European policy.[5]

Keeping in mind that the European Union[6] has not been allowed to deal directly with the minorities, an independent body was needed. In 1983 representatives of the minority NGOs in the EU Member States established a European network, called European Bureau for Lesser Used Languages (EBLUL). The title of the organization was a compromise, as the term 'minorities' would not be accepted by the EU and neither by some linguistic communities (Irish in Ireland, Catalans, Basques and others), which considered themselves nations or communities rather than minorities. The structure of EBLUL was very simple: in each EU member state a Member State Committee (MSC) was established, composed of the representatives of the NGOs dealing with linguistic minorities' issues. The presidents of all MSCs formed the Council of EBLUL, which elects the President and the Board of Directors. The activities of EBLUL, first established in Ireland (due to substantial financial support of the Irish government) and then moved to Brussels, were mostly funded by the European Commission, and some activities have been developed together by the EBLUL and the Commission. Among these, one has to mention the study visit programme consisting of exchange of more than 1,000 experts of linguistic communities visiting other communities for a week, sharing experience and collecting ideas about possible solutions to their problems. We refer to the time that communications between states were still very difficult, the internet did not exist at all and rudimentary telefax machines were the most modern office electronic supplies.

For many years EBLUL has dedicated itself to the affirmation of the cultural and linguistic diversity in Europe and in developing policies, which would help communities strengthen the use of their languages in all the domains. The role of such an organization was not temporarily related to specific political aspects; promoting and safeguarding the languages would always be an important task, as the languages are part of day-to-day life; they change and they develop, following the general development of the environment where they are spoken. So, as we could have expected that once peace would be established, the political tasks of protection of linguistic minorities would be over (and neither has this been yet achieved in Europe), we never could so affirm for the tasks related to protection and promotion of minority or lesser used languages.

The European Bureau for Lesser Used Languages (Brezigar 1998: 213-18)[7] has been implementing these tasks since the year 1984. It has been a hard job, even harder at the beginning when the minority languages were absolutely a taboo theme in most of the European countries. It took about fifteen years to reach the situation where there was only one European Union member state which does not recognize minority languages at all—Greece—while all the other states, at different levels, accepted the discussion about a sort of minimum standard to be recognized for minority language-speakers. This result has been achieved due to the increasing awareness of the importance of this problem at the pan-European level. It can be stressed that the European Bureau for Lesser Used Languages played an important role in achieving this awareness.

Let me now briefly explain what the European Bureau for Lesser Used Languages has been doing and what its main projects have been. EBLUL gave representatives of communities the opportunity of meeting and exchanging experience. Even if there does not exist any universal model for all the communities, there is always something people could learn from other people with similar problems. All the activities being developed by the linguistic groups at the European level now would have been unthinkable 25 years ago. People did not know one another, they had no contacts and also the few organizations existing since the 1950s were not able to give the communities the opportunity to meet, to exchange opinions about how they are dealing with problems and to try to resolve similar problems in a similar way. This task became even more relevant after the enlargement of the European Union in 2004 when connecting people, exchange of information and exchange of experience became ever increasing. Now everything seems normal and sometimes it would seem that there is no need of an organization to keep people together, as they do it themselves.

Further, one of the major tasks of EBLUL was to connect not only minority languages speakers and their associations, but also to extend this connection to regions and to public bodies interested in these languages or dealing with them. In Europe many regions have developed their policy in favour of minority languages and some of them have established official language agencies. Through a series of Conference, called Partnership for Diversity, EBLUL has promoted meetings of these bodies, proposing them to develop and produce their common policy. Later on regional authorities and linguistic bodies established their own network, which is still very active.

EBLUL made strong efforts for keeping the minorities informed. Most of the linguistic communities are very small and very far from the European institutions. EBLUL offered them information about what the European Commission and other institutions could do for them. The more important Europe became the more necessary it was that the communities were linked to where the decision-making took place in Europe. EBLUL produced an inventory of all the different EU programmes which could be of benefit to projects related to minority languages. As an NGO with observer status with the UN, ECOSOC, UNESCO and the Council of Europe, EBLUL has been continuously lobbying (the European Commission, European Parliament, the Assembly of the Regions, the Council of Europe, the OSCE), aiming to achieve better international protection for Lesser Used Languages. Certainly, there exist the basic documents, but the documents do not give linguistic rights, if they are not properly implemented. The monitoring of the implementation of these documents was one of the most important tasks of the European Bureau for Lesser Used Languages. It is important to stress that such work was not carried out in an adversarial manner against the states of the Union because it has been done in cooperation with the states and their regional and local authorities.

It has to be mentioned as well that EBLUL was the only minority organization invited to the hearings of two important EU Conventions: the Convention drafting the EU Charter of Fundamental Rights and the Convention drafting the Constitutional Treaty for the European Union. Among the results, it has to be mentioned that the Article 22 of the Charter of Fundamental Rights has been adopted on the specific proposal of EBLUL.[8] To ensure that majorities are not only supplied with negative information about Lesser Used Languages, EBLUL has established the Brussels Information Centre, with extensive documentation on Lesser Used Languages. Press releases, cultural presentations and publications form part of these activities. The initiative arose from the awareness that most information regarding minority languages is 'negative' information: it is often coupled with conflicts, tensions or problems. Newspapers and broadcasters rarely give any 'positive' information about the lesser used languages, their problems and their importance. On this basis EBLUL established the news agency Eurolang which has for years disseminated accurate information regarding minority languages, difficulties and troubles together with information on the role of EBLUL in maintaining the European cultural heritage. The main purpose of these activities was to get rid of the impression that the general public has accumulated, that is, that linguistic minorities are only a cause of trouble for the states and for Europe.

It has to be mentioned that on behalf of EBLUL three Mercator centres, dealing with education (Leeuwarden, Netherlands), media (Aberystwyth, Wales) and legislation (Barcelona, Catalonia) have been developed into the most important research network on minority languages in Europe. Among the projects, one more should be mentioned; the Euroschool project, meetings of children of minority languages all over Europe. On a two-year term some 400 children of at least 10 different communities met with hundreds of children of the hosting region and for a long weekend such a region became the capital of the minority language-speaking children: they lived together in the families, they attended the same lessons, they organized sport and cultural events. Euroschool was a great happening which gave children self-confidence and made them feel stronger. Unfortunately for lack of funding after 7 sessions the programme was abandoned.

The European Bureau for Lesser Used Languages has not produced a general policy for the protection and the development of the languages. It only assisted the communities in doing so within the framework of the aforementioned documents and agreements. EBLUL has never been a sort of European umbrella, establishing rules for everybody; it has been mostly listening to what people ask and what they need and transmitted to the European institutions of these needs. EBLUL still exists, but after 2004 the relevant budget line in the EU budget does no exist any more. So nowadays EBLUL has to refer to only its own sources and its activities have been reduced.

CONCLUSION

FUEN and EBLUL have been the most relevant NGOs dealing with minority issues in Europe. They have never established strong cooperation nor clashed with each other, mainly because they have always been different. FUEN has been a pan-European political organization, dealing with political rights of minorities all over Europe, while EBLUL has been established as a linguistic and cultural organization, focusing its activity on linguistic rights and on the promotion of linguistic and cultural diversity only in the EU Member States. Apart from these two important networks, there are in Europe some other internationally based NGOs dealing with minority issues, but they have never reached the political and social impact of FUEN and EBLUL.

NOTES

1. http://www.fuen.org/pages/english/e_1_2002.html, accessed 12 Oct 2009.
2. http://www.fuen.org/pages/english/e_1_2002.html, accessed 12 Oct 2009.
3. http://www.fuen.org/pages/english/e_1_2002.html, accessed 12 Oct 2009.
4. Official Journal of the European Communities n° C 287 of 09/11/1981, pp 106-107.
5. For the activities of the Intergroup see Csaba Tabajdi, ed. 2009. Minorities of Europe Unite! Dr István Kecskés. Budapest.
6. Art. 151 of the Consolidated version of the Treaty establishing the European Union, official *Journal of the European Communities* no C 325 of 24 Dec 2002.
7. The report on the activities of EBLUL has been updated upon the author's presentation at the Dublin conference in October 1998.
8. 'The Union shall respect cultural, religious and linguistic diversity'. *Official J* European *Communities* no C 364 of 18/12/2000, 99 1-22.

BIBLIOGRAPHY

Brezigar, Bojan. 1998. The role of the European Bureau for Lesser Used Languages within EU policy for the minority language communities. In International Conference on Language Legislation, Conference proceedings. Comdháil Náisiúnta na Gaeilge. Dublin.

Kühl, Jørgen. 2000. *The Federal Union of European Nationalities. An Outline History 1949 – 1999.* Danish Institute of Border Region Studies. Aabenraa, Denmark.

Tabajdi, Csaba, ed. 2009. Minorities of Europe Unite! Dr István Kecskés. Budapest.

Vade-Mecum. A Guide to International Documents on Lesser-Used Languages of Europe. Brussels: European Bureau for Lesser Used Languages, 2003.

10

REGIONAL/INTERNATIONAL FRAMEWORKS OF MINORITY PROTECTION IN EUROPE AND SOUTH ASIA

JAVAID REHMAN and HARRIET HOFFLER

DEFINITION OF MINORITIES

The issue of defining minorities in independent states has been problematic. In 1966 Special Rapporteur Francesco Capotorti was assigned the task of preparing a study pursuant to Article 27 of the International Covenant on Civil and Political Rights (ICCPR). In producing a detailed examination of the Rights of the Persons Belonging to Ethnic, Religious and Linguistic Minorities, Capotorti also formulated a definition, which is generally regarded as authoritative. According to his definition a 'minority' is a

> group numerically inferior to the rest of the population of a State, in a non-dominant position, whose members—being nationals of the State—possess ethnic, religious or linguistic characteristics differing from those of the rest of the population and show, if only implicitly, a sense of solidarity, directed towards preserving their culture, traditions, religion or language. (Capotorti 1991)

This definition proposed by Capotorti has been challenged and criticized on a number of grounds. The primary feature of the definition seems to be a combination of both objective and subjective elements in ascertaining a minority group (ibid). Objective criteria would involve a factual analysis of a group as a distinct entity within the state 'possessing stable ethnic, religious or linguistic characteristics that differ sharply from those of the rest of the population' (Shaw 2008).

The subjective criteria would be found on the basis that there exists 'a common will in the group, a sense of solidarity, directed towards preserving the distinctive characteristics of the group' (Sohn 1981). However, it could be argued that in view of the rather onerous considerations of evaluating both the objective and the subjective criteria, identification of a minority group might prove to be a difficult task.

The second proposition which needs to be addressed is that of the numerical strength of the group in question. It seems acceptable that the numerical strength must at least account for 'a sufficient number of persons to preserve their traditional characteristics' (UN Doc. 1953 Convention for the Protection of Human Rights and Fundamental Freedoms ETS No. 005 213 U.N.T.S. 222, entered into force Sept. 3, 1953, as amended by Protocols Nos 3, 5, and 8, which entered into force on 21 September 1970, 20 December 1971 and 1 January 1990 respectively). Hence a single individual could not form a minority group. On the other hand, it is contended that to put in place an absolute principle that in order to be recognized as a minority, an entity must necessarily be 'numerically inferior' places an unnecessarily heavy burden on the group and may well be factually incorrect. The minority concept, controversial as it is, cannot be treated in such a restrictive manner. A consideration of the case of the Bengalis of East Pakistan clearly reinforces this point. At the time of its emergence as an independent state, Pakistan was divided into two 'wings' of unequal sizes: East Bengal (subsequently renamed East Pakistan) and Western Pakistan. East Bengalis constituted nearly 54 per cent of the total population and in this sense the provincial population formed a numerical majority. On the other hand, the Bengalis had very little share in the political and constitutional affairs of the state. They were heavily discriminated against and suffered from the characteristic minority syndromes (Dinstein 1976). *The World Directory of Minorities* lists a number of states where it is difficult to isolate this straightforward majority-minority numerical relationship (Minority Rights Group 2008).

The third issue to arise out of the Capotorti definition is that of the position of non-nationals within the state (Weis 1979). Non-nationals could form a significant proportion of a state's population, and although the main thrust of the development of international law of human rights has devoted itself to a consideration of the plight of nationals within the state, the rights of the non-nationals, as individuals, are also increasingly becoming a concern of human rights law. Indeed, as Lillich correctly points out:

> The question of rights of aliens is inextricably linked to the contemporary international human-rights law movement because it poses a clear test of relevance and enforceability of international human rights norms which have developed since World War II (Lillich 1984).

Non-nationals include migrant workers, refugees and stateless persons and the phenomenal increase in their numbers in recent years has brought considerable attention to their position in international human rights law. *The travaux préparatoires* of the ICCPR are not extremely helpful on the matter, though whatever guidance that can be obtained points more in the direction of the exclusion of non-nationals from the category of minorities as envisaged in Article 27 (Capotorti 1991). The Special Rapporteur Capotorti has also taken the position that since foreigners are able to take advantage of protection bestowed upon them within customary international law and other international agreements, this provision should exclude non-nationals (Tomuschat 1983). On the other hand, it needs to be noted that Article 27 of the ICCPR, unlike Article 25, refers to persons, as opposed to citizens. It is also significant to note the views put forward by the Human Rights Committee in its general comment on Article 27. According to the Committee,

> The terms used in article 27 indicate that the persons designed to be protected are those who belong to a group and who share in a common culture, a religion and/or a language. Those terms also indicate that the individuals designed to be protected need not be citizens of the State party. In this regard, the obligations deriving from article 2.1 are also relevant, since a State party is required under that article to ensure that the rights protected under the Covenant are available to all individuals within its territory and subject to its jurisdiction, except rights which are expressly made to apply to citizens, for example, political rights under article 25. A State party may not, therefore, restrict the rights under article 27 to its citizens alone (ibid).

The Committee's views on the position of those groups whose degree of permanence could be questioned are also interesting. The Committee spells out its views in para 5.2 of the Comment,

> Article 27 confers rights on persons belonging to minorities which 'exist' in a State party. Given the nature and scope of the rights envisaged under that article, it is not relevant to determine the degree of permanence that the term 'exist' connotes. Those rights simply are that individuals belonging to those minorities should not be denied the right, in community with other members of their group, to enjoy their own culture, to practise their religion and speak their language. Just as they need not be nationals or citizens, they need not be permanent residents. Thus, migrant workers or even visitors in a State party constituting such minorities are entitled not to be denied the exercise of those rights (ibid).

Notwithstanding these views put forward by the Human Rights Committee, there remains a prevalent confusion as to the national status of claimant groups. Several of the recent minority rights instruments make reference to the term 'National'. This includes the United Nations Declaration on the Rights of Persons Belonging to National or Ethnic, Religious and Linguistic Minorities (1992). This has provided some states with the opportunity to claim a limitation on the scope of minority status; a criticism reiterated in the fifth session of the Working Group on Minorities (Report of the Working Group on Minorities on its fifth session, 1999). In the view of these states, nationality is the essential pre-requisite for making any claims to the status of a minority. South Asia provides a number of examples, including those of the Biharis of Bangladesh, the Tamils of Sri Lanka and the Nepali-speaking Bhutanese, where the relevant state has exploited the nationality issue in order to discriminate against and persecute a minority group.

Another area on which Capotorti's definition could be challenged is its narrowness by concentrating almost exclusively upon what has been termed as 'minorities by will' and overlooking the position of 'minorities by force'. 'Minorities by will' and 'minorities by force' are terms engineered by Laponce (Laponce 1960). Explaining the distinctions between the two kinds of minorities, he comments: 'two fundamentally different attitudes are possible for a minority in its relationship with the majority: it may wish to be assimilated or it may refuse to be assimilated. The minority that desires assimilation but is barred is a minority by force. The minority that refuses assimilation is a minority by will' (ibid).

INTERNATIONAL PROTECTION FOR MINORITIES

Minority Rights has been a problematic issue for international law to handle. Although international law primarily deals through the medium of states, and minorities generally have no locus standi, the treatment which minorities receive from their states has increasingly become a matter of international concern. International law, however, has historically found it difficult to deal with the problems around minorities. Like the poor, the weak and the inarticulate, minorities have historically fallen victim to persecution and genocide. Even in the contemporary period of relative tolerance and rationality, minorities are often subjected to persecution, discrimination and genocide. The stance of international law remains tentative and extremely cautious, for minorities pose questions of a serious nature; they exist in myriad forms, with their own social, political, cultural and religious particularities. Often transcending national frontiers, minorities are extremely capable of appealing to the sensitivities of their international sympathizers. Most national boundaries are arbitrarily drawn and a number of states contain turbulent factions artificially placed within their borders, often cutting across frontiers. This is evident specifically in South Asia.

At the time of the establishment of the League of Nations, an elaborate regime of minority rights treaties was established. The mechanisms that were adopted by the League of Nations to protect minorities were limited in nature and the minority protection regime collapsed well before the start of the Second World War. With the establishment of the United Nations, emphasis shifted to the position of individual human rights. The United Nations Charter contains several references to human rights. The Universal Declaration is committed to promoting individual rights and non-discrimination. There is no reference to minorities in either the United Nations Charter or the UDHR (Eide 1999). The Human Rights Commission, one of the principal functional commissions of the UN Economic and Social Council (ECOSOC), nevertheless, established a Sub-Commission whose specific mandate included the prevention of discrimination and protection of minority rights. In addition, within the UDHR, there is mention of a number of rights, which can be treated as forming the basis of minority protection. The Declaration specifically provides in Article 1 and 2 the right of equality and non-discrimination. The right to freedom of thought, conscience and religion is stated in Article 18, the right to freedom of opinion and expression is provided in Article 19, the right to peaceful assembly and association in Article 20, the right to education in Article 26 and the right to freely participate in the cultural life of the community in Article 27 (Henrard 2001). All these rights provide the necessary foundation for giving individual members a claim to autonomy.

Although the Universal Declaration has no explicit references to minorities, subsequent international instruments have provided greater attention to minority or group rights. The International Convention on the Elimination of All Forms of Racial Discrimination (CERD), while placing emphasis on the elimination of racial discrimination, also aims to protect racial minority groups. Article 1 of the Convention defines racial discrimination as 'any distinction, exclusion, restriction or preference based on race, colour, descent, or national or ethnic origin'. The inclusion of 'national or ethnic groups', adds to the protection afforded by CERD to minority groups. It provides an explicit recognition to affirmative action policies and allows minority groups to institute a complaints procedure. The International Covenant on Economic, Social and Cultural Rights (ICESCR) represents a strong recognition of the value of cultural rights in the human rights context (Craven 1995). According to Article 15 of ICESCR, states undertake to recognize that everyone has the right to 'take part in cultural life' (ibid). There is also recognition of legitimate differences in beliefs and traditions in Articles 13(3) and 13(4). Under Article 13, parents are given the right to establish and choose schools other than those established by public authorities. The most significant of international treaties in respect to protecting minority rights has been the ICCPR (Henrard 2001). Article 27 of the ICCPR is of special importance for minorities as it is the main provision in current international law which attempts to provide direct protection to ethnic, linguistic and religious minorities: Article 27 provides as follows: 'In those states in which ethnic, religious or linguistic minorities exist, persons belonging to such minorities shall not be denied the right, in community with other members of their group, to enjoy their own culture, to profess and practice their own religion, or to use their own language.'

The Article however does not take a straightforward approach in extending protection to minorities. It is drafted in an awkward manner and appears to suggest that while the majority of states comprise homogeneous groups, the issue of minorities is confined to only a few. The aim behind such wording appears to be to provide protection only to the long established minorities and to prevent or discourage the formation of new minority groups. This phraseology invites states to deny the existence of minorities within their boundaries. Many states have indeed not hesitated to do so. The obligations in the article require states 'not to deny the right [to persons belonging to minorities] to enjoy their own culture, to profess and practice their own religion, or to use their own language'. The wording of the provision, contrary to other articles, such as Article 18 (1) is negative in tone. The obligations that are to be imposed upon state parties have also been a matter of considerable debate. The text is not strong enough to place states and governments under the obligation of providing special facilities to members of minorities. The sole obligation that was placed on the states was not to deprive or deny members of the minority groups the status they were already enjoying (Caportorti 1991). Article 27 is not only weak due to not placing positive obligations on state parties, but it is also limited in scope as far as the issue of locus standi is concerned. The jurisprudence emanating from the operation of the First Optional Protocol confirms that the provisions of the article are limited to persons. Cases such Sandra Lovelace *vs.* Canada establish the possibility of vindication of minority rights using Article 27.

At the same time, the article has proved inadequate in satisfying many of the claims, such as Lubicon Lake Band *vs.* Canada. Minorities as groups are not entitled to bring actions before the Committee; however, minorities as a group of individuals who allege a violation of their rights are permitted to bring an action before the Committee (ibid). Nor has it been possible to claim violations of Article 1 under the Optional Protocol to the ICCPR.

The Human Rights Committee has dealt with Minority Rights in the context of Article 27 in a significant number of cases. The vast majority of these relate to ethnic minorities with very little jurisprudence relating to linguistic and religious minority groups. In Lovelace *vs.* Canada, a Maliseet Indian lost the rights and status associated with the minority after she married a non-Maliseet Indian man. The Human Rights Committee decided that as she was ethnically a Maliseet Indian and was brought up on a reserve and maintained ties to the reserve during her marriage, she must still belong to the minority. While there is no right to live on a reserve under Article 27, per se, her access to culture and to language was interfered with, as there was no place outside the reserve where such a possibility existed. Therefore, the loss of rights amounted to a violation of Article 27. In Länsman *vs.* Finland it was held that the quarrying of land traditionally used for reindeer breeding, which was also a sacred place in the Old Sami Religion, did not constitute a violation of Article 27, as the quarrying was of a limited nature and the reindeer herding had not been adversely affected. It is, however, important to note that in this judgment it was emphasized that ethnic communities have the right to use modern methods when carrying out traditional trades. In contrast in Lubicon Lake Band *vs.* Canada, it was held that the expropriation of land by the provincial government in order to lease it to private enterprise constituted a violation of Article 27. Economic and social activities, which are part of the culture of the community, are protected by Article 27. In Kitok *vs.* Sweden it was held that legislation with the reasonable and objective aim of the continued viability and welfare of the minority as a whole was not a violation of Article 27. The requirement of obtaining a fishing licence for fishing out of season on land not part of the reserve, especially when the reserve in question was abundant with fish, was not considered a violation of Article 27 in Howard *vs.* Canada.

In respect of religious minorities, the Human Rights Council (HRC) is yet to hear any cases in respect of Article 27. However, a number of cases have been brought in respect of Article 18 and Article 26. The rights of linguistic minorities have been dealt with in Ballantyne et al. *vs.* Canada, Guesdon *vs.* France and Cadoret and Bihan *vs.* France. In Ballantyne it was held that rules preventing the use of the English language in advertising in Quebec did not violate the rights of the English Linguistic minority, as they constituted the majority in Canada and, therefore, did not fall within the ambit of Article 27.

As a result of this deficiency there are now a number of notable initiatives. The UN Declaration on Minorities has been a positive step though much remains to be done. The Declaration needs to be converted in a binding treaty, and states must acknowledge more firmly their commitment to protecting minority rights. The appointment of the Independent Expert on Minority Issues (2005) with an extended mandate in 2008 is a positive step, as is the establishment of the Forum on Minority Issues by the HRC in September 2007; however, it is only with the passage of time that a fuller impact of these latter initiatives would become evident.

MODERN INITIATIVES IN INTERNATIONAL LAW

Since the adoption of the ICCPR a number of recent initiatives have reinforced the international provisions relating to minority protection. The primary instrument at the global level is the United Nations General Assembly's Resolution 47/135 of 18 December 1992. The Declaration represents a concerted effort on the part of the international community to overcome some of the limitations in Article 27 of the ICCPR (Dickson 1995). According to Article 1(1), states

> shall protect the existence and the national or ethnic, cultural, religious or linguistic identity of minorities within their respective territories and shall encourage conditions for the promotion of that identity.

Article 2(1) confirms and elaborates upon the position of Article 27 of ICCPR. The provisions of this article present a more positive attitude compared with the tentative position adopted by Article 27. It provides

> Persons belonging to national or ethnic, religious and linguistic minorities (hereinafter referred to as persons belonging to minorities) have the right to enjoy their own culture, to profess and practice their own religion, and to use their own language, in private and in public, freely and without interference or any form of discrimination.

Article 2(2) provides for wide-ranging participatory rights to persons belonging to minorities in 'cultural, religious, social, economic and public life'. The provision is significant as the recognition and authorization of such rights form an essential element of the concept of autonomy. Similarly, Article 2(3) provides for effective participation at national and regional levels and on matters which necessarily affect the position of minorities. Article 2(4) authorizes persons belonging to minorities to establish and maintain their own institutions, a matter indispensable to the autonomous existence of minorities. Hence, Article 2 as a whole could be taken to bear significant value in recognizing autonomy for minorities, even though the right to autonomy itself failed to be incorporated in the Declaration. Article 3 of the Declaration also carries a similar message. It reinforces the collective dimension with encouragement of the communal enjoyment of rights without discrimination of any sort. Article 4 provides that:

(i) States shall take measure to ensure that persons belonging to minorities may exercise fully and effectively all their human rights and fundamental freedom without any discrimination and in full equality before the law.
(ii) States shall take measures to create favourable conditions to enable persons belonging to minorities to express their characteristics and to develop their culture, language, religion, traditions and customs except where specific practices are in violation of national law and contrary to international standards.
(iii) States should take appropriate measures so that wherever possible persons belonging to minorities have adequate opportunities to learn their mother tongues.
(iv) States should, where appropriate, take measures in the field of education, in order to encourage the knowledge of the history, traditions, language and culture of the minorities existing with in their territory. Persons belonging to minorities should have adequate opportunities to gain knowledge of the society as a whole.
(v) States should consider appropriate measures so that persons belonging to minorities may participate fully in the economic progress and development in their country.

Articles 5, 6, and 7 also carry considerable value. According to Article 5, 'legitimate interests' of the persons belonging to minorities would be taken in account when formulating national policies or programmes of cooperation and assistance among states. The emphasis of Articles 6 and 7 is upon international cooperation in understanding the minority question in a more tolerant and rational manner. The Declaration has many positive elements. Aspects of ethnic, cultural and linguistic autonomy appear within the text of the Declaration and represent a considerable advance. The communal aspects of existence of minorities is more pronounced, the references relating to state sovereignty and territorial integrity although integral to the Declaration are framed in a more accommodating manner. They are less confrontational to aspirations of autonomy and distinct identity.

The Declaration, however, is a General Assembly Resolution and its impact on the development of international law is not clear. Many of the substantive provisions of the Declaration are themselves framed in a rather general manner, enabling a number of states to claim that they already respect minority rights. States may also prevent legitimate expression of minorities on the pretext of being 'incompatible with national legislation'. Even as a political and moral expression there have been controversies as to the rights of minorities and concern for state sovereignty and territorial integrity resurfaced frequently. The right to autonomy was not acceptable and even the 'lower level' right to 'self-management' failed to be incorporated (Thornberry 1994a). The manner and circumstances of the adoption of the Declaration, as its critics would argue, was probably more in response to the inability of the United Nations to take appropriate action to protect the rights of minorities, even after the East-West détente and the ending of the Cold War.

One ingenious method of overcoming historical weaknesses in the implementation of minority rights mechanisms was through the setting-up of a Working Group on Minorities. The Working Group, which was established in 1995, helped to eradicate some of the criticisms regarding the weaknesses existent in the practical realization and implementation of the Declaration before it was disbanded in 2006. The Working Group on Minorities was also influential in promoting the issue of minority rights at the global level and, notwithstanding its brief history, created a lasting impression within the United Nations as an effective forum for deliberation and producing mutual understanding between minorities and their governments.

The mandate of the Working Group was constituted as follows:

a. Review the promotion and practical realization of the Declaration;
b. Examine possible solutions to problems involving minorities, including the promotion of mutual understanding between and among minorities and governments;
c. Recommend further measures, as appropriate, for the promotion and protection of the rights of persons belonging to national or ethnic, religious and linguistic minorities.

The Working Group was able to enhance the overall jurisprudence of minority rights through a number of initiatives. Members of the Working Group produced commentaries on the Declaration, as well as on the various rights contained therein. Professor Asbjørn Eide, the chairman of the Working Group, made a substantial impression on the proceedings and continuing success of the Working Group (E/CN.4/Sub.2/AC.5/1998). Other members of the Working Group similarly provided valuable input. In March 1999, Mustafa Mehdi presented a working paper on Multicultural and Intercultural Education on the Protection of Minorities (E/CN.4.4/AC.5/1999) as did another member of the Working Group on Universal and Regional Mechanisms for Minority Protection (E/CN.4/Sub.2/AC.5/1999).

In the Working Group's session of May 1999, numerous significant proposals were put forward, including the establishment of a data-base on minorities and enhanced strategies for further involvement of regional and sub-regional agencies (E/CN.4/Sub.2/AC.5/1999). The Working Group on Minorities held its twelfth and final session in August 2006. However, it was not apparent at the time that this was to be the last session and consequently cooperation between the Working Group and the Independent Expert on Minority Issues was established (U.N. Doc. A/HRC/Sub.1/58/19 2006). In 2007, it was decided that the Sub-Commission on the Promotion and Protection of Human Rights was to be abolished, which led to the winding down of the Working Group. This development was of great concern to those involved in Minority Rights issues, who feared a weakening of the UN Human Rights framework and stressed the need for a similar mechanism in order to prevent conflict in addition to promoting and protecting Minority Rights (U.N. Doc. A/HRC/ 6/9 7 2007).

In its final session the Working Group in its recommendations,

> [proposed] that the sessions of the Working Group on Minorities or a similar future mechanism, if the Human Rights Council decides to establish one, should be intersessional and have a duration of five working days, and recommends that such a mechanism should ensure access to and participation by minority representatives from all regions of the world and serve as a forum for dialogue and mutual understanding on minority rights issues (U.N. Doc. A/HRC/Sub.1/58/19 24 2006).

The Working Group on Minorities during its time made a significant impact through its interpretation of the UN Declaration on Minorities, however, the mechanism itself was significantly weaker than other UN special mandate holders and it was not until the introduction of the concept of the Independent Expert on Minority Issues that there was a Minority Rights mandate on a par with the other Special Rapporteurs (Hadden 2007). The Working Group made a positive contribution to Minority Rights in so far as it allowed minorities that would usually be excluded from national and local decision-making to raise their concerns at an international level. It enabled minorities to learn about international standards, and in some cases allowed minority groups to engage in dialogue with governments (ibid). However, commentators have also criticized the Working Group for its lack of sustained discussion and government response; the ad hoc nature of the proceeding was a weakness as was the fact there was no consistency regarding the attending minorities. 'In more general terms, there has been an absence of any sustained agenda or programme and no clear objective in respect of the adoption or publication of agreed conclusions or recommendations by the Working Group' (ibid). It is likely that the issues of the Working Group were in part symptomatic of its weak mandate. Many of the difficulties which have characterized the United Nations approach towards minorities have been reflected at the regional level.

EUROPEAN PROTECTION FOR MINORITIES

European human rights and minority rights instruments are not the product of a single monolithic mechanism. At the supra-national there are several institutions which have established procedures for protecting human rights. These institutions sometimes act as parallels, while at other times they overlap with one another. The role of three organizations is worthy of consideration: the Council of Europe, the European Union and the Organization for Security and Co-operation in Europe. There is a range of national institutions within European states which are aimed at protecting and promoting human rights and minority right. State membership within the three organizations differs and the standard setting mechanisms also vary from one system to the other.

The Council of Europe, the oldest of these institutions, has also had the most significant role in promoting human rights and minority rights at the European level. It is an inter-governmental organization, established in 1949 with the objective, *inter alia,* of strengthening democracy, human rights and the rule of law. In its initial years, the membership of the Council of Europe was confined to the Western democratic European countries. It excluded Spain and Portugal until the mid-1970s. However, with the collapse of communism, several members of Central and Eastern Europe have joined the

Council. The current membership of the Council of Europe is forty-seven, including all EU member states. The Council of Europe has produced various important regional human rights treaties, the most prominent one being the European Convention on Human Rights (ECHR), the Framework Convention on National Minorities (FCNM) and the European Charter for Regional Minorities. The ECHR was adopted in 1950 and came into operation in 1953 and currently provides protection to well over 800 million people. The institutions of the ECHR, the Court and the Committee of Ministers are based in Strasbourg, France. As of November 1, 1998, when the eleventh protocol came into operation, the individual complaints procedure has become automatic, thereby providing individual complainants possibility of access before the newly re-constituted Court of Human Rights. The jurisprudence of the Convention is highly impressive in the sense that the judgments of the European Court of Human Rights have forced states to change their laws or to reformulate their administrative policies.

The ECHR and its Protocols do not cover several important rights. The Convention, unlike the International Covenant on Civil and Political Rights (1966), does not provide for the right to self-determination, which is recognized as one of the principal rights in international human rights instruments. There is also the failure to provide for economic, social and cultural rights. The vision of ECHR on minority or group rights is particularly thin. The provisions of the European Convention on Human Rights as well as the jurisprudence arising from the Strasbourg institutions have reflected the difficulties in advancing the cause of minorities as distinct entities; it is the absence of the focus on group rights that is problematic (Harris et al 1995). The ECHR contains a number of provisions relevant to protecting the interests of minorities. However, it is only in Article 14 (providing for a regime of non-discrimination) and Protocol 12 (providing for a general prohibition of discrimination) that direct references to minorities are made.

Some remedial action was taken by the Council of Europe to adopt a Framework Convention for the Protection of National Minorities. Despite these omissions in the protection of rights, in the past nearly six decades, the rights contained in the Convention have been utilized to protect individual rights. The Convention as a living instrument has been interpreted in keeping with the changing values and traditions of European society. It is described as a 'constitutional instrument of European Public Order'. The ECHR, although a regional instrument, has also had an enormous impact upon the development of norms in general international law.

Notwithstanding a considerable reluctance to engage with minority rights issues, in recent years, the Council of Europe has been successful in adopting two treaties which are directly relevant to minorities in Europe. The Framework European Convention for the Protection of National Minorities is the first binding instrument which has an exclusive focus on minorities. The treaty came into operation in 1998. As a major reference for the protection of minorities, to date 39/47 Member States from the Council of Europe have ratified this instrument.

There is little in the Convention for minorities from the standpoint of autonomy. The closest the Convention comes to the subject of autonomy is in the article which provides that 'the Parties shall create the conditions necessary for the effective participation of persons belonging to national minorities in cultural, social and economic life and in public affairs, in particular those affecting them.' The weak nature of obligations contained in the article has been a subject of criticism (Gilbert 1996) Furthermore, this article represents a retreat from the statements already advanced through Recommendation 1201 (1993) of the Parliamentary Assembly of the Council of Europe. However, considering the already restrictive approach taken by state parties to the FCNM, it is likely that including a provision on autonomy may have considerably limited the number of states willing to ratify the Convention, particularly as a binding right to autonomy can be considered as seriously infringing on state sovereignty. The final and most significant of weaknesses in the Convention is that it does not have a complaints' procedure. The Convention establishes general principles which are not directly applicable at national level, with implementation being the 'prerogative of the States' (Wheatley 1996). States parties are required to submit reports to an advisory committee of the Committee of Ministers on the measures, legislative and administrative, in order to ensure compliance with the treaty. The Advisory Committee also undertakes on-site visits as part of its investigations which allows the committee members to meet the officials from governments and others in non-governmental sectors. The reports submitted by the Advisory Committee is reviewed by the Committee of Ministers, which then adopts its conclusions with appropriate recommendations. It would be useful to further advance the possibility of NGOs and minority groups to comment or state reports to make suggestions when state practices are being considered by the Advisory Committee (Boyle, 2004). The flexible nature of the rights contained within FCNM and the margin of appreciation employed regarding the definition of a minority mean that the Convention itself does not lend itself to judicial interpretation or application (Hoffman 2008).

The Council of Europe has also adopted the European Charter for Regional or Minority Languages (1992). The Charter, a binding treaty, as its title suggests, aims to protect the regional and minority languages spoken within Europe. State parties to the Charter undertake to encourage and facilitate the regional and minority languages, inter alia, 'in speech and writing, in public and private life'. There is also an undertaking to encourage the usage of these languages in studies, in education, in administration of justice, public services, in media, in social and economic life, and to establish institutions in order to advise 'authorities on all matters pertaining to regional or minority languages'. Implementation of the treaty is to be conducted through periodic reports to the Secretary-General of the Council of Europe in a manner prescribed by the Committee of Ministers. The first report is to be presented within a year following entry into force of the Charter with respect to the state concerned and thereafter at three-year intervals. These reports are to be examined by a Committee of Experts, consisting of one member from each state party nominated by the relevant state, appointed for a six-year term and eligible for reappointment. Issues relevant to the undertakings of the state concerned may be brought to the attention of the Committee of Experts. France and Turkey, major states that are members of the Council of Europe, have as yet not signed the FCNM whereas Belgium, Iceland, Greece and Luxembourg have not ratified the FCNM.

In addition to work done by the Council of Europe, significant contributions in the field of minority rights are made by another inter-governmental organization, the Organization of Security and Co-operation in Europe (OSCE). The concern shown for the subject of minority rights within the OSCE stretches back to the Helsinki Final Act. The Copenhagen Document is valuable for the propagation of minority rights. There are important provisions relating to autonomy. Article 35 provides:

> The participating States note the efforts undertaken to protect and create conditions for the promotion of the ethnic, cultural, linguistic and religious identity of certain minorities by establishing, as one of the possible means to achieve these aims, appropriate local and autonomous administrations corresponding to the specific historical and territorial circumstances of such minorities and in accordance with the policies of the State concerned.

Similarly, the Oslo Recommendations regarding the Linguistic Rights of National Minorities and the Lund Recommendations on the Effective Participation of National Minorities in Public Life are also based around pre-existing legal standards. The Oslo Recommendations deal with subjects as far-reaching as 'names', 'religion' and 'the media'. The Lund Recommendations deal with two main topics, the participation of the National Minority in the 'governance of the State as a whole, and self-governance over certain local or internal affairs'. It is important to bear in mind when considering the Recommendations that their primary purpose is conflict prevention and as such

> The Recommendations do not propose an isolationist approach, but rather one which encourages a balance between the right of persons belonging to national minorities to maintain and develop their own identity, culture and language and the necessity of ensuring that they are able to integrate into the wide society as full and equal members (The Oslo Recommendations regarding the Linguistic Rights of National Minorities and Explanatory Note' 1998).

As the Recommendations are simply political documents, they do not contain any legal weight. That said, the 'although non-compliance with a non-legally binding commitment may not per se generate international legal responsibility, a violation of 'politically' binding agreements is thus as unacceptable as a violation of norms of international law' (Pentassuglia 2002). Despite their non-binding character, the Recommendations have frequently been used by policy and law-makers as a point of reference (Philips 1995). 'OSCE agreements not only often constitute 'progressive development' of existing legal norms, but also lead to the creation of law.' The Recommendations have even been used as if they were binding legal instruments by the High Commissioner on National Minorities, Max van der Stohl, when dealing with governments.

At the regional level, the Council of Europe's adoption of the Framework Convention for the Protection National Minorities and the European Charter for Regional or Minority Languages represent important developments. The OSCE has also brought the subject of minority rights to the forefront of its agenda, recognizing the importance of such rights in order to ensure peace and prevent future conflict. It is, however, an unfortunate reality that the regions where some of the worst minority rights violations take place, for example, South Asia, the Middle East and Africa, remain devoid of initiatives to protect minorities.

PROTECTION FOR MINORITY RIGHTS IN SOUTH ASIA

In the regional context of South Asia, human rights, including minority rights, present a major area of concern. Despite constitutional provisions protecting the rights of minorities within South Asian states, both domestic and international human rights obligations have often failed to materialize on the ground. Promotion of respect for universal values of human rights, the interdependence of rights and the indivisibility of rights are the key challenges which are facing human rights activists, organizations and governments in the region.

Aspirations of peace, security and respect for human rights within South Asia are confounded by the enormity of the region's historical and political problems. The political geography of the region reflects the mosaic and heterogeneous character of the nations from which it is formed. South Asia stretches from the Durrand Line (which separated British India from Afghanistan) in the northwest to the Burmese border in the east, from the Himalayas in the north to Dondra Head in Southern Sri Lanka. This densely inhabited region has a population of approximately one fifth of the world's total population, concentrated in about 3 per cent of the total landmass. A distinctive history is attached to South Asia. The region has the most ancient of the world's civilizations and is the birthplace of two of the most widely practised world religions. South Asia has braced waves of invaders, refugees and immigrants and has a greater number of followers of Islam than in any other country of the

Middle East or North Africa. With more languages spoken than the entire continent of Europe and having a population larger than Africa and Latin America combined, South Asia resembles a continent more than a set of countries.

The South Asian mosaic has also been a source of some of the gravest tragedies of human history, with a legacy of terrorism, violation of human rights and continuing threats to regional and international peace and security. The partition of British India and the emergence of Pakistan and India in 1947 were accompanied by the largest inter-country transfer of population of the twentieth century. Almost a million people were killed during this period. Approximately eight million people migrated from India to Pakistan, while there was a similar exodus of Hindus and Sikhs from both wings of Pakistan to India. What happened in India and Pakistan led to further decolonization. Ceylon (which adopted the name Sri Lanka in 1972) and Burma gained independence in 1948 and the Maldives in 1965. The new states that emerged, in common with those that had not been directly colonized, such as Afghanistan and Nepal, have had to face serious issues affecting peace, security and human rights. The existence of arbitrary boundaries; the absence of sound political cultures; the suppression of values including democracy and human rights; and the repression of ethnic, religious and linguistic communities have all contributed to threats to peace; extremism in Afghanistan and in Kashmir; the repression of Bengalis of East Pakistan; the scarcity of rule of law in Pakistan, Bhutan, Nepal and India; the discriminatory practices against the Tamils of Sri Lanka, and the nine-month civil war in East Pakistan present some of the unfortunate examples.

Several factors have led to the non-fulfilment of basic guarantees provided by several of the constitutions of the South Asian region. These include the suspension of fundamental rights as a result of military and civilian dictatorships (e.g., the Indian Emergency 1975-1977) and also a lack of political will to substantially implement the progressive legislation contained within the constitutional frameworks. A cursory survey of the states in the region reveal a range of assimilative strategies such as the treatment of Bengalis in Pakistan that amounted to a complete annihilation of a civilization, culture and language. In Nepal and Bhutan there is considerable evidence of the forced assimilation of minorities. Attempts to subjugate the Nepali-speaking southern Bhutanese and to eradicate their culture, along with other repressive measures, have resulted in the creation of more than 100,000 refugees. Pakistan and Bangladesh have had long periods of military dictatorships, which prevented any autonomous development on the part of ethnic minorities and indigenous peoples.

To illustrate; the nine-month civil war in East Pakistan (March-December 1971) resulted not only in grave violations of human rights, but also conceived the first (and until recently the only) successful secessionist movement of the post-colonial era. It is alleged that the conflict resulted in one to three million civilian deaths, with the civil war creating ten million refugees. Throughout the conflict, while the United Nations Security Council remained bitterly divided, unwilling and unable to take any form of action, the deliberations of the General Assembly and other United Nations organs reflected a concern more for state sovereignty than for regional peace and security or the protection of human rights. The Government of Pakistan remained adamant that the situation in East Pakistan was confined to Article 2(7) of the United Nations Charter; essentially a matter for the domestic jurisdiction for Pakistan. The majority of the states within the United Nations Security Council and the General Assembly agreed with the argument advanced by Pakistan.

There were serious political differences on the issue of East Pakistan in the Security Council and it was 'seized' of the matter only after active hostilities broke out between India and Pakistan in December 1971, nine months after the civil war had started. Ultimately when it did begin its deliberations on 4 December 1971, the political and ideological differences immediately came to surface. The issue became a pawn in the hands of the major powers, with the United States and China supporting Pakistan and asking for an immediate ceasefire and Indian military withdrawal, and the Soviets siding with India and insisting on immediate political settlement in East Pakistan. Ultimately these political and ideological differences prevented any form of action with a Resolution drafted by the Soviet Union failing to be adopted.

Given this impasse in the Security Council, the matter was then referred to by the General Assembly, which could take action under the Uniting for Peace Resolution. There was a sense of urgency in the General Assembly and a strong consensus on the ways things should operate. It must, however, be noted that this consensus suggests that the prime concern of the members was upon the insistence of the territorial integrity, and the retention of the status quo at the expense of democracy, human rights and regional peace and security. A similarly disappointing approach was adopted by the UN Commission on Human Rights and the Sub-Commission on the Prevention of Minorities and Protection of Human Rights (now replaced by the Human Rights Council).

The case before the International Court of Justice proved short-lived. The case did not proceed to a discussion of the merits. It was settled by an agreement between India and Pakistan in August 1973, leading Pakistan to drop the case against India. Through a subsequent agreement involving India, Pakistan and Bangladesh (signed in Delhi on 7 April 1974) it was agreed that no trials for crimes against humanity or genocide were to be conducted; all outstanding issues were to resolved through diplomatic channels instead of having recourse to courts, including the International Court of Justice.

Since the East Pakistan conflict, the foremost regional organization within South Asia is the South Asian Association for Regional Co-operation (SAARC). SAARC, which consists of eight states of South Asia, was formally established in December 1985. The current membership of SAARC comprises

Afghanistan, Bangladesh, Bhutan, India, Maldives, Nepal, Pakistan and Sri Lanka. In terms of its population, SAARC is the largest organization: the combined population of its Member States consists of over 1.5 billion people. SAARC, much like the European Union (during the European Union's initial phases), was devised as primarily a political organization with the objective of greater economic cooperation amongst member states. There was a similar institutional lacuna in SAARC for the promotion and protection of individual human rights or minority rights. That said, the institutional framework of SAARC has provided opportunities to debate and examine key issues relevant to human rights and minority rights of the region. Declaration on the Conditions of Minorities in SAARC Countries, adopted by the delegates to the workshop on this concern, discussed the issues of minority rights as a priority among the member states. The members reaffirmed their commitment to secure the rights to life, freedom, dignity and equality of all human beings under law and in reality. The members recognized that within each country there are minorities based on religion, language, ethnicity and nationality who are disadvantaged and vulnerable because of their inadequate share in power and decision-making. Realizing that owing to the majoritarian character of states and polities and denial of the right to equality to minorities in the common national domain and the right to preserve their distinct identity, minorities have generally faced varying degrees of threat to their existence, and to their language, religion and culture everywhere. A further, possibly more tangible contribution of SAARC is what has been termed as the 'Promotion of People-to-People Linkage'. Despite their close regional proximity, many states of the region have traditionally shown an inbuilt distrust of one another. The achievements are particularly significant given the violent and turbulent geo-political history of the region. Having said that, in practice, SAARC remains a minor player in so far as resolutions of regional disputes are concerned. The intransigence of the two larger states, Pakistan and India, over a number of issues including Kashmir, has been a major disappointment. Similarly SAARC has had an unimpressive record in dealing with notable conflicts such as those involving the Tamils in Sri Lanka, the Adivasis of the Chittagong Hill Tracts (in Bangladesh), Nepali-speaking Bhutanese (residing in Nepal) and the Maoist rebels (in Nepal).

A significant weakness in the work of SAARC is the absence of legislative powers, similar in nature to the European parliament. An inability to challenge administrative, political and legal decisions made by South Asian States remains a fundamental defect in the system; there is no European Style Court of Justice or Court of Human Rights. There are no effective enforcement procedures for the legal issues addressed by SAARC; enforcement is largely dependent on the goodwill of member states. Minority rights must be seen in the context of human rights, at the same time acknowledging both distinctions and convergence of the two. Minority rights do not have a meaning without a functioning democracy and good governance but to understand minority rights in South Asia one must address the alarming trends towards majoritarianism in the regional political arena. Currently, many of the South Asian minority groups find themselves in situations of great risk, let alone subject to routine discrimination due to weak constitutional safeguards, inadequate legal instruments and oppressive social and customary practices. The lack of regional supranational mechanisms aggravates the state of affairs.

REFERENCES

UN Documents

CCPR/C/33D/197/1985, 10 August 1988, Human Rights Committee, 33rd Session; Prior decisions CCPR/C/WG/27/D/197 1985; CCPR/C/29D/197 1985 (admissibility 25 March 1987).

Commission on Human Rights Res. 1995/24 (3 March 1995).

Communication no. 167/1984 (26 March 1990), UN Doc. Supp. no. 40 (A/45/40) at 1 (1990).

Communication no. 197/1985 UN Doc CCPR/C/33/D/197/1985.

Communication no. 511/1992, Views adopted on 26 October 1994, CCPR/C/52/D/511/1992.

Communication no. 879/1999, UN Do. CCPR/C/84/D/879/1999 (2005).

Convention on the Prevention and Punishment of the Crime of Genocide, adopted 9 December 1948. Entered into force 12 January 1951. 78 U.N.T.S. 277.

Convention for the Protection of Human Rights and Fundamental Freedoms ETS No. 005 213 U.N.T.S. 222, entered into force Sept. 3, 1953, as amended by Protocols Nos 3, 5, and 8 which *entered into force* on 21 September 1970, 20 December 1971 and 1 January 1990 respectively.

E/CN.4/Sub.2/AC.5/1998 WP.1 and observations thereon from governments, specialized agencies, non-governmental organizations and experts E/CN.4/Sub.2/AC.5/1999 WP.1.

E/CN.4/Sub.2/AC.5/1999 WP 6 May 1999.

ECOSOC Res. 1995/31 (25 July 1995).

Framework Convention for the Protection of National Minorities and Explanatory Report (1995) para. 13, 22.

GA Res. 45/41 UN GAOR, 45th. Sess. Supp. No. 49, p. 363, UN Doc. A/RES/45/41 (1990).

GA Res. 47/33 UN GAOR, 47th. Sess. 73rd mtg., at 3, UN Doc. A/RES/47/33 (1992).

GA Res. 2200A (XXI) UN Doc. A/6316 (1966) 993 U.N.T.S. 3, 6 I.L.M. (1967) 360.

Human Rights Council Resolution 7/6 on the Mandate of the Independent Expert on Minority Issues. para. 3.

Human Rights Commission Resolution 2005/79, para. 6.

Letter for the High Commission on National Minorities of the Organization of Security and Cooperation in Europe addressed to the President of the Human Rights Council. U.N. Doc. A/HRC/6/9 7 September 2007.

Report of the Working Group on Minorities on its fifth Session E/CN.4/Sub.2/1999/21 paras 19-20.

Report on the Working Group on Minorities on its Twelfth Session, U.N. Doc. A/HRC/Sub.1/58/19- 24 August 2006.

The Lund Recommendations on the Effective Participation of National Minorities in Public Life and Explanatory Note', 12 *IJMGR* (2005) 297, p.300.

The Oslo Recommendations regarding the Linguistic Rights of National Minorities and Explanatory Note' February 1998, 6(3) *IJMGR* (1999) 359, p.370.

UN Doc A/Res/47/135 Declaration on the Rights of Persons Belonging to National or Ethnic, Religious and Linguistic Minorities.
UN ESCOR, Commission on Human Rights, UN Doc. E/CN.4/SR. 368–71 (1951) para 37.

Cases

Ballantyne, Davidson, McIntyre *vs.* Canada, Communications Nos. 359/1989 and 385/1989, U.N. Doc. CCPR/C/47/D/359/1989 and 385/1989/Rev.1 (1993).
Cadoret and Hervé Le Bihan *vs.* France, Communication No. 221/1987, U.N. Doc. CCPR/C/41/D/221/1987 at 43 (1991).
Diergaardt *vs.* Namibia, Communication no. 760/1997, U.N. Doc. CCPR/C/69/D/760/1997 (2000)
Guesdon *vs* France. 25 July 1990. Communication No. 219/1986, U.N. Doc. CCPR/C/39/D/219/1986 (1990)
Kitok *vs.* Sweden, Communication No. 197/1985, U.N. Doc. Supp. No. 40 (A/43/40) at 221 (1988).
Länsman et al. *vs.* Finland, Communication No. 511/1992, U.N. Doc. CCPR/C/52/D/511/1992 (1994).
Lovelace *vs.* Canad*a*, Communication No. 24/1977 (30 July 1981), U.N. Doc. CCPR/C/OP/1 at 83 (1984).
Lubicon Lake Band *vs.* Canada, Communication no. 167/1984 (26 March 1990), U.N. Doc. Supp. No. 40 (A/45/40) at 1 (1990). Also see General Comment 23(50) Article 27, UN Doc. CCPR/C/21/Revs. 1/Add.5 (1994) at para 3.1

Books and Journals

Akehurst, M. 1987. *A Modern Introduction to International Law,* London: Harper Collins.
Alfredsson G., and Zayas, A.M. 1993. Minority Rights: Protection by the United Nations, *Human Rights Law Journal* 14:1.
Alston, P. 1995. The Security Council and Human Rights: Lessons to Be Learned from the Iraq-Kuwait Crisis and Its Aftermath (1990-91), *Australian Yearbook of International Law* 13: 107.
Bowring, B. 2008. European Minority Protection: The Past and Future of a 'Major Historical Achievement, 15 *International Journal of Minority and Group Rights* 413: 424.
Boyle, K. 2004. Europe: The Council of Europe, the OSCE, and the European Union. In *Guide to International Human Rights Practice,* edited by Hurst Hannum, Leiden: Brill and, Hotei Publishing: 143-70.
Capotorti, F. 1991. Special Rapporteur, *Study on the Rights of Persons Be-*

longing to Ethnic, Religious and Linguistic Minorities UN Sales no E. 78.XIVS.2, 96, para.568.

Cassese, A. 2003. *International Criminal Law,* Oxford: Oxford: University Press: 98–99.

Craven, M., 1995. *The International Covenant on Economic, Social and Cultural Rights: A Perspective on Its Development,* Oxford: Oxford: Clarendon Press: 340–44.

Crawford, J. 1995. Prospects of an International Criminal Court, *Current Legal Problems* 303: 319.

Dickson, B. 1995.The United Nations and Freedom of Religion, *International and Comparative Law Quarterly* 44: 354.

Dinstein, Y. 1976. Collective Human Rights of Peoples and Minorities, *International and Comparative Law Quarterly* 25, 102: 112.

Eide, A. 1999. The Non-inclusion of Minority Rights: Resolution 217C (III). In *The Universal Declaration of Human Rights: A Common Standard of Achievement,* edited by G. Alfredsson and A. Eide, The Hague: Nijhoff: 701–23.

Gilbert, G. 1996. The Council of Europe and Minority Rights, *Human Rights Quarterly* 18:160-89.

Hadden, T. 2007. The United Nations Working Group on Minorities, *International Journal of Minority and Group Rights* 14: 285.

Harris, R., et al .2002. The Burgeoning Minority Rights Jurisprudence of the European Court of Human Rights, *Human Rights Quarterly* 24, 3: 736-80.

Harris, R., M. O'Boyle and C. Warbrick et al, eds. 1995. *Law of the European Convention on Human Rights,* Oxford: Oxford University Press: 487.

Helsinki Document. 1992. rpt, *Human Rights Law Journal* 13: 284.

Henrard, K. 2001. The Interrelationship between Individual Human Rights, Minority Rights and the Right to Self-Determination and Its Importance for the Adequate Protection of Linguistic Minorities, *The Global Review of Ethnopolitic* 1, 1 (September): 41-61.

Hofmann, R. 2008. The Framework Convention for the Protection of National Minorities: An Introduction. In *A Commentary on the European Framework Convention for the Protection of National Minorities,* edited by M. Weller, Oxford: Oxford University Press: 6.

Ignatieff, M. 1993. Ugly Face of a New World Order, *The Sunday Times,* 7 Nov.

Kuper, J. 1994. Theoretical Issues Relating to Genocide. In: *Genocide: Conceptual and Historical Dimensions,* edited by G. Andreopoulos, Philadephia: University of Pennsylvania Press: 31-46.

Laponce, J.1960. *The Protection of Minorities,* Berkeley: University of California Press: 8-9.

Lillich, R., 1984. *The Human Rights of Aliens in Contemporary International Law, Manchester:* Manchester University Press.

Minority Rights Group, ed. 2008. *World Directory of Minorities and Indigenous Peoples* <www.minorityrights.org/directory> visited on 6th October 2008, see, for example, Uganda, Nigeria and Zambia.

Pentassuglia, G. 2002. *Minorities in International* Law, Strassbourg: Council of Europe Publishing: 144.

Phillips, A., and A. Rosas, eds. 1995. *Universal Minority Rights,* London: Cambridge University Press and Minority Rights Group International.

Poulter, S. 1997. The Rights of Ethnic, Religious and Linguistic Minorities, 2 *European Human Rights Law Review* 2: 254.

Rehman, J. 2008. Minorities. In *The New Oxford Companion to Law,* edited by P. Cane and J. Conaghan, Oxford: Oxford University Press: 791-93.

Rehman, R. 1999. Autonomy and the Rights of Minorities in Europe. In *Minority Rights in the New Europe,* edited by P. Cumper and S. C. Wheatley, The Hague: Kluwer Law International: 217-31.

Shaw, M.2008. *International Law,* Cambridge: Cambridge University Press: 298.

Sohn, L. 1981. The Rights of Minorities. In *The International Bill of Rights: The Covenant on Civil and Political Rights,* edited by L. Henkin, New York: Columbia University Press: 270-89.

Thornberry, P. 1991a *International Law and the Rights of Minorities,* Oxford: Clarendon Press.

Thornberry, P. 1991b. *Minorities and Human Rights Law,* London: Minority Rights Group.

Tomuschat, C. 1983. Protection of Minorities under Article 27 of the International Covenant on Civil and Political Rights. *Völkerrecht als Rechtsordnung, Internationale Gerichtsbarkeit, Menschenrechte, Festschrift für Herman Mosler:* 945: 960.

Weis, P. 1979. *Nationality and Statelessness in International Law,* Alphen aan den Rijn: Sijthoff and Noordhoff.

Wheatley, S. C. 1996. The Framework Convention for the Protection of National Minorities, *European Human Rights Law Review* 1: 83.

Wirsing R., ed. 1981. *Protection of Minorities: Comparative Perspective,* New York: Pergamon.

Wright J. 1996. The OSCE and the Protection of Minority Rights, *Human Rights Quarterly* 18: 190.

LIST OF CONTRIBUTORS

Paula Banerjee specializes on issues of conflict and peace in South Asia, publishing extensively on gender, forced migration and peace politics, and is vice president of the International Association for Study of Forced Migration.

Thomas Benedikter is an economist and senior researcher in Bozen (Italy) and writes on minority rights and ethnic conflicts; currently engaged with the EURASIA-Net programme.

Bojan Brezigar is a journalist and political scientist and has spent more than twenty years working in NGOs for minorities; former president of EBLUL.

Samir Kumar Das is professor of political science, University of Calcutta, and a member of the Calcutta Research Group.

Andreas Eisendle is a junior researcher at the Institute for Minority Rights, European Academy Bolzano/Bozen (Italy) and a law student at the University of Innsbruck.

Benedikt Harzl is a junior researcher at the European Academy, Bolzano/Bozen (Italy) and a PhD candidate at the department of political science, University of Innsbruck.

Harriet Hoffler is researcher on the FP7 EURASIA-Net Project with a special interest in the philosophy of human rights law and lecturer in international human rights law at Brunel University.

Emma Lantschner is a researcher at the Institute for Minority Rights at the European Academy, Bolzano/Bozen (Italy) and the Centre for Southeast European Studies at the

University of Graz. She has published widely on the protection of minorities with a special focuson the mechanisms of the Council of Europe.

Joanna Pfaff-Czarnecka is professor of social anthropology and pro-vice-chancellor for organizational development, Bielefeld University; a visiting fellow at many international institutes; she has published widely her most recent work, *Nationalism and Ethnicity in Nepal, is* co-edited with D. Gellner and J. Whelpton (Vajra, 2008).

Javaid Rehman is professor of Islamic law and international human rights law at Brunel Law School and its head; he has written extensively on Islamic law, human rights law and minority rights.

Ranabir Samaddar is director, Calcutta Research Group and is known for his critical writings; his most recent book is *Emergence of the Political Subject* (Sage, 2009).

INDEX

B&S

B&S